DRYLAND GARDENING
Plants that survive and thrive in tough conditions

DRYLAND GARDENING

Plants that survive and thrive in tough conditions

JENNIFER BENNETT

FIREFLY BOOKS

A FIREFLY BOOK

Published by Firefly Books Ltd. 2005

First printing

Publisher Cataloging-in-Publication Data (U.S.)
Bennett, Jennifer.
    Dryland gardening : plants that survive and thrive in tough conditions / Jennifer Bennett.
[192] p. : col. photos. ; cm.
Includes bibliographical references and index.
Summary: Guide to selecting plants for dry climate conditions with extensive plant lists and how-to-grow information.
ISBN 1-55407-031-7 (pbk.)
1. Plants–Drought tolerance. 2. Drought-tolerant plants.
3. Gardens–Irrigation. 4. Xerophytes. I. Title.
635.95 22   SB439.8B46   2005

Library and Archives Canada Cataloguing in Publication
Bennett, Jennifer
    Dryland gardening : plants that survive and thrive in tough conditions / Jennifer Bennett.
Includes bibliographical references and index.
ISBN 1-55407-031-7
1. Drought-tolerant plants. 2. Xeriscaping. I. Title.
SB439.8.B46 2005   635.9'525   C2004-906894-6

Published in the United States by
Firefly Books (U.S.) Inc.
P.O. Box 1338, Ellicott Station
Buffalo, New York 14205

Published in Canada by
Firefly Books Ltd.
66 Leek Crescent
Richmond Hill, Ontario L4B 1H1

Printed in Canada

PHOTO CREDITS

ACKNOWLEDGMENTS

This book represents the commitment and cooperation of several individuals. They include Michael Worek at Firefly Books, Tracy Read and Susan Dickinson of Bookmakers Press, designer Sari Naworynski and editorial associates Deborah Viets and Laurie Coulter. I would also like to express my thanks to Arizona Sonora Desert Museum in Tucson, Arizona; Desert Botanical Garden in Phoenix, Arizona; Cedar Valley Gardens, Port Hope, Ontario; Mason Hogue Gardens, Uxbridge, Ontario; Van Dusen Botanical Garden, Vancouver, British Columbia; and Devonian Botanic Garden, Devon, Alberta, for the opportunity to take photographs in their beautiful gardens.

CONTENTS

INTRODUCTION

INTRODUCTION

The statistics are sobering, the conclusions inescapable. During the last century, the average surface temperature of our world rose about 1 degree, whether measured Fahrenheit or Celsius. During the same period, the concentration of carbon dioxide in the atmosphere — largely the product of industry and the automobile, worsened by deforestation — rose about 25 percent. This is the gas that produces the "greenhouse effect" which holds the sun's heat within the atmosphere. In an article in the British magazine New Statesman, *Mark Lynas estimated that in England global warming "is equivalent to your garden moving south by 20 meters (65 feet) every day."*

An overall rise in global temperature doesn't necessarily mean that your own garden will be 1 degree warmer this summer than it was last summer, or even than it was 5 or 10 years ago. What it means is that the weather will be less predictable. In 2003, the World Meteorological Organization (WMO) announced that a record number of weather extremes worldwide show that climate change is under way. In June 2003, in Geneva, where the WMO is based, Genevans had the hottest June they've had for at least the past 250 years. Spring of 1999 in the northeastern United States was the driest spring since weather records began. Snowdrifts are deeper, winds are stronger, floods more devastating, droughts more severe.

The changing climate favors adaptable and drought-tolerant garden plants.

Water used for landscaping can be reduced by half when drought-tolerant plants are grown in a dryland garden.

Tornadoes are more frequent — a record 562 tornadoes in the United States in May 2003, which beat the previous record by 163. The WMO stated, "New record extreme events occur every year somewhere in the globe, but in recent years, the number of such extremes has been increasing."

Meanwhile, freshwater supplies are in crisis, not so much because of the changing climate as because of our increasing demands. Long-standing water reservoirs are shrinking. Where the Colorado River enters the Gulf of California, it is now a trickle instead of the wide river it used to be. The Ogallala aquifer below the Great Plains is being utilized far faster than it can be replenished. So is the aquifer under Mexico City, causing buildings to sink. While the average American uses 100 gallons of water a day, more than a billion people worldwide do not have clean drinking water at all.

GARDENING IN A NEW CLIMATE

It might seem that your backyard garden doesn't have much to do with such enormous changes, but there are adjustments you can make in attitude and practice which will make your garden more weatherproof and will also help conserve energy and water, whether you garden in a desert or your dry spell lasts only a week. We can emulate the farmers in dry areas who are turning to drip or trickle irrigation, which uses one-third to two-thirds less water than sprinkler systems, while increasing yields. Demonstration gardens utilizing low-water techniques are springing up across the continent in places like Montecito, California; Tempe, Arizona; Dallas, Texas; Greene County, Missouri; Stone Ridge, New York; Victoria, British Columbia; Wallingford, Connecticut; and Wichita, Kansas.

DROUGHT

A garden designed to withstand drought can withstand other climatic extremes as well. What is drought? What is dryland gardening? David Phillips writes in *The Climates of Canada* (1990), "There are no universally accepted definitions of drought. Any extended dry weather that is worse than expected and that leads to measurable losses can correctly be called a drought." So when the corn doesn't grow past knee-high because there's been no rain for six weeks, that counts as drought, even though the spring weather was wet. In fact, climate change in North America has meant a slight rise in precipitation, but it tends to be concentrated in fall and winter. If it comes as a deluge in October, it's not much help in July. And because days are longer and hotter in July and August, the soil dries out roughly twice as fast as it does in spring. Because dryland gardens depend upon well-drained soil, they are better able to withstand periodic heavy rains than gardens with heavy soil.

On the other hand, there are desert or semi-desert places where the year's rainfall is measured in fractions of inches or millimeters, and scarce

Cacti are the plants best adapted to drought.

water is a fact of life. Mediterranean climates such as California and South Africa and parts of South America and Australia (zones 8-10) generally have moist winters and hot, dry summers. Gardeners everywhere are looking to the plants native to these places (and to dry slopes and meadows worldwide) to find what will grow for them when the rains fail. The term xeriscaping — from the Greek word for dry — was coined in the Arizona desert, where water used for landscaping was reduced by half when gardeners and landscapers chose xeric — drought-tolerant — plants and used water-conserving methods.

This book will outline the methods and some of the plants that have been found most successful in gardens — or even parts of gardens — where the soil is dry for days, weeks or months at a time. It concentrates on zones 4 through 7, although some of the listed plants will grow in places warmer or colder than that.

Using the techniques in this book and growing these plants, you will not only have a garden better able to survive extreme weather but a garden that conserves water and is easier to mind and manage.

CACTI AND SUCCULENTS

Whether in the wild or in the garden, cacti and succulents are the plants best adapted to drought and least tolerant of wet ground.

Cacti are native to the Earth's western hemisphere, so they were unknown in Europe and Asia before Europeans arrived in America and took some of them back to Europe. There, these odd plants were given the Greek name *kaktos*, meaning cardoon or thistle. In his Herbal of 1597, John Gerard described "Thistle of Peru": "It doth much resemble a fig in shape and bignesse, but so full of sharpe and venomous prickles, that whosoever had one of them in his throat, doubtlesse it would send him packing either to heaven or to hell."

Cacti are supremely adapted to drought. The stem — the body of the cactus — is enlarged to hold water. It shrinks and withers after prolonged dry periods or in overly wet ground but stretches out full, like a balloon, when the plant is again content. Flowering happens soon after the rainy season. The leaves are mere thorns or hairs that do not lose precious water and, at the same time, help shade and protect the stem. The skin is leathery or waxy, the sap thick or milky. The root system is usually fibrous and shallow to take advantage of rainfall over as wide an area as possible. All cacti have unique structures called aureoles on their stems and branches. The aureole has two buds: the lower usually makes spines; the upper produces new branches or flowers.

There are a few species, especially of the genus *Opuntia* (page 119) that are hardy to temperatures as low as minus 40 degrees F (–40°C). These are among the favorite cacti for gardens everywhere, but for desert or semidesert gardens, there are hundreds of species and cultivars that can create a beautiful and varied landscape.

Succulents — plants with fleshy stems and leaves, not spines — are more adaptable in the garden than cacti, but they also do best where the soil is mostly dry.

In desert gardens and arid rock gardens, cacti and succulents dominate. In wetter places, succulents such as sedum can be used quite freely in well-drained soil, but cacti are perhaps best treated as conversation pieces. Keep them away from passing hands and feet and from competition from grasses or plants that might shade them. One of the best ways to show off cacti is in a small area of sand or gritty soil in a rock garden or traditional stone trough or in a large container with drainage holes. Pots should be at least 2 feet (60 cm) wide to accommodate the plants. Purchase special cactus mix, which is available in garden stores, or mix your own soil with 20 to 50 percent sand. Be sure to keep the pot weeded, but otherwise, do nothing; cacti need little or no fertilizer — at most, a small amount once in spring. A mulch of gravel or stone chips will help reflect heat and light onto the plants.

Cacti and succulents grown as houseplants can move outdoors for the summer, but like any other plant, they need hardening off between moves indoors and out. Put them in shade at first, and, of course, bring them back indoors if frost threatens. Prolonged temperatures of 41 degrees F (5°C) or colder can damage many species.

Given the few things they require, cacti and succulents are among the easiest and most interesting plants in a low-water, low-maintenance garden.

CHAPTER ONE

THE NEW DRYLAND GARDEN

Water is the lifeblood of the garden, even the dry garden. Since water is so critical to the survival of not only plants but all other living things, it needs to be managed carefully. How you water, when you water, if you water — these are critical questions in the dry garden, questions that will determine what plants you can grow and where and how you can grow them. The less water you have, the more careful about conserving it you must be.

Plants need an almost constant supply of water, and virtually all of that is taken in through the roots. The soil may look dry to you, but a heavy dew can refresh roots that grow near the surface, while those deeper underground search for enough moisture to keep their cells plump even in the midsummer heat. A fresh leaf is about 80 percent water, as are we, but plants, unlike humans, must constantly take in water from the bottom to replace what is lost out the top through pores that are always at least partially open. Weight for weight, plants need about 17 times as much water as humans do. Stop the intake of water for long, and most plants soon wilt, then die. Only cacti and succulents, which carry their own water supply — kind of like botanical camels — can survive long periods of excessive drought. Otherwise, the deeper-rooted the plant, the more self-reliant it is.

A pot of *Opuntia* 'Crystal Tide' blooms in a bed of *Achillea* 'Paprika.'

Once trees are established, gardeners can pretty much forget about watering them, and there are many shrubs and even perennials that likewise seldom require watering once their root systems have grown.

Watering needs depend upon many things. Plant choice, soil quality, exposure to sun or shade and even the garden's location all play a part. For instance, *Rudbeckia hirta* (black-eyed Susan, gloriosa daisy) will grow without watering most summers in Atlanta, Georgia, but it needs regular watering in drier, sunnier Albuquerque, New Mexico.

USING RAINWATER

Making the most of rainwater is an important survival strategy of the dry-summer gardener. Rainwater has several advantages over tap water:

- It is free.
- It is soft. Hard tap water not only leaves a whitish residue of calcium or magnesium carbonate on leaves, soil and plant pots but can also interfere with the uptake of nutrients from the soil.
- It is the ambient temperature. Water that is colder than the air slows seed germination and plant growth. In hot weather, cold irrigation can actually cause wilting.
- It is not treated with chlorine, fluorine or other tap-water additives. Fluoridated tap water normally contains about 1 part per million (ppm) fluorine, but as little as $1/4$ ppm can damage many plant species, in the garden or in a vase. Symptoms range from burning of leaf tips to leaf death. Chlorine, too, is toxic to plants in sufficiently large amounts, although it is very volatile and will dissipate into the air if the water is allowed to sit for a few hours.
- Rainwater is naturally acidic. Due to carbon dioxide and other acid-producing substances in the atmosphere, rainwater has a pH of less than 7,

A rain barrel collects precious runoff from the roof.

generally 5.6 to 5.7, an ideal pH for most garden plants. On a scale of 1 to 14, pH 7 is neutral. Numbers higher than 7 indicate increasing alkalinity; numbers lower than 7, increasing acidity. In industrialized regions, such as the northeastern United States, the pH of rainwater can be as low as 4.1, because sulfur and nitrogen oxides from the burning of fossil fuels react with raindrops to form sulfuric and nitric acids.
- Using rainwater in the garden means that precious, expensive treated tap water can be used for the purposes for which it is intended: drinking and washing. One of the reasons the Denver, Colorado, water department began an extensive xeriscaping plan was that 40 percent of its treated water was going to residential landscape use.

MEASURING WATER

Most watering is done in summer, of course, when all needs are highest but water supplies are generally lowest. In Georgia, where summers are relatively humid and gardening goes on year-round, household water use in summer is about double that in winter. In Kamloops, British Columbia, a semidesert city where only about 10 inches (25 cm) of rain falls each year and where cold weather prohibits winter gardening, the figure for midsummer water use is about five times that for midwinter. There is a program in that city to reduce summer water use by 25 percent. The most effective way to do this is to decrease landscape use, which accounts for at least half of the residential water supply.

You probably don't need to know how much rain falls on your garden. It's enough to know that sometimes your garden is dry. But you may want to keep track — to give a lawn its allotted 1 inch (2.5 cm) per week, for instance — so that you can make up the difference from a sprinkler. Some hardware stores and garden-supply sources sell rain gauges, or you can make one from a large can set just deep enough into the garden soil that it stays securely upright. After each rainfall, simply measure the water level with a ruler, then empty the can before replacing it. For an ongoing record of water accumulation, mark a plastic drinking straw from the bottom in inches or centimeters. After a rain or after sprinkling, insert the straw to the bottom of the can, put a finger on top, pull the straw out, and read the level.

How can you tell when to water? Mostly by the appearance of the soil and by wilted plants. The most needy plants will wilt and may even die before more drought-tolerant ones show any signs of stress at all. Wilting in the evening can be caused by a day of hot, windy weather and can even occur when there is moisture in the soil, but wilted leaves in the morning are a sign of dry soil and imminent damage to plants unless they are watered immediately. Another way to gauge dryness is with one of the soil-moisture meters on the market. When the meter is inserted into the soil, a bimetallic tip generates electricity in the presence of moisture, causing the pointer to move. In experiments in California, even inexpensive meters were somewhat effective, although salts in the soil made the meters indicate more moisture than was present. The California researchers concluded that gardeners should get to know their own soil-moisture levels and plant responses before relying on meters.

Watering is best done when the air is calm and relatively cool — that means morning or evening. Evening is best, because most plant growth occurs at night, the seeds of many desert species germinate in darkness, and plant cells can take time to plump up and prepare for the heat of the following day. The only caution about evening watering is that you should water the ground, not the foliage. Foliage that stays wet all night is easy prey for fungal diseases. If you use a sprinkler, choose the morning instead.

Never overwater by watering so heavily that it leaves puddles on the ground. Too much watering weakens plants, making them more vulnerable to diseases, to future drought and to winterkill.

WATERING PRIORITIES

Don't have a set schedule for watering, because the garden's needs will vary from place to place and time to time. Prioritize your plants according to their water requirements. They are as follows, starting with those with the greatest need:

- Young plants. Watering priority goes to any plant in its first year in your garden, even drought-tolerant perennials, shrubs and trees. Shrubs and trees under stress may look perfectly fine until they reach the point of death, when the leaves wilt. By then, it is likely too late. As

HOUSEHOLD WATER CONSERVATION

Water-conservation practices are seldom limited to the garden alone but are connected with saving water in other areas of life. If children want to play in the water, give them a wading pool rather than letting them play with a sprinkler or hose.

Use a bucket of water to wash the car rather than using a sprinkler or going to a commercial car wash, an extravagant water waster.

Swim in a natural body of water rather than a swimming pool. Residential swimming pools lose enormous amounts of freshwater through evaporation and backwash. And swimming-pool water cannot be recycled, as it is contaminated with chlorine.

If you do have a swimming pool, fill it to 6 to 8 inches (15-20 cm) from the top to reduce the water loss from splashing. Also, a swimming-pool cover will cut down on evaporation while it holds in heat and keeps out dirt.

Install a water-saving device in your toilet tank. Old models can use as much as 7 gallons (26 L) of water per flush, while most modern toilets use less than half that amount. Old toilets can be retrofitted with toilet-tank banks that lessen the tank capacity.

Make sure your plumbing is not leaking. A dripping toilet, for example, can waste as much as 17 gallons (64 L) of water a day.

An automatic dishwasher uses about 12 gallons (45 L) per run. Make sure it's fully loaded before turning it on.

Store a jug of ice water in the refrigerator rather than letting the water run until it's cold every time you want a drink.

Take short showers rather than baths, and if you do have a bath, don't fill the tub to the top. Install a water-saving showerhead.

Many washing machines use 40 gallons (150 L) or more per load. Wash a full load rather than a few items, or set the water level lower.

How Much Do You Use?

About 10 percent of American water usage occurs in the home. Your water meter will record the amount of water your household uses in cubic meters, gallons or cubic feet. If it measures in cubic feet, multiply the number by 7.5 to translate into gallons. One cubic meter equals 220 gallons. Turn on your sprinkler or other watering device for a minute, and record how far the meter turns. Multiply the number of gallons times the number of minutes you usually leave the sprinkler running. You can use the same method to calculate the number of gallons used in the shower, the dishwasher or the washing machine. If all appliances are turned off and the meter continues to turn, there is a leak somewhere in the system.

You can also measure the flow rate by collecting and measuring the water that flows from, say, your shower in 10 seconds. Multiply by 6 to arrive at the total number of gallons per minute, then figure out how many minutes you generally spend in the shower to arrive at the total.

these plants represent your greatest garden investment in terms of time, space and probably money, they must be considered top priority at planting time and then watered deeply once a week during dry weather. Thorough watering helps roots go deeper, making the plant more self-reliant. A tree needs soaking to a depth of about 14 inches (35 cm). If the ground is really dry and you don't want to haul buckets of rainwater, place a hose near the trunk and let the water trickle gently for several hours. If there is runoff, the water is either flowing too fast or the ground is saturated. In experiments in California, privet plants given the most frequent watering developed 18-inch (45 cm) roots, compared with 12-inch (30 cm) roots on plants watered half as often. By their second year, drought-tolerant trees, shrubs and perennials should be able to get by with watering no more frequently than every two weeks in dry weather.

• Annuals. Like all plants in their first year of growth, vegetables and annual flowers also demand high priority. Most vegetables do best with about 1 inch (2.5 cm) of water per week, although drought-tolerant annuals require watering only during the first few weeks after seeding or transplanting. Self-sown annuals need even less. Annuals that are not drought-tolerant should be grown only in areas with shade, deep soil and easy access.

• Plants in containers, other than cacti and succulents. Because their root systems are restricted, container plants can't draw water from as large an area as plants in the ground. Also, once container-plant foliage becomes dense, any rain that falls may be shed outside the container, making the plant totally dependent upon the gardener. Adding wetting agents — hydrogels — to potting soil may help. These water-absorbing polymers take in large amounts of water and, in theory, gradually release it to plant roots.

Research on their effectiveness has been controversial, but trials at the University of Georgia indicated that hydrogels enhanced the growth of summer annuals in nonirrigated soil.

• Plants that are not drought-tolerant. You may decide to grow a group of thirsty plants, even though you know they'll require more attention during dry weather.

• Lawn. Some people like to have a lush, green lawn all summer and are willing to make it a watering priority. Sprinkler systems are the only practical way to water a lawn, and such watering is best done first thing in the morning. Even the thirstiest types of lawn grasses need only 1 inch (2.5 cm) of water per week. If it rains that much, no more water is needed. See the directions on page 19 for making a simple water-measuring device. See Chapter 4 for suggestions about cutting down on watering by planting drought-tolerant grasses and alternative ground covers.

WATERING SYSTEMS

How you water your garden will depend on many considerations: How big is it and how dry? How thirsty are your plants? How often are you away? How much time and money do you want to spend?

• Watering can. A watering can may be old-fashioned, but it is the cheapest water-conserving device available. Needless to say, it doesn't suit every situation. Lugging water around by hand takes time and energy, and somebody has to be around to do it. If your watering needs are modest, however, this is your most valuable piece of gardening equipment, especially when combined with rain barrels. Using a watering can has the double benefit of giving you a good excuse to wander through your garden.

• Rain barrel. When 1 inch of rain falls on 1 square

foot of roof, that equals a little over $^1/_2$ gallon (U.S.) of water. If $^1/_4$ inch of rain falls, then 1,000 square feet of roof collects about 150 gallons of water. (In metric terms, 1 centimeter of rain on 10 square meters of roof provides 1,000 liters.) So it doesn't take much of a rainfall to fill a barrel placed at each downspout from the gutters, or eavestroughs. Make sure your barrel has a lid or is screened to prevent mosquitoes from breeding. Some have a tap near the base, and some can be connected together for added capacity. If these barrels dry out in summer, you can fill them from the hose and let the water warm to air temperature before using it in the garden. Where winters are cold, empty the barrels in late fall and lid them or turn them upside down to make sure ice doesn't form, causing them to crack or swell.

- Cistern. At one time, farmhouses often had a cistern in the basement, filled by runoff from the roof. Water could be pumped out whenever it was needed. A cistern may be aboveground or buried and may be made of plastic, wood, metal or concrete.

- Subirrigation. Subirrigation means that the soil under the surface is watered. The usual method is to insert topless cans or other open containers in the soil near plants, with just the rims above the soil surface. Punch a few small nail holes in the cans before you bury them, then fill with water. The water will soak into the soil at root level, where it is most useful. You can also buy subirrigating watering fixtures that can be attached to plastic soda bottles whose bases have been removed.

- Furrows. Furrows are ditches that direct water between rows of cultivated plants. Not particularly attractive, furrows are most practical in the vegetable garden. You must follow the contours of the garden, and the water supply must be plentiful enough to reach the end of the furrows.

Water from a rain barrel is easily directed to the thirstiest plants with an old-fashioned watering can.

HEATPROOFING THE GARDENER

Heatstroke is a potentially deadly condition that can arise from working for hours in the hot sun, causing the body's core temperature to rise. There are many warning signals that cooling is needed. Early symptoms of heat stress are mild dizziness, fatigue, irritability, decreased concentration and impaired judgment. Heat rash, heat cramps and heat exhaustion can be followed, finally, by heatstroke. Heat cramps are caused by loss of body salt in sweat. If they occur, rest in a cool place and drink a lightly salted beverage. There are a few ways to avoid heat stress:

- Do your midsummer gardening in the morning or evening, especially on days that are hot and humid.
- If you do garden during the heat of the day, wear a hat and loose, woven clothing that admits air.
- Drink enough water to replace body fluid lost by sweating.
- Take periodic breaks in a shaded or air-conditioned place.
- If you notice any of the above symptoms in somebody else, take that person immediately to a cool place. One symptom of heat stress is a resistance to treatment. Make the person rest for at least half an hour. If heatstroke occurs, take the person to a shaded place, wrap him or her in a wet sheet and arrange transportation in an air-conditioned vehicle to a hospital as quickly as possible.

The advantages of furrows are that they are inexpensive, they water the soil only, not the foliage, and they allow you to leave a hose in one place and get on with other things while gravity does the work.

- Soaker, drip or trickle irrigation. In a way, these are simply more expensive, more attractive forms of furrowing. Again, water goes onto the soil, not the foliage, and the system is relatively or totally automated, so you don't have to stay in the garden while watering is going on. Rather than flowing down an open furrow, however, water flows down a perforated hose or tube. Most hoses can be hidden with mulch, so these systems are appropriate for ornamental as well as vegetable gardens. The greatest advantage of these systems is water conservation. Also, they can be automated. There are a few disadvantages:
  - Equipment may be expensive, and the initial setup can be labor-intensive.
  - It is not frostproof, so the system must be emptied where winters are cold.
  - Rodents, insects or foot traffic can cause damage.
  - The water from such a system is likely to be cold.
  - Overwatering is possible.

Drip and trickle systems both utilize smaller feeder tubes plugged into the larger tube where needed. These systems are commonly used on large commercial acreages, but on the other end of the scale, plant pots on a balcony or rooftop can be connected with drip hoses. Some systems can handle normal household water pressure.

Made from recycled tires, the soaker hose is the most economical choice for a smaller garden. Tiny pores in the hose allow water to seep from it slowly and evenly; about half a gallon (2 L) of water per minute from every 100 feet (30 m) of hose. The chief disadvantage of the soaker hose is that because of the small size of its pores, it can easily clog from hard or alkaline water or from solids in the water, even if you install a filter. Treated tap water or fresh rainwater from

An elaborate drip irrigation system is used to water the gardens at a commercial daylily farm.

a lidded barrel are among the best sources of water for a soaker hose. If you are in doubt about the clarity of your water, try a short length of hose for a season to see how it works for you. These systems operate at lower water pressure than normal household water pressure, so you must have the tap only partially turned on or install a pressure regulator next to the filter on the line leading to the hose.

If you are interested in a soaker, drip or trickle system, ask several manufacturers for descriptions of their products (see Sources). Also, most hardware and garden stores sell basic home-garden systems in spring. If you buy from more than one manufacturer, make sure that all the components are compatible.

- Sprinklers. These are widely available, but they are inefficient watering devices. About half of the water applied by sprinklers can be lost to evaporation, especially if you use a fine spray on a windy day. However, sprinkling is the most practical method for shallow-rooted plants like grasses and for large areas like lawns, especially if water is plentiful. To conserve water when you

do sprinkle, settle for a coarse spray rather than a fine one. Spray during calm weather, preferably first thing in the morning. Because spraying wets foliage, it should not be done in the evening, which can encourage fungal diseases.

An underground sprinkler system can be professionally installed. Make sure the application rate suits the absorbing ability of your soil; otherwise, runoff will occur. Keep track of the amount of water your sprinkler uses by placing three or four rain gauges in the irrigated area for a certain length of time, usually an hour. See the directions for making a rain gauge on page 19. Average the water level among the gauges.

- Household and gray water. Water used for cooking and washing is called gray water, as opposed to "white" drinking water and "black" sewage water. Gray water cannot legally be used in all places, especially in cities, so check with local officials before you redirect your wastewater.

Where it can be used, gray water is especially good for lawns and flower beds. It should not be used on vegetables and fruits or new plantings because of possible bacterial contamination. As it is likely to be alkaline, do not use it on acid-loving plants. Dilute it with freshwater whenever possible, and don't always use it on the same area. A certain amount of soap does not harm most plants, including grasses, and can even act as a fertilizer and pesticide. Too much soap, however, can burn the foliage of sensitive plants.

If you intend to use your gray water, use simple soaps rather than detergents containing softeners and whiteners. Dish-washing or cooking water should be allowed to cool, then poured into the soil around plants near the kitchen. Water from a dehumidifier is pure and safe to use. Water from the rinse cycle of the washing machine is better for the garden than water from the wash cycle, which may contain chlorine bleach, borax or other substances that can harm plants. Boron (borax) is especially dangerous — it is sometimes deliberately used as a herbicide. In any case, gray water should be applied directly to the soil, not the foliage. Regularly test soil watered with gray water to measure salt or boron accumulation.

Do not use gray water:

- if it is contaminated with black water. For instance, do not use water in which diapers have been washed.
- if it has been softened, because softened water contains too much sodium.
- if it comes from a swimming pool, because it will contain too much chlorine and/or bromine.
- if it comes from a sink where a garburetor has been used.
- if you intend to direct it into a drip-irrigation system, unless you install both a filter to remove suspended particles and a grease trap for kitchen-sink water.
- if it has been sitting any length of time, because bacteria in it may multiply. Handle carefully.

- if soil drainage is poor, because salts may accumulate in the soil.

Garden-Water Conservation

Anything that will hold rain near roots, rather than letting it flow away, will maximize the efficiency of watering. On flat or slightly sloped ground, make a ring dike a few inches high around each plant. Slopes are best terraced if you can manage it. This gives plants the ideal conditions of good drainage, water retention and relatively deep soil. Support the terrace banks with rocks, boards or logs, and build the flat surfaces up with compost or topsoil.

Soil drainage is critically important for many plants that can survive drought, especially in gardens which may be soggy for weeks in spring. Gardening on a slope helps plants survive, especially xeric plants. In places where water collects, grow tough plants — or nothing at all.

Plant Choice

How can you tell whether a plant will survive without water? There are many ways. Much of this book consists of lists of plants that survive dry stretches of varying length and severity. Most nurseries and seed catalogs give some indication of relative needs for moist or dry ground, and that ubiquitous term "well-drained soil" applies to virtually all the probable drought survivors. Some companies specialize in dryland plants. Plants native to dry places or developed there are usually good bets. And, of course, experimentation is worthwhile and often rewarding, but you must be prepared to accept a few losses.

Here are five things to consider when choosing plants for the dry garden:

- Plants that other people consider weedy might be just right for you. Goutweed (*Aegopodium podagraria*), for instance, is considered too weedy

INVASIVE PLANTS

Some of the most reliable plants for dry places are invasive in certain climatic areas and certain types of soil. These plants, especially imported species, termed aliens, are receiving increased attention and are discouraged or banned in some places. The following species recommended in this book are considered invasive in some areas of the United States or Canada or in the northern United States, according to two sources. One is Brooklyn Botanical Gardens publication number 149, Invasive Plants (100 Washington Avenue, Brooklyn, NY 11225-1099). The other is a survey by 35 botanists reported in *Invasive Plants of Natural Habitats in Canada* (Canadian Wildlife Service, Environment Canada, Ottawa, 1993).

Although the following species are sometimes invasive, their cultivars may be fine. Check with local government agencies and plant nurseries. Several internet sources for further information are listed in Sources.

Aegopodium podagraria; Artemisia absinthium; Berberis thunbergii; Caragana arborescens; Centaurea cyanus; Coronilla varia; Cytisus scoparius; Euonymus alatus; Euonymus fortunei; Gypsophila paniculata; Hesperis matronalis; Lonicera maackii; Lonicera tatarica; Miscanthus sinensis; Phalaris arundinacea; Poa compressa; Poa pratensis; Polygonum cuspidatum; Sedum acre; Spiraea japonica; Syringa vulgaris; Verbascum thapsus; Vinca minor.

for a manicured border, but it is beautiful and reliable in the dry shade under trees or under the gutters, or eavestroughs, against a house wall. So are certain grasses, bellflowers, yarrows and plants that drop their seeds after blooming. Fast-spreading species are best kept in their place by mowing or paving.

- The deeper and longer-lived the root system, the more self-sufficient a plant is likely to be, so plants are drought-resistant in roughly this descending order: trees, shrubs, perennials and annuals, including vegetables.
- Almost anything that has survived two winters in your garden, whether it comes back in spring by self-sown seeds or from a perennial root, will be better able to take care of itself than anything freshly planted.
- Lawn grasses can be difficult, expensive and environmentally harmful to keep pristine, but they are among the easiest plants if you choose the right grasses and accept summer brownness or occasional weediness.
- Just because a plant can live in dry ground doesn't mean it can put up with anything. Many plants that will survive drought are intolerant of extended wetness.

Remember, too, that while many plants can survive with little or no watering after they have been established in your garden for a year or two, all must be watered regularly when newly sown or planted. And if a plant looks wilted first thing in the morning, it needs watering right away.

Choosing plants that will grow in your climate and in your garden is a first step to success in a drought-prone place. Plants not sufficiently hardy for your climatic zone (see the map on page 179) may survive until they are polished off by a so-called test winter, one with record low temperatures or seesaw variations. In the meantime, you will probably have to contend with winter-killed shoots each spring. If you have acidic soil, it is best to grow plants that prefer acidity — the same with alkaline soil. You can fight nature, of course, but be prepared to work hard and to put up with discouragement.

Sowing Seeds

The easiest way to obtain some unusual plants for your garden is to grow them yourself from seed. Some perennials and shrubs can be a bit tricky from seed, but many are as easy to grow as tomatoes, especially if you have a simple fluorescent light fixture which can be raised or lowered so that it is always just slightly above the plant tops. Seed catalogs and packets give instructions about seed depth and any special needs the seeds have. Many prairie species, for instance, require light to germinate, so the seeds should be sprinkled on top of the soil, rather than buried.

For seeding, use a special seedling mixture, such as the type made from peat and vermiculite, which is available in garden stores. Any pots or containers that will hold soil securely and drain from the bottom can be used, but stay away from terra cotta, which dries out too quickly. The soil mixture must be kept thoroughly moist until the seeds sprout, then misted whenever the surface dries. Hardy species can begin to spend part of the day outdoors in their pots in partial or full shade as soon as the temperature rises above freezing. Gradually increase their outdoor exposure until planting time.

Some seeds can be sown directly in the garden. These are divided into two groups: seeds that should be sown before the last spring frost date and seeds that wait until later. Many annuals are most easily grown this way, and most of the hardy ones can be sown anytime after the snow melts. They germinate as soon as the soil is warm enough and sprout in the moisture left from winter. Seeds of frost-tender species — those which have to wait until after the last spring frost — are best sown directly in the garden in early summer soon after a rain, but if this is not possible, wet the ground before seeding. To catch water, the seeded area should be slightly lower than the surrounding soil. If you are seeding in rows, sow the seeds in shallow

Where winters are harsh, seeds can be sown indoors.

ditches and mark the row ends with small twigs.

If you are seeding in drifts or patches, you may want to draw a perimeter around the planting with white flour or string; seedlings can take a week or more to emerge, and identification can be tricky when they do. Check the seeded area every day, and water with a fine spray if it dries out. Once the seedlings emerge, they quickly develop a deep root system if watering is limited to no more than once a day. Self-sown seeds of hardy annuals take care of themselves, sprouting when conditions are best.

Cuttings

Many of the plants in the dry garden can be multiplied from softwood cuttings. Artemisia, lavender, rosemary and penstemon are a few. In early summer, when the new growth is still soft, take a stem tip about as long as your finger, strip off all but the top couple of leaves, dip the base in rooting hormone, and plant the cutting to about half its length in a pot of damp sand or seedling mixture, several cuttings per pot (you will probably have some failures). Place the pots in a shady spot outdoors, water them, and cover with something transparent.

Single cuttings can be covered with drinking glasses; flats can be covered with the plastic domes that protect baked goods. Weight the top down so that it will not blow off. When new growth starts, remove the lid, but replace it if the cuttings wilt. As soon as they can survive without the lid, transplant each cutting into its own pot. Let it grow for another couple of weeks before planting out. Then follow the rules as for any potted transplant, whether purchased or homegrown.

Transplanting

Make sure the soil in the plant pot is wet, then tip the plant out. If the plant is root-bound — roots circle round and round inside the pot — tease the roots away from the soil ball before planting. Pour water into the planting hole, and set the plant at the same depth it grew in its pot. Press the soil down around the roots, and water again.

Healthy root growth of seedling marigolds.

The general rule with transplants, including annuals, perennials, shrubs and trees, is to water them regularly until new growth begins — the sign that roots have grown into the surrounding soil. This may not mean daily watering (in fact, watering too frequently encourages shallow root growth, and you want the roots to grow deep), but it may be as often as twice a week for shrubs and trees, every second day for annuals and perennials. At Prairie Habitats Nursery in Manitoba, owner John Morgan marks with red flags anything newly planted to remind himself that these plants need close watching and may need watering. Fall-planted trees, shrubs and perennials need deep soaking, just as they would if planted in spring. Do not fertilize them. It is no longer recommended that top growth be pruned back after planting, but dead or damaged branches should be trimmed off. Perennial plants need as much foliage as possible for root development.

Shading transplants in sunny places for the first few days will help them adjust to the stress of planting. Temporary shade can be provided by cut fern fronds, evergreen branches or a portable lath roof. The only trees and shrubs that require staking are any which are top-heavy or are growing in windy places. In most cases, the stake should be removed after one growing season. The trunk will strengthen if the tree is allowed some movement in the wind.

Planting Time

In the dry garden, all planting and transplanting are best done in spring or fall. In spring, the soil will likely have some moisture from winter. The northern plant-nursery business hits its stride in spring, and most mail-order shipping is done then. But hot, dry summer weather may soon follow planting time, making it difficult for new plants to become established. Fall planting often works better, from August through October, or at least six weeks before freeze-up in cold climates. Soil temperatures are still high enough for root growth, fall rains may arrive, and the new roots will have all next spring to grow. Also, plant prices are usually marked down in fall. In zones 6-10, fall planting is a matter of course.

Fall planting is not wise for any species considered only marginally hardy in your area. These plants need the advantage of an entire growing season before they must endure their first winter.

Antidesiccants

Evergreens should be watered in late fall the year they are planted and, thereafter, following a very dry summer. Otherwise, they should be able to survive the winter on their own, although they may suffer some browning and needle loss. To help prevent this, some growers use antidesiccants, waxy products that coat the leaves of evergreens in winter to minimize moisture loss. Although antidesiccants are sometimes used on needle evergreens, they are most valuable on broad-leaved evergreens — few of which are adapted to dry-summer, cold-winter gardens. The antidesiccants themselves are difficult to use where winters are cold. They must be reapplied at least once during the winter and can be applied only when the temperature stays above 40 degrees F (4.5°C) long enough for the substance to dry without freezing, a winter intermission that may not occur in your garden.

Windbreaks

Any object, however small, on the windward side of a plant will provide that plant with a certain amount of drought protection. Most windbreaks are hedges or rows of wind-tolerant plants situated on the side of the garden that faces the prevailing winds. The higher the windbreak, the farther the protected area extends on the leeward side (away from the wind) — up to 30 times the height of the windbreak. Windbreaks that allow about half the wind to pass through are more effective at preventing turbulence on the leeward side. Windbreaks also help keep snow around the garden.

Windbreaks have a couple of side benefits. Trees and shrubs screen roadside dust and absorb sound, providing a pleasant rustle of their own. They protect wildlife, affording nesting sites for birds as well as food for birds and other animals. And they cut down the wind around any buildings in their wake, lessening the need for heat in winter and shading the buildings in summer. According to the USDA Forest Service, homes protected by shade trees or windbreaks may use 15 to 30 percent less heating energy in winter and 10 to 20 percent less cooling energy in summer.

This effect can be especially dramatic in a city. The average temperature of city cores is rising 1 Fahrenheit degree (0.5°C) per decade relative to the surrounding countryside. Near a reflective surface or paving, temperatures may soar. Preliminary data indicate that an increase of 5 percent in a landscape's tree canopy in city or country can lower July temperatures by 2 to 4 Fahrenheit degrees (1-2°C), while reducing wind speeds by about 10 percent.

In cold-winter places, it makes sense to plant deciduous trees on the southerly side of the yard. These will lightly screen the house and garden during the summer but will allow solar heat and sunlight to pass through in winter, when the trees are leafless. For a rural or prairie property that needs extensive windbreaks, ask for current species and spacing recommendations from the nearest Extension Service in the United States or from the relevant provincial department or ministry of agriculture in Canada.

Some of the genera commonly used for low windbreaks are caragana, cotoneaster, euonymus, lonicera, physocarpus, pinus, potentilla, prinsepia, prunus, ribes, spiraea, syringa, taxus, thuja and viburnum. Any of these plants can be used for an informal hedge, one that requires minimal pruning. For a formal hedge, one with a geometric shape, avoid fast-growing plants and plan to prune at least once a year or as often as every two weeks during the growing season. Do not prune coniferous evergreens beyond the current year's growth, as they will not recover. Only evergreens offer good windbreak value year-round.

Sun and Shade

Windbreaks also provide shade to the garden. Most drought-tolerant plants are described as needing full sun, but full sun in a place with blue sky from horizon to horizon every day is quite different from full sun in a place that is often overcast. All plants need a certain amount of sunlight, even if it is reflected from a nearby surface, but almost all appreciate a bit of shade too, and some shade can allow you to grow plants that would otherwise be impossible. While daylong shade makes any garden difficult, the dappled shade provided by trees, shrubs and tall perennials — or, for that matter, the intermittent shade afforded by a fence, porch railing or slatted roof — provides the best environment for healthy plant growth, especially in a sunny, windy place.

Obviously, some balancing has to be done. Trees provide shade and shelter, but they are water hogs themselves, and those with a lot of feeder roots near the surface will take water you might want for other plants. In a small garden, grow only shrubs or trees that mature at a reasonable height, and provide additional shade with fences, gazebos and other landscape features.

Soil, Fertilizer and Compost

Soil in the dry garden should be improved before you begin planting. Good drainage is especially important. If you are working with an existing weedy garden or a garden that does not thrive, consider salvaging whatever plants you can by digging them up with big root balls, watering them and temporarily putting them in big pots in the shade or heeling them into a cleared area. Then remove all the weeds in the bed, and start fresh by working plenty of organic matter such as compost into at least the top 12 inches (30 cm) of soil.

One inch (2.5 cm) of water will penetrate clay soil 4 inches (10 cm), loam 6 to 8 inches (15-20 cm) and sandy soil 12 to 14 inches (30-35 cm). Sandy soil encourages deeper rooting and drains well but needs watering more frequently than loamy soil. Clay soil holds water longer, but drainage is poor, and once dry, clay is difficult to rework. Compost or another type of organic matter will improve all soil types and their ability to retain water without interfering with drainage. In the *Journal of Soil and Water Conservation*, Berman Hudson states that soils high in organic matter have a significantly higher available water capacity (the amount of water available to roots). The available water capacity of a silt loam containing 15 percent organic matter by volume is more than twice that of a silt loam containing 5 percent organic matter. "Other factors being equal," says Hudson, "soils containing more organic matter can retain more water from each rainfall and make more of it available to plants."

It's tempting to apply fertilizer, but plants that tolerate drought don't need much, if any, and fertilizer, especially nitrogen, can easily do more harm than good. The vegetable garden is an exception. It benefits from plenty of water as well as regular fertilization, but otherwise, err on the side of moderation. Phosphates are often required, so a transplant fertilizer used initially will help plants become established, but a high-nitrogen diet encourages plants to grow lush, green and leggy. Then, when dry weather comes, they quickly wilt. Organic matter is what a dry garden needs — the more, the better. Well-rotted manure that has a balanced nutrient analysis, such as .5-.5-.5, is also excellent. And for most gardeners, organic matter means compost.

If you have a dry garden, you need a compost pile. Compost, a decomposed mixture of vegetable scraps and garden clippings wetted and layered with soil, is free and will help the soil absorb and retain water. It is also a gentle fertilizer. Compost can be piled in the open or within an enclosure.

If you don't have much compost or livestock manure, green manuring is a method of adding the same quality of nutrients and humus. A crop such as ryegrass or buckwheat is allowed to grow just a few inches high, then turned into the soil. In a vegetable garden, the rotation of crops can include one bed devoted to a green-manure crop each season. In a flower garden or wildflower meadow, green manuring must be done the season before the bed is planted.

Mulch

Mulches are blankets, usually of organic materials, laid between plants. Suitable mulch materials include grass clippings, bark chips, salt hay (stiff grass that grows in some coastal marshes), ever-green needles, seaweed and leaf mold (partially composted leaves from the previous fall). The leaves themselves can also be used directly: Run a lawnmower through piles of leaves to shred them, or put the leaves in a garbage can, then chop them with a string trimmer. Leaves make a better soil additive, however, if left to compost for a year. To compost them, add them in small amounts to a compost pile or pile them on their own within an enclosure made of wire or snow fencing. A sprin-kling of high-nitrogen fertilizer or a layer of manure will speed composting. Grass clippings are most easily handled if they dry before use. Evergreen needles make an ideal mulch in dry areas with alkaline soil, but where soils are naturally acidic, they should be confined to acid-loving plants. A power chipper/shredder will turn all weeds, vines, leaves and branches into a good mulch.

There are two types of mulch: summer and

A mulch of fallen leaves helps prevent winter damage.

winter. Both should be at least 2 inches (5 cm) deep. Each offers somewhat different advantages.

Summer Mulch: Summer mulches of organic materials hold in moisture, limit weed growth and moderate temperatures. Recent research in North Carolina has shown that mulches reduce the maxi-mum daily temperature at the soil surface by 4 to 6 Fahrenheit degrees (2-3°C) and increase the mini-mum daily temperature by around 2 to 4 Fahrenheit degrees (1-2°C). The temperature is not affected by the type of organic mulch; the North Carolina test used pine bark, hardwood bark, cedar chips and pine needles. There are additional advantages of a summer mulch. While bare soil can lose three-quarters of the rain that falls on it to runoff and evaporation, almost all that rainfall can be saved by summer mulches. In the vegetable garden, mulching greatly reduces the incidence of fungal-disease infection, especially on tomatoes and potatoes.

Soil splashing onto foliage as a result of rain or watering is the cause of most fungal infections.

To apply the mulch, wait until the soil has warmed in spring and the plants are tall enough to stand above the mulch. Organic mulch applied too early keeps the soil cool. If you have an unexpectedly wet summer, remove any mulch. It can hold too much moisture against plant roots and will attract slugs and snails.

Winter Mulch: Winter mulches also hold moisture in the soil, but their main function is to help protect roots during cold winters. They are most valuable on new plantings or on plants that are only marginally hardy for your area. They are best applied after the ground freezes. If you are mulching trees, make sure the mulch does not come into contact with the bark, or it can cause rotting of the bark and may attract pests and rodents. Remember that snow has been called the poor man's mulch. When the air temperature is minus 22 degrees F (–30°C), 6 feet (1.8 m) of snow can maintain a soil temperature of 32 degrees (0°C), whereas without snow, the soil would freeze to a depth of 4 feet (1.2 m). Anything you can do to concentrate snowdrifts on planted areas will help protect roots from low winter temperatures and provide more soil moisture in spring. Leave perennial stems in place in fall to help hold snow.

Year-Round Mulches: In some gardens, mulches remain more or less permanently around trees and shrubs and are simply augmented whenever necessary. For instance, there are permeable landscape polypropylene fabrics that are meant to be used around perennials, shrubs and trees. The mulches are covered with gravel, wood chips or another covering that looks attractive and prevents ultraviolet degradation of the mulch. The fabric, in turn, increases the durability of the organic mulch above it. But these mulches are not for everyone. They are expensive, and some growers have had problems with mice tunneling under-

neath. Not only that, but in some studies, these mulches have been found ineffective against perennial weeds. An organic mulch at least 4 inches (10 cm) deep has been shown by the Denver Water Department to be just as effective.

Mulch steadily composts into the soil, so if you want a permanent mulch, you must add to it in spring and fall. Because mulch keeps the soil cool in spring, early growth will be delayed.

Truly xeric plants such as cacti, succulents, artemisias and perennial salvias are better left without a mulch, which can keep too much moisture around the roots.

Additional Winter Protection

Dry winters can be hazardous to plants — especially evergreens, anything newly planted and anything only marginally hardy — which is one reason to apply a winter mulch. Evergreens that turn brown in winter may be losing moisture more quickly than their roots can take it up. Desiccation progresses from buds and needle tissues inward from the edges and tips. Pine and spruce needles turn yellow, then brown. Branch tips of junipers and cedars may die. Sometimes, severe or even complete defoliation follows and may lead to the death of the plant the following spring or summer.

As soon as the ground thaws in spring, damaged evergreens should be given a good watering. Deciduous trees and shrubs may lose branch tips, which appear brown and dried out and may not blossom or leaf out properly in spring. Do not prune away branches until you are sure they are dead. Then prune carefully to restore a balanced shape to the plant.

As well as mulching after the soil freezes, there are other ways to prevent cold and drought injury:

• Grow plants suited to your climatic zone.
• Make sure the soil is reasonably well drained.
• Avoid poor planting locations. Trees and shrubs

TREES UNDER STRESS

Trees have different growth patterns and so show drought damage in different ways. Some trees, including spruce, hemlock, beech and certain ashes, maples and pines, are described as having predetermined growth. This means that their buds develop one year and expand the next. Therefore, if there was drought when the buds were forming, it will show up the following year in stunted growth of new leaves. Another group of trees described as heterophyllous have winter buds that grow during the current season. These species, including birch, poplar, elm, apple, silver maple and some ashes, show the effects of drought the season it occurs by leafing out sparsely.

Other shrubs or trees, including junipers, produce several flushes of growth each year and can stop or start growing as the weather changes, so they may look normal. In many species, mild water stress stimulates flower production. Browning of the needles of evergreen trees and shrubs in winter or during hot summer weather may be unsightly but is not serious unless it carries on for two or three seasons. All evergreens show some browning by fall. Lost needles do not grow back, but if the plant is healthy, it will continue to grow from branch tips. To minimize winter losses, soak the ground around the stem in fall before the soil freezes.

near white or aluminum-sided buildings may be damaged by reflected heat. Only the toughest plants should go in places that are very windy or have poor soil drainage.

- Water trees and shrubs deeply before the ground freezes, especially if the summer or fall has been dry. Plants near the house will probably be especially dry.
- In late summer or fall, do not fertilize, especially with nitrogen, and do not prune plants. Both practices encourage growth that is less winter-hardy. Wait until spring.

The Vegetable Plot

Vegetables require plenty of water. Most are annuals that grow quickly from seed to harvest in a season and when harvested are more than 90 percent water. The few vegetables that are perennials — asparagus, rhubarb, Jerusalem artichoke — are among the most drought-tolerant because they can take advantage of the wet ground of early spring. There are a couple of lesser-known perennial vegetables. One is sea kale (*Crambe maritima*),

with edible young shoots that are generally blanched under pots and beautiful big leaves ornamental enough for a flower bed. Another is Good King Henry (*Chenopodium bonus-henricus*), which produces a huge crop of somewhat spinach-like spring greens and edible seeds on stems sometimes taller than 9 feet (2.7 m).

But the vegetables almost everyone wants to grow are more demanding of water and care. The National Gardening Association estimates the following season-long water requirements for vegetables:

- 9 inches (23 cm): spinach and leaf lettuce
- 12 inches (30 cm): cabbage family
- 18 inches (45 cm): cucumbers, onions, pole beans, beets, carrots, eggplants, peas, peppers, squashes, muskmelons, sweet potatoes
- 24 inches (60 cm): tomatoes
- 25 to 30 inches (64-75 cm): potatoes, celery

This water must be provided all season. The general rule for the vegetable garden is that it needs 1 inch (2.5 cm) of water per week, which translates into

Most vegetables need deep, frequent watering, even those like bell peppers, which thrive in warmth and sun.

64 gallons (240 L) per 100 square feet (9.3 m²). You will probably have to water deeply every two days. A vegetable garden will survive with much less, provided it is mulched, the soil is high in organic matter and spot watering is done on plants at their neediest times, especially right after transplanting and then while fruit is enlarging and ripening.

Too little water at critical growth periods can mean undersized plants, fallen blossoms, fallen fruit or small, tough, misshapen or bitter-tasting fruit. Leaf vegetables are undersized. Onions and radishes become hot and ornery, potatoes develop hollow hearts, and beets, radishes and carrots are small, pale and woody.

All this may mean that if your garden is dry and apt to be neglected, you will be better off buying vegetables from the supermarket or at a pick-your-own farm. But if you have any water at all — enough, at any rate, to get seedlings under way early in the season and to water sporadically — you can grow most vegetables. You probably have at least one thing going for you: Dry gardens are often sunny gardens, and most vegetables thrive in sun. Desert areas like California's Imperial Valley are among the most productive places for vegetables, provided the ground is plentifully irrigated.

No Raised Beds

While raised beds can be attractive and easy to tend, they are not practical for vegetables in a dry garden, because they quickly dry out. Instead, vegetables should grow in flat or gently hilled ground, in soil improved with as much compost as possible and mulched roughly 4 inches (10 cm) deep as soon as the plants are tall enough, usually early June, and preferably after a good rain or watering.

In a small garden, the ring method, in which plants are grown in a circle around a central cage filled with compost, helps concentrate water and nutrients in one spot. Watering is done into the compost reservoir.

Walk only in pathways, even if these are nothing more than indentations in the soil between beds of vegetables. Leave the area directly around the plants untrampled; loose soil aids root growth and holds water better. Also, keep up with weeding, because weeds can grow faster than vegetables and are good at grabbing whatever water is available. Leave pulled weeds in the pathways as extra mulch. Remember, too, that some common garden weeds, including purslane, lamb's-quarters, pigweed and nettle, are drought-tolerant and as edible and at least as nutritious as lettuce or spinach.

CHAPTER TWO

THE PLEASURE PRIORITY

Dryland gardening isn't just a matter of choosing the right plants and techniques; it's also landscaping. Everyone wants to be able to look at, wander through and spend time in a garden that looks beautiful. We may plan the most water-efficient garden possible, a garden geared for survival no matter what the climate offers, but our garden still has to fulfill our desires for peace and renewal.

Landscaping a dryland garden isn't very different from planning any garden. As always, you are limited by the size of your space and its many features, including trees, fences and buildings, not only your own but also those around you. Your garden site may be sunny or shady, windy or calm, sloped or flat, rocky, sandy or gifted with deep loam. While you may have to rein in your plant choices according to what is practical, you can still choose your favorite leaf and flower colors and combine them in ways you find most attractive, whether you want them to be as bright as a gypsy dance or as subdued as a forest glade or a wedding in white. Install paths and flagstones to define garden areas, while allowing you and your visitors to walk through the garden without damaging plants or compressing the soil.

A drought-tolerant bed includes spirea, daylilies, cranesbills and annual poppies.

In a dry climate, a small water feature can provide intriguing visual and textural contrast.

What makes designing a dryland garden different is that you have priorities in addition to horticultural indulgence. You can't simply buy anything at the local nursery. For the most part, you need plants that are self-reliant. You may be grouping plants with similar preferences, such as the need for more irrigation, better-drained soil or a position closer to the water barrel. You may be installing a drip or trickle watering system. As described in the next chapter, you may be reducing or eliminating lawn in favor of other ground covers, whether plants or paving.

Choose a mixture of annuals, perennials, shrubs and, if space permits, trees. Also, a blend of evergreens and deciduous plants will provide welcome color and visual interest all year. Broadleaf evergreens can be grown in southerly zones, while there are many coniferous evergreens for the coldest climates. Use ground covers, both herbaceous and evergreen, to unite taller garden elements with blankets of color and texture.

A pond can make a pleasing thematic and environmental contrast. Even a small water feature that requires only a few gallons of water will provide a rest for the eyes and drinking water for pets as well as birds and other wildlife. Introduce a goldfish or two to gobble any mosquito larvae that hatch.

You may also want to incorporate garden furniture, statuary, wind chimes, bird feeders and bird houses. Choose their positions carefully so that your garden becomes an extension of your home, an outdoor room with features that attract wildlife and welcome visitors.

BEGINNING STRATEGIES

The object in a perennial bed is to have plants just touching or slightly overlapping, but the first year after they are planted, perennials may not bloom at all, and it could be three or four years before you have a satisfying clump. In the beginning, there will be tiny plants here and there with gaping spaces between. It makes sense, in the first year or two, to fill these spaces with annuals that will give the border an overall impression of completeness, even though those plants may not be there again the following season.

If you find that when the perennials do start to bloom or grow larger, they are growing in the wrong places, make a note to move them in the fall or the following spring. It is best not to disturb them in summer. If the weather is still dry at moving time, water the transplants thoroughly and cover them during the day with large flower pots or bushel baskets to provide shade until they are rooted well enough so they don't wilt during the day.

Using Rocks

Rocks suit dry gardens aesthetically and practically. Many drought-tolerant plants are native to rocky or scree areas. Consider rocks not only as accents, borders and mulches but also on their own — in the establishment of gravel paths or stone patios. The soil under and shaded by rocks stays cooler and wetter than the surrounding ground, and large rocks act as windbreaks, enabling high-alpine plants, for instance, to survive bright sun and constant wind. Lowland plants can benefit in the same way. On arid sites, the placement of a few large rocks around each transplant increases rooting success. If your soil is rocky, the initial planting can be difficult, but plants that demand well-drained soil, whether they are directly seeded or set in place when small, will send their roots through the rocks and may ultimately be tougher than those in deep soil.

There are a few things to keep in mind when working with rocks. Remember that it is difficult to mow or keep weeds down directly around rocks. Leave an area of bare ground or low ground cover between rocks and mowed lawn. Rocks exposed to the sun should not be used as mulches near the

Stones and xeric plants such as sempervivum make attractive and reliable partners in a dryland garden.

south side of a home in places where summers are hot. They can act as a heat sink, heating during the day and releasing heat at night, contributing to the warmth of the house. Gravel or larger stones make an attractive mulch for the dry garden, but fallen leaves and other organic matter will eventually create soil pockets between the stones, and where there is soil, weeds will follow. Rake or clean your stone mulch at least once a season.

Containers

Containers can be attractive and useful in any garden, including a dry one. Roots confined within a small area, such as a container, are more dependent than ever upon the gardener for their water supply, but containers afford the possibility of gardening in places like patios and porches and can be the best way to show off thirsty or otherwise demanding plants you want to highlight, such as azaleas or miniature roses. This can also be a way

A strawberry pot holds a selection of trailing sedums.

to grow common, colorful bedding annuals such as petunias and geraniums in such a small space that they won't need much water, even though you'll likely have to water them daily.

Place containers of water-demanding plants in partly shaded places. The black plastic pots that nursery trees and shrubs are sometimes sold in can heat to over 120 degrees F (48°C) in the summer sun, hot enough to bake the roots. Containers that are set into the ground, to their rims, will stay cooler, cutting down on watering needs. They may even root through the drainage holes into the soil. If you have to leave the containers untended for more than a day, take time to place them in a shallow basin of water in an area that is shady all day.

For moisture-loving plants, any sort of container that is porous, from a basket to wood or terra-cotta clay, should be lined with plastic to retain soil moisture, unless the container is partially buried. Drainage holes are usually not needed for moisture-loving plants, except when the containers are placed in deep shade.

Containers can also display drought-tolerant plants, and in this case must be porous or have drainage holes. Troughs made of traditional stone or a lightweight copy called hypertufa — a mixture of peat, vermiculite and Portland cement — are perfect for cacti and succulents. Drought-tolerant plants that are content with relatively little soil are good choices for containers such as pottery bowls, clay pots and strawberry planters. Place pots in sun or part shade. A few examples of plants which require very little watering but are decorative all season, include:

- any of the trailing types of sedum
- upright sedums such as 'Autumn Joy'
- any of the sempervivums, echeverias or jovibarbas
- artemisias such as the low 'Silver Brocade' and tall 'Valerie Finnis'
- variegated Solomon's seal (*Polygonatum odoratum*)
- tall succulents such as yucca and agave
- cacti, whether houseplants or hardy types
- ribbon grass (*Phalaris arundinacea* 'Picta') and blue fescue (*Festuca glauca*)

Even if perennials are winter hardy in the garden, they may not survive the winter in a container. Take the plants out of the pots in fall, and plant them in the ground to ensure winter survival.

CHAPTER THREE

HERBS

One traditional type of garden that is by its nature suited to low-water landscapes is the herb garden. Many of its plants belong to two plant families that have strong survival instincts: the mint family (Labiatae) and the dill family (Umbelliferae). The former group includes many natives of dry, sunny places, while the latter has taproots that descend quickly to moister depths. Many additional herbs have ancestors that grow wild near the Mediterranean, an area known for its dry summers.

While there are plants in other chapters that have historically assumed positions in a medicinal garden, the plants listed in the following pages can also be grown beyond the herb garden, especially in containers or shoulder to shoulder with perennial flowers. Annuals such as basil and summer savory can be watered frequently if grown in a large pot. Tender perennial herbs such as rosemary, lemon verbena and bay, all of which are safely wintered outdoors only in zone 7 or warmer, can live in a pot year-round in cooler zones. Give them a sandy soil mixture, and when they are indoors, allow the soil to dry between waterings. They need plenty of light in a place that is preferably cooler than 70 degrees F (21°C) by day and even cooler but above freezing by night. Hardy potted herbs left outdoors should be buried up to their rims in fall, then mulched.

The classic perennial herb garden is a geometrically designed plot that is walled or defined by pathways or hedges and a central eye-catching feature.

AGASTACHE 'GOLDEN JUBILEE'

Agastache foeniculum; A. anisata

Anise-hyssop, licorice mint
Annual

The usual green-leaved version of this mint relative has the distinct scent of licorice, and makes a delicious tea either on its own or blended with other herbs. Foliage and flowers can also be used as edible garnishes. Although perennial in zones 8 to 10, it is generally grown everywhere as an annual, since it self-sows so plentifully that its constant survival is assured. It grows 2 to 3 feet (60-90 cm) tall, looking much like its relative catnip, with 4-to-6-inch (10-15 cm) spires of lilac-colored flowers for four to five weeks in summer. There is also a white-flowered version. Like catnip, it will wilt during a long dry spell but revives quickly after a brief watering and can even be grown in sand. It is easy from seeds sown directly in the garden anytime in spring. For a more ornamental effect but no licorice scent, look for 'Golden Jubilee,' a Fleuroselect and All-America winner, also easy from seeds, which has sunny yellow-green foliage all season and bears spires of lilac flowers. It is excellent in flower arrangements.

Additional ornamental versions of agastache, all good in tea, include 'Firebird,' with maroon markings and orange flower spikes, and 'Heather Queen,' with lilac-colored flowers. *A. barberi* 'Tutti Fruiti' has grayish foliage and red flowers. Where the frost-free season is sufficiently long, it can reach 6 feet (180 cm).

Allium species

Chives, garlic
Zones 3 to 10

Chives (*A. schoenoprasum*) thrive in moist, fertile soil but will also survive in dry ground, although the leaves will be smaller and more slender. Whether the soil is dry or moist, give the herb a spot with some sun. Chives are decorative in a flower garden, with their tubular deep green foliage and lilac umbels, which keep their color for a month or so in late spring and lure bees and butterflies. Grow them from seed or bulbs. Once it takes hold, this plant can be divided easily anytime during the year. Chives will self-sow if some flowers are left to go to seed, but seedlings are easily pulled out where they are not wanted.

A similar species, but with the addition of a distinctive garlic flavor, is garlic chives (*A. tuberosum*), which is a little less vigorous than regular chives but ornamental enough for a flower bed. Garlic chives have flatter leaves and taller stems bearing white flowers.

A. sativum (garlic) is not ornamental and requires rich, well-watered soil, so it should be confined to the vegetable garden. The arching leaves grow about 18 inches (45 cm) tall, and the seed heads of some types grow taller than 5 feet (150 cm). Garlic needs a long season to fill out fully, and if planted in late fall, it can take advantage of the cool, moist soil of winter and early spring to get a head start. Plant locally grown cloves if possible. Mulch plants after they sprout in spring.

ALLIUM SCHOENOPRASUM

Anethum graveolens
Dill
Annual

Dill thrives in rich, moist soil, where it may reach 3 feet (1 m) in height, yet it will grow, although not as tall, in very dry soil, provided the seeds have enough moisture to germinate in spring and the seedlings can get their taproots down before the soil dries. Even in a dry garden, dill often self-sows to reappear the next year. The ferny foliage is used in salads, the seeds in pickles and vinegars. 'Dukat' is an especially leafy variety. If you need dill in quantity for pickling, broadcast the seeds anytime in spring and thin the seedlings to 4 inches (10 cm) apart. Dill is also pretty enough to grow as a green-topped ornamental in flower beds and in arrangements, so several cultivars were developed for that purpose; 'Vierling' has thicker stems than most, and plenty of foliage. The dwarf 'Fernleaf' is about 18 inches tall.

Armoracia rusticana
Horseradish
Zones 3 to 10

The thick, fleshy taproots that are grated to make a pungent sauce carry horseradish through all kinds of inclement weather, from floods to deep freezes to summer-long droughts. In other words, horseradish can be very hard to get rid of once you have it in the garden, and if you till the roots, you will have it everywhere. The coarse green leaves may be taller than a foot (30 cm) from the ground. For the strongest flavor, harvest the roots when the ground is cold, either just before it freezes in fall or just after the

ground thaws in spring. Horseradish can be immediately grated and made into sauce — beware its eye-stinging powers — or it can be washed and stored whole for several weeks in a plastic bag in the refrigerator.

Artemisia species
French tarragon, wormwood
Zones vary

Artemisias are dependable inhabitants of the dry garden, and *A. dracunculus sativa* (French tarragon) is no exception, despite a delicate anise flavor that suggests haute cuisine. The plant is unimpressive-looking, with slender green leaves on a bushy, lax plant 12 to 18 inches (30-45 cm) tall. It can be grown only from plant divisions or cuttings. If your tarragon has been grown from seed or has no flavor, it is probably Russian tarragon, a plant not worth including in the herb garden. French tarragon is hardy in zones 5 to 10, preferably in well-drained, slightly alkaline soil. In zone 5, mulch it in fall to ensure its survival. Leaves can be harvested at any time.

   A. absinthium (wormwood), hardy in zones 3 to 10, has an ancient reputation as a medicine for both internal and external use, but its power gained notoriety in Europe a century ago when absinthe, a liqueur that contains it, proved addictive and physically and mentally destructive. There are a few ornamental forms, all around knee height, with bright silver leaves that are eye-catching from summer until early winter. 'Lambrook Silver' is widely available. 'Powis Castle' has performed especially well at the Xeriscape Demonstration Garden in Plainview, New York. Wormwood is a short-lived

ARTEMISIA ABSINTHIUM

perennial whose woody stems do not die back to the ground in winter. It puts up with any well-drained soil in sun or part shade. In some areas, it is invasive.

Borago officinalis
Borage
Annual

Borage is grown mostly for its sky-blue flowers, but the fresh young leaves can also be used as edible decorations or in salads. There are also pink- and white-flowering varieties. Borage does best in well-drained, even sandy soil in sun or part shade where it grows 1 to 2 feet (30-60 cm) tall. Sow seeds in spring directly where they are to grow, since borage does not transplant well. Keep the soil moist until the plants are well established. It often self-sows.

Calendula officinalis
Pot marigold
Annual

This is the plant called marigold in England, although it is not a close relative of *Tagetes*, the plant called marigold in North America. *C. officinalis* has a long history of medicinal and "pot" (cooking) use in Britain and Europe. The usual flower colors are orange and yellow, although the flowers, single or double, can also appear in shades of cream and apricot. There are many cultivars, from tiny to 30 inches (75 cm) tall. All are edible; the fresh petals can be used as a saffron substitute. Deadheading prolongs the production of blooms. Calendula is easily grown from seeds sown 1/4 inch (6 mm) deep directly in the garden in early spring in zones 2 to 7; in late summer or early fall in zones 8 to 10. It can tolerate poor, dry soil but does best in partial shade and appreciates cool weather. Deadhead spent flowers.

CALENDULA OFFICINALIS

Chamaemelum nobile; Anthemis nobilis
Roman chamomile
Zones 5 to 8

Chamomile is a decorative perennial. Its relaxed stems grow about 1 foot (30 cm) long with feathery, gray-green foliage and small white daisies in summer. Outside the herb garden, it can grow anywhere in sun or light shade, provided the soil is well drained. The flowers are used to make a relaxing tea in the same way as the annual version *Matricaria*. Start seeds indoors several weeks before the last frost date or buy plants. The double-flowered 'Flore Pleno' is just 3 inches (7.5 cm) tall. There is a creeping, non-flowering variety 'Treneague,' selected for use as a ground cover. It can be underplanted with bulbs but can't compete with weeds or grasses. Mulch it in zone 5. Since 'Treneague' does not flower, it must be grown from cuttings or divisions and has no culinary use.

Cichorium intybus
Chicory
Zones 3 to 10

Chicory is a noxious roadside weed throughout much of North America, proving its adaptability to neglect and poor, dry soil. The blue daisy flowers that bloom along 4-foot (1.2 m) or taller stems are pretty, however, and can be used as edible decorations or in teas and salads. There are also white- and pink-flowered varieties. The long taproot can be cleaned, chopped and roasted to extend coffee beans or to make a substitute for coffee — in appearance if not fragrance or flavor. The strains of chicory developed for the vegetable garden, some of which are forced into the tender, pale green delicacies known as Belgian endive, need plenty of water and care.

Coriandrum sativum
Cilantro, coriander
Annual

Coriandrum is a plant with two kitchen names; one for its leaves, another for its seeds. As a leafy vegetable it is called cilantro, indispensable in the cuisine of China, the Middle East and Central and South America. The deeply notched leaves, which resemble those of parsley, can be harvested as soon as the plant is sufficiently robust and should be picked regularly to promote new growth. 'Santo' is a bolt-resistant variety for gardeners who want mostly leaves. Leaf production stops when the tiny flowers bloom, followed by small capsules — coriander — that must be gathered as soon as they turn brown, before they drop from the plant. Drop entire seed heads into a paper bag, allow to dry and then shake off the capsules.

Coriander needs average, well-drained soil and prefers sun. Sow the seeds in late spring, after frost danger. If the plants are allowed to go to seed, they may self-sow.

Hyssopus officinalis
Hyssop
Zones 3 to 7

Hyssop is one of many ancient herbs rarely used today in either medicine or the kitchen. Fortunately, it has several aesthetic virtues. It forms a neat shrub about 1 foot (30 cm) tall in sun or part shade; it is covered with tiny dark green leaves that persist for most of the winter, and in late summer, spikes as tall as 2 feet (60 cm) are decorated with whorls of small flowers, usually blue but sometimes white or pink. Hyssop is an ideal plant for edging a herb bed. It will put up with clipping and is easy to propagate from spring cuttings, so you can make a row from a single plant in a season. Hyssop prefers well-drained, slightly alkaline soil in sun. It is hardy but short-lived, so cuttings should be taken every two or three years to renew it.

Lavandula species
Lavender
Zones vary

Lavender's gray-blue foliage denotes a plant that likes to dry thoroughly between waterings. It needs well-drained soil, preferably alkaline and sandy. In areas that are wet in winter, lavender should be grown in a raised bed, on a slope or in a container of sandy soil. Give it full sun or a bit of shade and little or no fertilizer. In places where it is not hardy, it can be confined to a pot and wintered

LAVANDULA ANGUSTIFOLIA

indoors, where it should be grown in a sunny spot and allowed to dry thoroughly between waterings. Lavender forms a bush of fragrant, very narrow foliage and, in summer, produces spikes of flowers that are typically lavender-blue, although there are also pinks and purples.

L. angustifolia (English lavender) is the hardiest species, zones 5 to 10. 'Twickle Purple' is deep purple. 'Pink Perfume' is 2 feet (60 cm) tall with pink flowers. 'Rosea' also blooms pink but grows only half as tall. 'Lady' is an All-America Selection that flowers the first year from seed. The cultivars 'Hidcote' and 'Munstead' may survive in zone 4, but in zones 4 and 5 all should have a winter mulch.

L. dentata (Spanish lavender) is a tender perennial (zones 8 to 9) that can survive only light frosts. It grows 1 to 3 feet (30-90 cm) tall with densely hairy, strongly aromatic gray leaves. There are many cultivars with different flower colors.

The hybrid *L.* x *intermedia* (*L. angustifolia* x *L. latifolia*), sometimes called lavendin, is slightly less hardy than *L. angustifolia*, and needs mulching in zone 5. Cultivars include 'Grosso' and 'Provence.'

In trials involving six varieties

of lavender at Ohio State University in Columbus, Ohio, where winter temperatures fell to minus 24 degrees F (−31°C), the best survivor was 'Hidcote,' followed by 'Munstead.' More than half of the *L.* x *intermedia* plants survived but all the *L. dentata* plants died.

Levisticum officinale
Lovage
Zones 3 to 10

Looking like the jolly green celery plant that managed to grow as tall as 7 feet (2.1 m), lovage is as much a lover of rich, moist soil as its better-known cousin. But perhaps because it is a perennial, lovage will survive far drier conditions than celery, especially if given rich, deep soil. It will grow in sun or shade. In late summer, the dry stalks should be broken off at the base and discarded.

Leaves and young stems can be used as a strongly flavored substitute for parsley or celery; the leafy stems are especially good as stir sticks in tomato drinks. Known in Europe as the magi plant, lovage is a good seasoning for vegetable and meat soups. Leaves can be frozen or dried for winter.

LEVISTICUM OFFICINALE

Lippia citriodora; Aloysia triphylla
Lemon verbena
Zones 7 to 10

This tender, semi-evergreen shrub has woody stems and smooth, pointed foliage that smells strongly of citrus; you'll know if you brush past it. The foliage tastes like lemon, too, so it makes a delicious tea whether fresh or dried. Lemon verbena is evergreen in zones 9 and 10, where it can grow as tall as 10 feet (3 m), and deciduous in zones 7 and 8. In colder zones, it can be kept year-round in a large container that is taken outdoors after spring frosts and brought back indoors before fall frosts. Indoors, this shrub does best near a sunny window where nights are cool. It may drop its leaves, but they will regrow.

Marrubium species
Horehound
Zones 4 to 9

Not popular as a kitchen herb, horehound is best known for horehound "candies," bitter-tasting confections occasionally prescribed for colds and sore throats, probably consigned to the same dreaded spot in the medi-

MARRUBIUM VULGARE

cine cabinet as castor oil. But horehound earns its place in the herb garden today due to its appearance; its grayish, hairy ("hoary") foliage is handsome all season. In poor, dry soil, plants grow about 1 foot (30 cm) tall and from late summer through fall, clusters of tiny white flowers bloom at intervals up the stems. *M. vulgare* is the usual herb-garden occupant. The cultivar 'Green Pompom,' used in flower arrangements, has greenish flower clusters. *M. incanum* (woolly horehound) is more ornamental and drought-resistant, with woolly white foliage. In colder zones, mulch horehound after the soil freezes to help ensure survival. Propagate by division or from cuttings.

MATRICARIA RECUTITA

Matricaria species
Chamomile
Annual

The annual type of chamomile (*M. recutita, Chamomilla recutita*), called German, Hungarian or wild chamomile, self-seeds profusely, producing a tangle of willowy stems about 1 foot (30 cm) tall, topped by small white-petaled daisies in early summer. The chamomile-tea fragrance is noticeable after every

MELISSA OFFICINALIS

rain or if you brush by the plants. Annual chamomile will survive with practically no care once the seeds have germinated, but it does need weeding and an open area where it can grow without interference. Seeds can be sown in fall or spring. Handpick the flowers in summer, and use them fresh or dry them to store. They can be used on their own or combined with other herbs to make tea.

Melissa officinalis
Lemon balm
Zones 4 to 8

Lemon balm looks much like its close relative mint and is similarly rambunctious, growing 2 or 3 feet (60-90 cm) tall and spreading rapidly by rhizomes. You may want to surround it with lawn or confine it in a large container. The main difference is in the flavor and fragrance of the wrinkled leaves, not mint but distinctly lemon. Use them fresh as edible garnishes, boil them as tea, or dry them for later use. Lemon balm does best with some winter cold. Give it sun or shade and dry, poor, preferably slightly alkaline soil.

MENTHA SPICATA

Mentha species
Mint
Zones 3 to 10

The hardy perennial mints have a reputation for being not only tolerant of soggy ground but water guzzlers as well — these plants will thrive under a drippy gutter, or eavestrough, or in a bog garden, where they are apt to grow about 2 feet (60 cm) tall and spread thickly and rapidly by rhizome. Even when the soil dries out, mint survives, although it stays smaller and curtails its invasive ways. One species, *M. rotundifolia* (apple mint, woolly mint), is sometimes dubbed dryland mint because it is especially amenable to dry conditions.

Because of their wandering rhizomes, mints should be kept away from smaller plants and are good candidates for a big pot, but the pot must be protected in winter beyond zone 6 by being buried up to its rim in fall. If you grow mint in a pot, water it regularly and prune it back to keep it looking lush and neat. Divide the plant when it is crowded. For best flavor, pick leaves and stem tips before flowering. Leaves can be dried till they are crisp, then stored in airtight jars. The best-flavored

mints are grown from cuttings or plant divisions, not from seed. Most commonly available are *M.* x *piperita* (peppermint), whose leaves have smooth edges, and *M. spicata* (spearmint), whose leaves are jagged. Other species and varieties have subtly different flavors and foliage that may be silver or variegated.

Nepeta cataria
Catnip
Zones 3 to 8

Catnip is a mint relative that grows wild and weedy where it is content. Its early-spring sprouting is heralded by sniffing cats. As it grows, the cats chew it and later roll in it. Eventually, plants reach as tall as 3 feet (1 m) and are topped with spires of pink flowers. Catnip grows despite season-long neglect, although it can look threadbare and seedy by late summer. It resembles anise-hyssop and has a similar tendency to self-sow profusely. Harvest shoot tips while they are still lush and green in spring and early summer, let them dry on trays in the sun or in a barely warm oven, then stuff them into small cloth bags for cat toys. Or use fresh or dried catnip to make a soothing herbal tea for humans.

Origanum species
Oregano; sweet marjoram
Annual or perennial

Perennial oregano spreads into an attractive 1-foot (30 cm) mound that makes a good ground cover around taller plants or at the front of a sunny herb garden in dry, well-drained, somewhat alkaline soil in zones 5 to 10. The small, grayish leaves can be used fresh or dried for

ORIGANUM VULGARE

dishes such as pizza and other Mediterranean foods. The regular variety is decorative, but even more attractive are selections or species meant for edging flower beds. 'Hopleys' has rose-colored flowers. 'Aureum' is golden, although not strongly flavored. 'Compacta' and *O. pulchellum* grow just 6 inches (15 cm) tall, the latter with pale pink flowers.

Oregano needs well-drained soil to survive the winter and is dependably hardy only to about zone 5, so where winters are colder, it should be mulched heavily or brought indoors for the winter. There, it should be allowed to dry thoroughly between deep waterings done only often enough to prevent wilting.

The annual version is *O. majorana* (sweet marjoram), which has a more delicate flavor. Its seeds can be lightly covered directly in the garden after the last spring frost.

Portulaca oleracea sativa
French purslane
Annual

The cultivated form of a common weed also grows into a spreading mat of small, succulent leaves in hot, dry weather and in the driest sandy ground. The young foliage, rich in vitamin C and antioxidants, is very nutritious and can be cooked in soups or added to salads. Purslane grows easily from seeds sprinkled on the ground in spring and often self-sows if allowed to flower. 'Aurea' is a decorative golden-leaved form that needs more moisture.

Rosmarinus officinalis
Rosemary
Zones 7 to 10

Where it is hardy, rosemary forms a fragrant, drought-tolerant evergreen ground cover or shrub as tall as 5 or 6 feet (1.5-1.8 m). In winter and early spring, small lilac-colored flowers bloom. In cooler zones, rosemary is generally grown in a large pot where it may reach 1 foot (30 cm) or taller and will need watering whenever the soil dries out. Give it a spot in partial shade, with the container partly buried to help insulate the roots and cut down on watering needs. Before the first fall frost, bring the pot indoors to a cool, bright location. Branch tips can be cut at any time for use in the kitchen. The pot can go back outdoors after the last spring frost.

To start a new plant, strip the foliage from a bottom branch and bend the stem gently where it will contact the ground. Make sure this layer is held firmly in place, and stake the branch tip to hold it upright. It should root by the end of the grow-

ROSMARINUS OFFICINALIS

ing season and can then be cut from the parent plant. There are several varieties. The 2-foot (60 cm) 'Salem' has blue flowers. Both 'Huntington Carpet' and 'Prostratus' are low-growing. 'Miss Jessup's Upright' can reach 6 feet (180 cm), excellent for hedging where it is hardy.

Ruta graveolens
Rue, herb of grace
Zones 4 to 10

This herb has a strong, bitter, musky fragrance once thought to counteract sadness, unpleasantness, evil and rue, or regret. But rue is not the way to banish sadness from every garden; it is poisonous if ingested in large amounts, and merely handling the plant gives some people an itchy rash and blisters that are intensified by exposure to sunlight. Wear gardening gloves unless you know that you are not sensitive to it. On the plus side, it is a conversation piece, and rue's deeply indented bluish foliage and yellow summer flowers make it a beautiful 1-foot-tall (30 cm) shrubby perennial that can be used as a herb-garden hedge. It needs sun and good soil but tends to be short-lived.

Salvia officinalis
Sage
Zones 5 to 9

Many sages there are, but only this one carries the species name *offici-nalis*, designating it as an official plant of the herbalists and apothe-caries — a medicinal staple. The genus name *Salvia* means a plant that saves, and our own word "sage" suggests wisdom and goodness. An old saying asks, "Why should a man die while sage grows in his garden?" Now, sage is primarily a cooking herb. It is also beautiful, with wrin-kled, grayish "sage green" leaves on sprawling woody stems that grow about 18 inches (45 cm) tall. In summer, spikes of pale blue flowers bloom. Sage is a short-lived peren-nial that does better in well-drained, dryish, sunny soil than in dampness or shade. Renew it frequently from seed or tip cuttings.

There are several varieties of *S. officinalis*, and many other species and varieties of culinary and medici-nal salvia, most of which are less winter hardy than *S. officinalis*. Golden sage ('Aurea,'), with green-and-gold variegated foliage, purple sage ('Purpurascens') and tricolor sage ('Tricolor'), which is variegated purple, pink, cream and green, are all hardy to zone 6 or 7. Pineapple sage (*S. elegans*) is generally grown as an annual. It is hardy in zones 9 and 10. Equally tender is *S. lavandifolia* (Spanish sage), which forms a clump of aromatic whitish leaves and 10-inch (25 cm) spikes of pale violet flowers, excellent for the herb garden or rock garden. There are many other species available from herb specialists (see Sources). Strictly ornamental types of salvia are described on pages 125 and 149.

Satureia species
Savory, summer savory
Annual or perennial

There are two distinct types of savory, both of which grow best in well-drained, preferably alkaline soil in sun. Summer savory (*S. hortensis*) is an annual grown from seeds sown about ¹/4-inch (1 cm) deep any time in spring or summer. After the seeds germinate, the wiry stems grow quickly to 1 foot (30 cm) or taller, with tiny, dark green leaves that can be stripped off and added to salads, sausages and cooked vegetable dishes. Harvesting is best done before the small pink or white flowers open. Its flavor is generally more esteemed than that of its perennial cousin winter savory (*S. montana*), hardy in zones 5 to 10 and reaching about 12 inches (30 cm) tall and wide. In the warmer zones, it is evergreen, but in zones 5 and 6 should be cut back and covered with mulch after the ground freezes. The creeping form (*S. spicigera; S. repandra*) is a good ground cover for a sunny herb garden. *S. biflora* is a lemon-scented tender perennial from Africa. All perennial types can be grown from seed or propagated from cuttings.

Symphytum grandiflorum
Comfrey
Zones 3 to 10

A herb of ancient reputation, comfrey excels as a garden plant, although it is no longer recommended for internal use because it contains alkaloids that may be carcinogenic. Long, hairy, pointed green leaves form a rounded mound 3 feet (1 m) or more high and even wider, reminiscent of its cousin borage. Arching spires of bell-shaped flowers, usually pink or white, bloom in summer. Comfrey is a strong plant that will grow in either sun or shade. If it is badly wilted after your summer vacation away from the garden, it can be cut back and will regrow. Situate the plant carefully at the outset, because it is difficult to eradicate once it is settled. It can be divided easily in spring before flowering.

TANACETUM PARTHENIUM

Tanacetum species
Feverfew, tansy
Zones 3 to 10

T. parthenium (*C. parthenium, Matricaria eximia, M. parthenium*), known as feverfew, has fragrant, ferny foliage once used as a bitter-tasting seasoning and occasionally used now to control migraine headaches or to repel rodents from gardens and houses. The small yellow daisies, which bloom in clusters, can be cut and dried as everlastings. It tends to self-sow.

Tansy grows about 2 feet (60 cm) or taller in any soil in sun or part shade. It spreads by rhizome and grows in even the most inhospitable places so it can become a pest. Rather than living to regret planting tansy, confine it to a large pot. The attractive cultivar 'Fernleaf,' which cannot be grown from seed, is less invasive but, nevertheless, should not be trusted among delicate plants. Grown in masses, feverfew can create a ground cover 1 foot (30 cm) high that is green all winter. There is a double-flowered form and another with golden foliage, sometimes called golden feather.

Teucrium chamaedrys
Germander
Zones 5 to 10

Along with lavender and santolina, germander is a common edging plant for the sinuous beds of English knot gardens. It is seldom used today as a medicinal herb, yet it remains decoratively useful because it is a compact, evergreen shrub that takes shearing well. It seldom exceeds 1 foot (30 cm) tall and has woody stems, small, glossy green leaves and purplish flowers in summer. For hedging, space plants 1 foot (30 cm) apart and shear them lightly every spring. There is also a creeping form.

Germander grows in any well-drained soil in sun or part shade. Where the climate is too cold for it to overwinter in the garden, a few cuttings should be kept in a cold frame or a cool place indoors until spring. Germander is easy to grow from seeds that should be given an early start indoors.

THYMUS X CITRIODORUS

Thymus species
Thyme
Zones 4 to 10

Easy, hardy and possessed of a wide spectrum of flavors — from citrus to caraway to unmistakably thyme — the thymes are low-growing, small-leaved herbs that will put up with neglect in terms of watering but not weeding. Most are easily outpaced by grasses and other weeds. They do best in well-drained, slightly acidic soil in sun. Ground-covering species are described on page 72. Among culinary varieties, the standard is *T. vulgaris* (common thyme), which forms a low bush 6 to 12 inches (15 to 30 cm) tall. There are two strains: English (German or winter) thyme, which has broad, dark green leaves, and French (summer) thyme, which has narrow grayish leaves and a sweeter flavor. The form 'Argenteus' is shrublike, about 8 inches (20 cm) tall with variegated gray-and-cream foliage. Just as hardy are caraway thyme (*T. herba-barona*) and the distinctly citrus-scented lemon thyme (*T. x citriodorus*), which has upright, bushy growth and variegated golden foliage. There are additional flavors and leaf colors in perennial thymes, but not all are hardy. If in doubt, take entire plants or root cuttings indoors in winter and keep them in a cool, bright place.

Valeriana officinalis
Valerian, garden heliotrope
Zones 4 to 10

This somewhat carrotlike plant, whose roots are used to make a sedative, produces a clump of ferny foliage above which 3-foot-tall (1 m) self-supporting stems hold showy umbels of white or pink flowers in late spring when few other lacy flowers are available to fill out vases and perennial beds. The flowers are sweetly fragrant and attract bees, butterflies and the small wasps that feed on insect pests. Cut the flower stems back to the ground after the blooms fade. Altogether a lovely and totally dependable plant, valerian is equally suited to a flower bed or a herb garden, although it will need regular dividing, preferably in spring.

According to British plants-woman Kay Sanecki, it is possible to make a compost accelerator by combining approximately equal portions of fresh valerian, dandelion, chamomile, nettle, yarrow and oak bark. Spread a thin layer of leaves, bark or whole plants, fresh or dry, between other compost ingredients, then add water.

VALERIANA OFFICINALIS

CHAPTER FOUR

GRASSES AND GROUND COVERS

North Americans love lawns. It is said that if all the lawns in the United States were joined together, they'd add up to an area the size of Indiana. That should make for acres of drought resistance; grasses are, after all, the plants that dominated the dry, windy prairies for thousands of years. But lawns are very different things. We've selected and pampered certain grasses until they can no longer survive without special care. Bluegrasses and ryegrasses kept unnaturally juicy and bright green no matter how hot and dry the weather are among the greatest water wasters on the continent. At 18 gallons per square foot (7 L/0.01 m²) per year, a bluegrass lawn may use more water in a summer than the swimming pool it surrounds. Lawn grasses also need regular fertilizing, and they're susceptible to many insects and diseases.

Gardening for a changing climate may mean less watering — or simply less lawn.

Dianthus sylvestris and sempervivums fill pockets of soil between rocks.

EXISTING LAWNS

If you already have a lawn but want to do less watering, the Turf Resource Center in Rolling Meadows, Illinois, offers the following tips:

- Reduce or stop fertilizing at least one month before you expect hot weather. Lush, recently fertilized grass is less able to withstand high summer temperatures.
- Gradually raise the height of your mower blade as the temperature increases. Longer grass shades the soil and encourages deeper roots.
- Mow often enough so you never remove more than the top third of the grass at a time. Make sure your mower blade is sharp.
- If you do water, do it late at night or early in the morning so that the water can soak deeply into the soil. Thorough, infrequent watering encourages deeper roots.
- Confine watering to areas that are more often seen or receive the most traffic.
- In fall, aerate, dethatch, if necessary, and apply a balanced fertilizer. If your soil is deficient in potassium, add this nutrient, as it improves rooting and therefore heat tolerance.

If you want your lawn to stay green in dry weather, soil depth is important. For a lush green lawn of bluegrass, for example, soil must be at least 4 inches (10 cm) deep to avoid the need for daily watering. About half an inch (1 cm) of compost sifted over the lawn every fall will gradually increase the soil level. Otherwise, consider a lawn substitute.

If you have fallen heir to a labor-intensive lawn, the most sensible course of action is to replace what you don't need with something like a patio or a different ground cover, such as a wildflower meadow (pages 79-80), or any of the plants listed on pages 58-73. Lift the unwanted sod in chunks, and, if you have space, turn them upside down in a pile to compost into good topsoil, which they will do in about a year. Add garden topsoil to the depth needed. Difficult lawn can also be replaced with easier lawn. Seeds of fescue or white Dutch clover can be sprinkled on an existing lawn about a month before the first mowing in spring. Clover (*Trifolium* species), not a grass at all but a legume, contributes nitrogen to the soil; it also tolerates medium-to-low mowing and some shade. It is deep-rooted, drought-tolerant and green all summer. In cold-winter areas, it will winter-kill if there is insufficient snow cover, but it can be reseeded easily. On the negative side, clover stains clothing and shoes worse than grass, and if it is not mowed, it will grow tall and lush, creating sprawling bunches that can crowd out lawn grasses during wet weather.

NEW LAWNS

A lawn of mixed plant species is more able to put up with varying weather conditions than a lawn of nothing but grass. If you don't use herbicides, a mixed plant population will develop naturally, but if you want to get off on the right foot, there are also self-reliant mixtures on the market, especially if you are starting a lawn from seed rather than sod. One recommended mixture for prairie lawns that are not watered contains 35 percent Kentucky bluegrass, 35 percent creeping red fescue and 30 percent wheatgrass. There are also ecological mixtures (ecolawns) on the market, such as Fleur de Lawn and Fragrant Herbal Lawn, both developed by Tom Cook of Oregon State University. Cook's lawns include low ornamentals such as English daisies (*Bellis perennis*), yarrow (*Achillea millefolium*) and strawberry clover (*Trifolium fragiferum*). Dwarf perennial ryegrass keeps the lawn green through winter. Ecolawns must always be hand-weeded; they cannot be treated with herbicides.

In a study of low-maintenance turf alternatives

by the University of Minnesota, the mixtures No Mow, Ecology Lawn Mix and Fleur de Lawn required mowing only twice a season and provided good color, good cover and overall ratings equal to traditional lawns.

Sodding or Sowing

Large lawns, such as those around newly built homes, are usually grown from sod, which is purchased in rolls like carpet and laid directly on cleared, raked ground. Different grass mixtures are available in sod form, just as they are in bags of seed, so if you have any say in the matter, ask for a drought-tolerant easy-care mixture. Even if the grass mixture is drought-tolerant, however, the sod must be watered deeply and regularly until it roots into the soil underneath it.

A lawn grown from seed requires regular watering too. Prior to seeding, the soil should be enriched with compost, rotted manure or fertilizer. Lawn seed is best sown during the last two weeks of August. Temperatures then are still warm enough for fast germination, and fall usually brings the cool, rainy weather that gets the grass off to a good start before a winter's rest and the cool, moist conditions which allow rapid growth in spring.

Thoroughly weed, smooth and rake the ground, apply seeds according to package directions, then roll or press the area under boards. Water thoroughly and frequently to maintain the surface moisture. Don't step on the area until the grass is well established, usually about two months after sowing. A small amount of extra nitrogen should be applied six weeks after germination.

Mowing

Lawn grasses develop deeper, more drought-resistant roots if they are kept at a height of about 2 1/2 inches (6.3 cm). Grass clippings are best left in place if you have a mulching mower or the clippings are small. According to turf-grass experts, leaving grass clippings in place can reduce nitrogen-fertilizer requirements by as much as 30 percent below the application rates for lawns from which clippings are removed. Grass clippings do not contribute to thatch (a layer of stems and roots that decomposes slowly) but instead help maintain soil fertility and quality.

Fertilizing

In places where summers are dry, fertilizing is best done only in late summer or fall. Certain grasses, especially buffalo grass and wheatgrass, should not be fertilized at all. Otherwise, they become lush and more susceptible to damage by drought, diseases and pests.

Weeds

Lawn grasses compete poorly with most weeds, which will quickly colonize empty spots. In very hot, dry weather, cool-season turf grasses go dormant while weeds flourish. Crabgrass, for instance, can grow almost half an inch (1 cm) a day during a drought severe enough to cause Kentucky bluegrass to go dormant. A thick, healthy lawn that includes not only grasses but a mixture of different ground covers to fill in the empty spaces is therefore the best defense if you are opposed to herbicide use and don't want to spend your life on your knees. Perennial ryegrass sprouts quickly and is thus a good choice to fill in empty spots in a lawn. When weeds do appear, hand-digging is the most environmentally friendly remedy. The definition of a weed, of course, is in the eye of the beholder.

Hardscape Ground Covers

The ultimate solution to a ground cover problem may be no plants at all. A stone, concrete or brick patio, for instance, can be beautiful and requires no mowing, no fertilizing and no watering. Maintenance? If the patio is made properly, weeding, even between patio stones, should be minimal. Other than that, all you may need to do is sweep off the fallen leaves once in a while.

The lowest plants to go in the cracks include antennaria, any of the creeping sedums, sempervivums and hardy thymes listed on the following pages. A little taller but also good are thrifts, small dianthus and in zone 6 or warmer gardens, mondo grass (*Ophiopogon*) or lilyturf (*Liriope*). If a patio or path is edged by lawn, leave a bare area or install a barrier around the patio to prevent the grasses from invading the cracks between the stones and the ground covers from invading the lawn.

BROADLEAF GROUND COVERS

Ground covers are plants that spread outward, usually forming a sufficiently dense cover to prevent most annual weeds from sprouting. While ground covers could be any height, the plants in this chapter are mostly under 1 foot (30 cm) tall. All can be considered substitutes for lawn in places where there is little or no foot traffic, but only lawn grasses can take frequent trampling. If there is to be foot traffic through an area planted with other ground covers, install a path. An even more important consideration is hardiness for your climate.

Ground covers are meant to cover the ground densely, providing a weed-free mat. But in their first year or two, there will be gaps that invite weeds to take root. During this inevitable period of waiting, there are several things you should do:

- Make sure the ground is absolutely weed-free before you plant.
- To cover a large area in a hurry, buy enough plants so that they will be touching by the end of the second season. If crowded, remove some.
- Water the plants when necessary to keep them growing strongly.
- Pull weeds as soon as you see them. The smaller and airier ground covers never become impenetrable to grasses that spread underground.
- Herbaceous ground covers should be divided as soon as they are big enough. Two small plants will cover an area faster than one large plant. With any ground covers, including woody perennials, you may speed up the multiplication process by starting plants with cuttings taken from new growth.

Many ground covers need shearing when they finish blooming, since the bare flower stalks look unattractive. These include alchemilla, arabis, cerastium, dianthus, geranium, helianthemum, iberis, lamium, nepeta, phlox and veronica.

Note that although some perennial ground covers are listed as suitable for zones 9 and 10, they may not do well in southern Florida and along the Gulf Coast because of the combination of high humidity and warm winters.

Ground covers elsewhere in this book include species of: *Armeria, Euonymus, Euphorbia, Genista, Gypsophilia, Helianthemum, Hemerocallis, Hypericum, Oenothera, Penstemon and Potentilla.*

Aegopodium podagraria

Goutweed, bishop's weed, goat's foot
Zones 1 to 9

A neat mound about 16 inches (40 cm) tall of dense, mostly pest-free foliage is often used to soften the edges of walls or fences. Goutweed grows in wet or dry soil and spreads by underground runner, so it should be confined to places that can be defined by mowing or architectural features or allowed to colonize places where little else will grow, such as the ground under maples and other deciduous trees. It does best with some shade. Dill-like umbels of white flowers that appear on long seed stalks in late spring can be cut back, since it is the leaves that look best. In good soil, goutweed can be a ruthless spreader that chokes out smaller plants and is almost impossible to remove.

FAVORITES
There is a plain, dark green form of this easy ground cover, but the variegated form, 'Variegatum,' is better known. It has handsome green-and-white-patterned leaves.

Ajuga reptans

Ajuga, bugleweed
Zones 3 to 10

This thickly growing ground cover is only a few inches tall and capable of smothering smaller plants. It puts up with wet soil or dry in sun to considerable shade. Flat rosettes of shiny, pointed leaves form on runners. During the season, the foliage changes color from reddish to bronze and green. Five-inch (12 cm) spires of blue flowers bloom in spring.

FAVORITES
The most ornamental forms are hybrids with variegated, silver or purple foliage. The following all have blue flowers:

'Burgundy Glow' is variegated scarlet, green and white; 'Silver Carpet' has silvery foliage; 'Braunherz' is dark purple-bronze. There are also white and purple-flowered forms.

ALCHEMILLA MOLLIS

Alchemilla mollis

Lady's mantle
Zones 2 to 8

Lady's mantle is best known for its roundish leaves as wide as 6 inches (15 cm), which are uniquely pleated and covered with tiny hairs that can hold drops of water upright like pearls. These drops were prized by alchemists, hence the genus name. The sprays of greenish yellow flowers are prized by flower arrangers. Lady's mantle loves deep, rich soil but will survive, although smaller, in poor, dry soil if given shade and watered occasionally. It spreads modestly, forming rounded clumps 1 foot (30 cm) tall, suitable at the front of a border, on the shady side of large rocks or under shrubs.

AEGOPODIUM PODAGRARIA 'VARIEGATUM'

Antennaria species
Pussytoes; cat's paw
Zones 1 to 9

These native plants of the North American prairies have small, fuzzy leaves that form a solid ground-hugging carpet less than 1 inch (2.5 cm) high. They spread slowly but surely, filling the spaces between paving stones or between the rocks in a rock garden. As is the case with many ground huggers, flowering is a surprise. Pussytoes erupts into what, considering its diminutive size, are gigantic seed stalks 4 to 6 inches (10-15 cm) tall. White daisy flowers bloom to be replaced by woolly seed heads. The variety *A. dioica rosea*, which has silvery foliage and pink spring flowers, is less tough and spreading. Set rooted pieces 6 inches (15 cm) apart; the plants will fill in the spaces between them within a season. Pussytoes must have perfectly well-drained ground and should be planted in absolutely weed-free soil, unless you are not bothered by seeing other plants grow through it.

Arabis caucasica
Rock cress
Zones 3 to 9

This old-fashioned creeper is a blanket of white star flowers in early spring. It grows about 8 inches (20 cm) tall, best in well-drained soil in sun or part shade.

FAVORITES
The ordinary single white version makes a fine filler between taller perennials. Double white 'Plena' keeps its flowers about twice as long. 'Compinkie' has pink flowers. 'Variegata' has green leaves edged with white. Pull out any shoots that are all green.

    A. x *sturii* is a hybrid that grows just 4 inches (10 cm) tall with glossy green leaves and white flowers.

ARABIS CAUCASICA

ARCTOSTAPHYLOS UVA-URSI

Arctostaphylos uva-ursi
Bearberry, kinnikinick
Zones 2 to 9

This handsome shrubby plant is especially prized for shiny, ever-green leaves about half an inch (1 cm) wide. Small white or pink-tinted flowers are followed by a summer crop of beautiful red berries that last through fall. Bearberry needs organically rich, well-drained soil, preferably acidic, and some sun. It grows slowly at first but may eventually cover a circle 5 feet (1.5 m) wide and 1 foot (30 cm) deep. The leaves turn bronze in winter. If not covered in snow, they may suffer from wind-burn and desiccation. Trim off damaged foliage in spring.

FAVORITES
'Vancouver Jade,' zones 4 to 9, is more vigorous than the species, with pink flowers and bright red fall color.

Artemisia species

Mugwort, sagebrush
Zones 3 to 10

Known for their attractive, fragrant grayish leaves and their tolerance for heat, drought, sand and gravel, artemisias are a rugged group perhaps best represented by a few species native to the prairies and rangelands — pasture sage (*A. frigida*), prairie sage (*A. ludoviciana*) and big sagebrush (*A. tridentata*). These plants perfume the air of western cattle country on breezy summer days. Sagebrush is one group among hundreds of artemisias, only a handful of which have been tamed for the garden. But even the elegantly named cultivars are tougher than they look, provided the ground is well drained. No matter how hot and dry the weather, artemisias look respectable, although their spikes of white flowers are not especially attractive and best pruned off. Artemisias are useful in dried wreaths and floral arrangements. All are easy to multiply from cuttings. Two additional artemisias, French tarragon and wormwood, are listed with the herbs on page 45.

FAVORITES
Some of the best artemisia ground covers for dry soil are:

A. ludoviciana, zones 4 to 9, especially 'Valerie Finnis,' 18 to 24 inches (45-60 cm) tall with wide, white leaves. Although all the selections spread by underground runner, both 'Silver King,' about 3 feet (90 cm) tall, and the similar 'Silver Queen,' are more invasive. They are easy to multiply by division or from cuttings.

A. pontica (Roman wormwood), zones 4 to 9, forms an attractive cloudy mound, 2 feet (60 cm) tall, of pale bluish green, feathery foliage. This species is hard to find, perhaps

ARTEMISIA 'SILVER BROCADE'

because of its invasiveness, but its spreading habit is an advantage on poor ground where little else will grow, even under trees or next to buildings, and it is easily rooted out if it goes too far. It looks best if the flowering stems are cut back, and it can be clipped once or twice during the season to maintain density.

A. schmidtiana, zones 1 to 9, especially 'Silver Mound,' also known as 'Angel's Hair,' forms a neat rounded clump of finely divided bluish silver foliage about 1 foot (30 cm) tall. It must be mass planted to be used as a ground cover. When it blooms, cut it back to a few inches above the ground to encourage new dense foliage. Divide plants or take cuttings every three years or so; otherwise, clumps eventually die out in the center.

A. stelleriana, zones 2 to 9, has bright white, evergreen foliage and recumbent stems that root where they touch the ground. One of many plants known as dusty miller, it is good at the front of a border or as a ground cover in small areas. 'Silver Brocade' grows about 6 inches (15 cm) tall and has deeply indented, almost

pure white leaves. 'Broughton Silver' is similar but taller. Trim plants back when flowering to encourage the growth of new foliage.

A. vulgaris 'Oriental Limelight,' zones 4 to 8, looks very different from the others, 4 to 6 feet (120-180 cm) tall with variegated green-and-yellow foliage. It spreads by underground runners so can be invasive. Cut it back if it grows too tall. It is best in part shade and a good candidate for a container.

AURINIA SAXATILIS

Aurinia saxatilis;
Alyssum saxatile
Basket of gold, gold dust
Zones 3 to 7

Still sometimes known as golden
alyssum in honor of its former
botanical name, this hardy perennial covers its gray foliage with a
blanket of bright yellow flowers on
1-foot (30 cm) stalks in late spring.
Best used to tumble over walls or
down rocky steps in sun or part
shade, it needs well-drained soil
and will die in ground that is too
wet, although it may leave seedlings.
It is one of the favorites at the xeric
garden of the Denver Botanic
Gardens.

FAVORITES
'Compactum' is the most popular
selection, with bright yellow flowers.
'Citrinum' has paler flowers. 'Dudley
Neville Variegated' has foliage variegated cream-and-green, with pale
yellow flowers. 'Sunny Border Apricot'
has orange-yellow flowers.

Calluna vulgaris
Scotch heather
Zones 4 to 5

Think of the Scottish Highlands
when situating this plant. Cool, misty
mornings and perfectly drained
acidic soil on a slope or in a raised
bed in sun or light shade suit it
perfectly. Heather is fussy. It does
not like hot, humid conditions or
wet ground. If it is not content, it
soon perishes. Where it is happy, it
forms a mounding ground cover
that looks best when various flower
colors are grown close together.
The summer flowers bloom in
shades of white, pink and lavender
on the tips of shrubby plants about
1 foot (30 cm) high and twice as
wide. It has become naturalized in
parts of the United States.

FAVORITES
There are hundreds of named cultivars, all of which must be grown from
plants or cuttings.

Campanula species
Bellflower, rampion
Zones vary

Campanula means bell, because all
the members of this genus have
lovely bell-shaped flowers, charac-
teristically blue or purple, although
there are also whites and pinks. The
flowers decorate slender stems.
Non-spreading types are described
on page 102. Ground-cover types
range from tall to small and from
the delicate to the aggressively
weedy. They do best in well-drained
soil with some shade.

If you live in an old farmhouse,
you may have inherited a patch of
C. rapunculoides, called creeping or
rover bellflower, a pioneer favorite
that will survive decades of neglect
and no watering at all and will
rebound and spread as soon as the
perennial beds are weeded by an
unsuspecting newcomer. It grows
about 2 feet (60 cm) tall and is
topped in summer by spires of
smallish purple bells. *C. rapunculoides* is almost impossible to get rid
of — roots break when you are digging, and the smallest bits will
resprout. It spreads by underground

CAMPANULA CARPATICA

rhizome and by seed. If you have fallen heir to *C. rapunculoides*, be ruthless to keep it within bounds. Mowed lawn will contain it, as will pavement. This is not a plant to share with a friend.

FAVORITES

C. carpatica (Carpathian bellflower), zones 2 to 9, forms a 6-inch-tall (15 cm) dome of pointed leaves topped by 1-inch (2.5 cm) blue or white flowers in midsummer. It does not spread quickly, so for a ground cover, you will need several plants. Clumps are easy to divide in spring. Among the best cultivars are the blue 'Blue Uniform' and 'Blue Clips' and the white 'Bressingham White' and 'White Clips.'

C. glomerata (clustered bellflower), zones 2 to 9, is somewhat coarser than *C. carpatica* but is a better ground cover, spreading a little faster without being invasive. Blue flowers top 18-inch (45 cm) stems in mid-summer. 'Superba' has violet-purple flowers.

C. poscharskyana (Serbian bell-flower), zones 3 to 8, is a trailing plant about 4 to 8 inches (10-20 cm) tall with starry lilac-blue flowers in late spring. It roots where the stems touch the ground. 'E.H. Frost' has white flowers with a pale blue eye.

C. takesimana (Korean bellflower), zones 5 to 8, forms a spreading clump about 2 feet (60 cm) tall with pale lilac flowers in summer. It will toler-ate the dry shade under shrubs. 'Beautiful Truth' has split petals that are recurved.

CERASTIUM TOMENTOSUM

Cerastium tomentosum
Snow-in-summer
Zones 2 to 9

Best in sun, this invasive plant is not suitable for growing among small, delicate things, but given a place where little else will grow and where it can be contained by paving or lawn — or where it can substitute for lawn — it is beautiful all four seasons of the year and a lovely con-trast to plants that have green or maroon foliage. Midwinter thaws reveal sterling-silver foliage as eye-catching as in spring. Snow-in-summer forms a mat about 6 inches (15 cm) high topped by pure white flowers in June. After blooming, it should be clipped back. The seed pods are unattractive and con-tribute to the spread of the plant. It can be divided in spring or fall and can be easily dug out where it is not wanted.

Ceratostigma plumbaginoides; Plumbago larpentae
Leadwort
Zones 6 to 9

From late summer to early fall when other flowers are fading, the brilliant blue, 1-inch (2.5 cm) blooms of ceratostigma are a welcome sight. It grows 9 inches to 2 feet (20 to 60 cm) tall and spreads rapidly by under-ground roots, a good thing if you have a large area to cover in either sun or light shade. The leathery, lance-shaped leaves turn bright reddish bronze in fall. In cooler areas, it does best if grown fairly close to a south or southwesterly wall for wind protection and greater warmth. Wet soil in winter and early spring can be deadly, so ensure that soil is well drained. In zone 6, mulch in fall. It emerges fairly late in spring, so mark its place to prevent damage.

CONVALLARIA MAJALIS

Convallaria majalis
Lily of the valley
Zones 1 to 9

Although its waxy little bells look delicate and smell ethereal, lily of the valley can be a pest in rich, moist soil. Too low to crowd out weeds except in the shadiest places where few weeds grow, it can itself invade plantings around it, including surrounding lawn, although mowing will keep it in check. It spreads by means of thick underground rhizomes. The waxy white bells are tiny, born on slender 6-inch (15 cm) stalks, but the leaves resemble tulip foliage. Give it a spot in shade, dry to moist, even the deep shade under a deciduous canopy, or grow it in a container or in a patch of ground where it can be contained by a lawn or patio. 'Rosea' has pink flowers.

Coronilla varia
Crown vetch
Zones 3 to 10

You may see this legume along steep highway embankments, where it has been planted to hold the soil in place with its spreading underground runners. Its fernlike foliage and clusters of 1-inch (2.5 cm) white to lilac or pink summer flowers are pretty, and because it is a legume, crown vetch improves the soil by enriching it with nitrogen. The arching branches form a tangled mat about 2 feet (60 cm) high that tumbles over other plants and down hills, no matter how dry and sunny. Valuable in its place and useful as a green manure if it is plowed under before flowering, crown vetch is too aggressive for most garden situations. Confine it to dry hillsides and rocky outcrops where little else will grow. Crown vetch can be divided in spring or fall.

FAVORITES
Improved cultivars include the tidier, 2-foot-tall (60 cm) 'Penngift,' 'Emerald,' recommended for the Midwest, and 'Chemung,' recommended for the Northeast.

Cotoneaster species
Cotoneaster
Zones vary

Cotoneasters are shrubs, plants with woody stems. Some types grow more or less upright (page 159), and others are reclining, but both types are valued for their spring flowers, summer berries and tiny, waxy green leaves that turn red in fall. Where winters are warmish, cotoneaster is evergreen. It does best in alkaline soil in full sun. Stems can be layered — pinned down and buried — to root, then cut from the mother plant.

FAVORITES
As well as the listings below, see *C. apiculatus* and *C. salicifolia* 'Repens,' page 159.

   C. adpressus (creeping rockspray), zones 4 to 7, grows about 2 feet (60 cm) tall, with short, rigid branches that may root where they touch the ground. For *C. adpressus praecox*, see *C. nanshan.*

   C. dammeri (bearberry cotoneaster), zones 5 to 9, is almost completely flat, a good choice for slopes or for use as a lawn substitute. Best known is the variety 'Skogholm' (Skogholm cotoneaster), which grows a little taller than the species. It forms a

CORONILLA VARIA

1-foot-tall (30 cm) mound of small green leaves and white flowers, followed by bright red fruits. The cultivar 'Coral Beauty' has orange berries. 'Eichholz' can spread wider than 10 feet (3 m). All do best with a good snow cover in the colder zones. After a difficult winter, *C. dammeri* may revive from the base upward. In warm zones, it is evergreen.

C. horizontalis (fishbone or rock-spray cotoneaster), zones 5 to 8, is a popular foundation plant, useful as a spacer between taller shrubs or as a ground cover on uneven slopes. It is usually deciduous. The flowers are pink. It grows 2 to 3 feet (60-90 cm) high and as wide as 8 feet (2.4 m). The cultivar 'Variegatus' is prized for its cream-edged, green leaves that turn reddish in fall.

C. nanshan was, until recently, labeled *C. adpressus* var. *praecox*. It is more vigorous than *C. adpressus*, with especially large, dark orange fruit and bright red fall color. 'Boer' has even larger fruits. In the garden of the University of Maine at Orono, this shrub suffered a small amount of winter damage, so it should be mulched in zone 4. It grows at least 18 inches (45 cm) high and can spread 4 feet (1.2 m) wide. In warmer places, it is evergreen.

Dianthus species
Pink, carnation
Zones vary

Pinks are among the best flowers for dry places, especially if the soil is alkaline. Almost all bloom in shades of pink, from pale to screaming, but there are also whites and purples. Some of the taller-growing types are described on page 105. Low-growing species can create cushions of narrow foliage and bright summer flowers between patio stones, in containers or near the front of perennial beds. All should be given well-drained, preferably alkaline soil in sun, although in very dry gardens, they appreciate some shade. They may self-sow if not entirely dead-headed and are easy from seeds started indoors.

FAVORITES
D. arenarius (sand pink), zones 1 to 8, grows just 4 inches (10 cm) tall, forming a mat of needlelike gray-green leaves and fragrant, fringed, white 1-inch (2.5 cm) flowers, some spotted with pink.

D. deltoides (maiden pink), zones 2 to 9, is one of the easiest to find. It forms a low, spreading mat about 6 inches (15 cm) high with small single flowers in summer.

D. sylvestris, zones 5 to 8, forms a low tuft or mat of 5-inch (13 cm) stems and pink flowers in summer.

Erica species
Heath, florist's heather
Zones vary

Much like *Calluna vulgaris* (page 62) but capable of blooming all year, provided several overlapping species are grown, this mostly shrubby, evergreen genus also colors the rounded mountains of the Scottish Highlands. Flowers bloom in shades of white, pink, rose and magenta on the tips of slender stems circled with tiny green leaves. The species look similar and are identified mostly by hardiness and blooming time, from late winter or early spring through summer and fall. There are tree heathers 10 feet (3 m) or taller, but the toughest types grow about 12 to 20 inches (30-50 cm) tall and about twice as wide. They need poor, perfectly drained, somewhat acidic soil, preferably amended with sand and peat. Do not fertilize. Cool weather in a partly shaded rock garden or raised bed sheltered from winter winds suits them best. In the colder extremes, a good snow cover helps survival. Prune after flowering, and mulch with pine needles.

FAVORITES
There are several species and scores of cultivars, so choose from what is available, either locally or by mail order. *E. carnea*; *E. herbacea* (winter heath, spring heath), zones 5 to 7, is the least finicky and one of the hardiest species. With a good snow cover, it may survive in zone 3. It blooms in late winter or early spring and tolerates somewhat alkaline soils. *E. cinerea* (bell heather), zones 4 to 6, blooms in summer or fall. *E.* x *darleyensis* is less hardy, zones 6 to 8.

Genista pilosa

Broom; silky woadwaxen
Zones 4 to 7

A genus with wiry stems, tiny leaves and masses of pea flowers in summer, usually bright yellow. *G. pilosa* is similar to the earlier-blooming *G. tinctoria* (common woadwaxen) and the popular Lydia woadwaxen (*G. lydia*), page 161. After flowering, cut back the new growth that has flowered, but do not cut into old wood.

Broom likes poor soil and can become invasive.

FAVORITES

'Vancouver Gold,' zones 4 to 9, is an outstanding carpet-forming, ever-green, fairly drought-resistant cultivar that can be grown on slopes or as a substitute for lawn. It grows 6 to 8 inches (15-20 cm) tall.

Geranium species

Cranesbill
Zones vary

There are hundreds of species of true geranium, or cranesbill, more and more of which are appearing in perennial catalogs as their admirers increase. There is at least one for every garden. Some of the more upright or mounding forms are described on page 110. There are others that spread outward to form a good ground cover, although none are badly invasive. All are low enough to grow at the front of a border or under roses and other shrubs.

Unlike many perennials, cranes-bills have beautiful foliage that lasts all season, and some have a long blooming time as well. Many are drought-tolerant and hardy to zone 4 or even colder gardens, provided the soil is well drained. One of their best features is an ability to flower in shade. Deadhead all of them after blooming to keep them looking neat and encourage more flowering.

FAVORITES

Newly discovered species and new cultivars come on the market every year. These are a few good, easily available choices.

G. x *cantabriense*, zones 5 to 8, is a hybrid that includes *G. macrorrhizum* in its parentage. It grows just 4 to 6 inches (10-15 cm) high and can be used as a ground cover for small areas. The glossy green foliage turns bright red in fall. Cultivars include pink-flushed white 'Biokova,' dark pink 'Biokova Karmina' and rose 'Cambridge.'

G. macrorrhizum, zones 4 to 8, has become the choice ground cover for difficult areas, replacing ivy, pachysan-dra and several others. What it offers is fragrant, softly fuzzy foliage as wide as 4 inches (10 cm) in a dense, weed-excluding clump about 1 foot (30 cm) tall, with pretty, long-lasting magenta flowers in late spring. The flowers, about 1 inch (2.5 cm) wide, have a protrud-ing center. The clump is easy to divide and is capable of surviving in the dry shade under deciduous trees, on a slope or alongside a driveway, where it looks good all season. There are several cultivars, including clear-pink-flowered 'Ingwersen's Variety,' deep magenta 'Bevan's Variety' and white 'Spessart,' which has pink stamens. 'Variegatum' has pink flowers and grayish green foliage marked with cream.

G. sanguineum, named bloody cranesbill for the dramatic fall color of the foliage, zones 3 to 9, forms a neat dome about 1 foot (30 cm) tall. It can spread into a clump about 3 feet (1 m) wide in a few years, making a mounding weed-smothering carpet for shade or sun in any soil. The magenta flowers, as pretty as small single roses, are persistent, and the small, deeply divided leaves turn scarlet in autumn. It is easy to divide. Cultivars include red-flowered 'Alpenglow,' reddish purple, compact 'Max Frei' and purple and bright pink 'Shepherd's Warning.'

GERANIUM SANGUINEUM

Glechoma hederacea
(Nepeta glechoma)
Creeping Charlie, ground ivy,
gill-over-the-ground
Zones 1 to 9

In its green form, this is an extremely invasive, weedy creeper that roots from its stems and can grow happily in a lawn, tumbling over and through the grasses, or just about anywhere else short of a busy highway. It should not be intentionally introduced into a garden unless you are sure you can control it. A cutting in a hanging basket trails attractively and needs minimal care. It grows about 4 inches (10 cm) high, has fragrant foliage and pretty purple flowers in late spring. The green-and-white variegated and golden forms, both zones 4 to 9, are less invasive and are sometimes grown in wild gardens.

Juniperus species
Juniper
Zones vary

The junipers are a varied group, from tall trees to wide shrubs to spreaders that hug the ground. Some of the vertical forms are described on page 164. In downtown office gardens, scrunched between concrete sidewalks and walls, the lower-growing junipers create a reliable and refreshing spread of green, whether bright, dull, bluish or gold. An all-juniper design is too static for a home garden, but junipers used as specimens or planted among other shrubs and perennials can provide dependable points of reference that look good all year. The females are distinguished among coniferous evergreens by their blue, black or reddish berries. Those of common juniper (*J. communis*)

are used to flavor gin, which takes its name from the Old French name of the plant, genevre.

The spreading junipers need plenty of room, although not necessarily when they are first planted. You can keep moving perennials farther out as the shrubs widen from year to year or transplant the junipers when they outgrow their space. Some spring pruning may be necessary. Wearing gloves, cut away dead needles and trim broken branches back to the closest joint. You may choose to cut off the lowest branches to allow underplantings to be seen. Plan your cuts carefully, because juniper will not regrow from old wood. In colder areas, juniper is susceptible to infection by snow mold, which develops on foliage covered by snow until late spring. Remove the gray mats of fuzzy mycelia before they turn black and tarry. Junipers should be given full sun or a little shade and are best in well-drained, even dry soil.

FAVORITES

J. communis var. *depressa* (dwarf common juniper), zones 2 to 7, is a prostrate form that grows about 2 feet (60 cm) tall and 5 feet (1.5 m) wide with ascending branches. The soft green to blue-green foliage turns bronze in winter. 'Depressa Aurea' is a golden form. 'Hornbrookii' grows 16 inches (40 cm) tall and 5 feet (1.5 m) wide. 'Repanda' is even lower, about 1 foot (30 cm) tall.

J. horizontalis (creeping juniper), zones 3 to 9, is native to the Canadian prairies and the Midwest, where it colonizes dry, sandy hillsides. There are green, gold and blue cultivars, from a few inches to 2 feet (60 cm) tall and as wide as 8 feet (240 cm). Among the greens are 'Bow Dak' (Prairie Elegance™), 'Emerald Spreader,' 'Lime

JUNIPERUS HORIZONTALIS

Glow,' 'Prince of Wales,' and 'Plumosa Compacta,' better known as Andorra juniper. Among the blues are 'Blue Chip,' 'Bar Harbor,' 'Hughes,' 'Yukon Belle,' 'Wiltonii' (Blue Rug™), 'Monbec' (Blue Ice™) and 'Monise' (Turquoise Spreader™). 'Douglasii,' called Waukegan, is a very hardy carpeting juniper that is blue in summer and plum in winter. One of the best for gold foliage is 'Motherlode.' 'Variegatus' has white markings.

J. x *media* (hybrid juniper), zones 4 to 9, is a variable group of hybrids represented by several cultivars that grow about 4 feet (120 cm) tall or taller and somewhat wider, including yellowish 'Gold Coast' and 'Old Gold.'

J. sabina (savin juniper), zones 3 to 7, has a distinct resinous fragrance. Savins relocate easily. In the coldest, windiest gardens, savins can suffer from winter browning in full sun but usually recover in spring. In dry places, they can become infested with spider mites. Most grow about 5 feet (150 cm) tall and as wide as 15 feet (4.5 m), although some are much lower, including the bright green 'Arcadia' and 'Broadmoor.' 'Buffalo' stays bright green through the winter and is a good spreader. These cultivars do best with a generous snow cover.

Mahonia species

Creeping mahonia
Zones 5 to 8

The mahonias, sometimes called Oregon grapes, are evergreen shrubs native to the Pacific Coast yet capable of growing in dry soil and tolerating cold winters, provided there is shelter from wind and hot sun. The foliage of *Mahonia aquifolium* is particularly susceptible to winter damage because this species can form a shrub as tall as 6 feet (180 cm). In sunny gardens, mahonias should be grown in part shade. Deep snow will help protect the foliage from winterburn. Prune off damaged foliage in spring. They spread by underground stolons. Prune away unwanted suckers.

FAVORITES
The best ground cover is *M. repens* (creeping mahonia), which grows less than 1 foot (30 cm) tall and spreads fairly rapidly. In colder zones, it should be mulched unless the snow cover is dependable.

MAHONIA AQUIFOLIUM

MICROBIOTA DECUSSATA

Microbiota decussata

Russian arborvitae, Siberian carpet
Zones 2 to 7

Microbiota looks like flattened cedar. Bright green in summer, it spreads over low rocks and carpets the ground to form a circle that can eventually measure 10 feet (3 m) wide and 1 foot (30 cm) thick. In winter, it turns purplish brown. It is one of the few needle evergreens that thrives in shade.

Nepeta x faassenii

Faassen's catmint, Persian ground ivy
Zones 4 to 10

Although not a plant for really windy, dry places, *N.* x *faassenii* (*N. mussinii*) forms a foot-high (30 cm) gradually spreading mat that can tolerate drought for several weeks, provided it has moisture in spring and fall, humusy, well-drained soil and some shade. It self-seeds freely and looks fine in containers, tumbling down a set of stairs or near the edge of a perennial border. There are white and pink varieties, but the flowers are typically lavender-blue, appearing above grayish green foliage in late spring and early summer. Shear nepeta after it flowers, and it will probably bloom again. Shearing also helps avoid rampant self-sowing. A member of the mint family closely related to catnip, this plant is also appealing to cats.

FAVORITES
An old favorite is 'Dropmore Blue,' whose deep lavender flowers are sterile and thus will not drop seeds. 'Snowflake' has white flowers. 'Walker's Low' grows just 10 inches (25 cm) tall. 'Six Hills Giant' is about 3 feet (90 cm) tall and wide.

N. sibirica, zones 2 to 9, grows about 15 inches (40 cm) tall and wide. The usual offering is 'Blue Beauty,' ('Souvenir d'Andre Chudron') with clear blue flowers.

NEPETA 'DROPMORE BLUE'

Phlox subulata

Moss phlox, moss pink

Zones 3 to 9

This rock garden favorite creates an almost unbroken carpet of color in spring, around the same time as the early tulips. The needlelike foliage is evergreen. Plants grow only 4 to 5 inches (10 to 12 cm) tall, with flat five-petaled flowers about an inch (2.5 cm) wide in shades of white, pink, red, blue, lavender and bi-colors. Shear back the plants after flowering and they may produce additional blossoms later in the season. Moss phlox does well at the front of a border, on a terraced slope or between the stones on a rock staircase. Divide clumps in spring after flowering. It is not the most drought-tolerant of ground covers but enjoys well-drained soil, whether in full sun or part shade.

SEDUM KAMTSCHATICUM

PHLOX SUBULATA

FAVORITES

Good cultivars include the vigorous white 'Snow Queen,' blue 'Benita,' light pink 'Laura,' dark pink 'Marjorie,' rose 'Atropurpurea' and pink-and-white-striped 'Candy Stripes.'

Sedum species

Stonecrop

Zones 2 to 9, except as noted

There are more than 100 species of sedum in cultivation, evidence of the suitability of this genus of succulents for many gardens, not just dry ones. But it is in the dry garden that sedums take the limelight, since they can survive in full sun and baked soil, although they will grow more lush with some watering. There are upright forms (page 126) and creepers just a few inches tall, the latter being some of the best ground covers for rock gardens and perennial beds and for covering slopes in dry sun. All the trailing sedums are excellent choices to trail over the edge of a container in sun. They root at stem nodes, forming a fairly dense cover, and are easy to divide. Foliage may be green, variegated or purple. The starry flowers may be white, yellow, pale pink or brilliant magenta. Shear off the flower stems when the flowers dry to show off the foliage again. Like other succulents, sedums' chief demand is well-drained soil; prolonged wetness causes root decay. In their native habitat, they usually grow over or between exposed rocks, surroundings easily copied in the garden.

FAVORITES

Sedums are often mislabeled in nurseries and are easily confused. Foliage that is bright green in spring may turn drab green in summer; grays turn to beige, maroons to green. Among the most commonly available are the following:

S. acre (showy stonecrop) is one of the smallest, just 1 to 3 inches (2.5-7.5 cm) tall. It is a European species that spreads so easily, even in the shallow patches of soil on exposed rocks, that it can invade lawns and has become naturalized throughout much of North America. In trials at Colorado State University in Fort Collins, however, *S. acre* was the only tested ground cover deemed a suitable alternative to Kentucky bluegrass in terms of attractiveness and water conservation. (The other ground covers tested were *Potentilla neumanniana* and *Cerastium tomentosum*.)

S. acre has sunny yellow summer flowers, but the variety aureum (golden stonecrop, also known as the cultivar 'Aureum' and as the species *S. aureum*) has paler flowers. All should be managed carefully because of their invasiveness.

S. album has shiny, cigar-shaped green leaves and light pink flowers. The form 'Murale Cristatum' has white flowers. Both are flat creepers that can overrun a garden bed and should be handled carefully, in the manner of *S. acre*.

S. divergens (old man's bones) has spherical, pearl-like green leaves and yellow flowers. It forms a rapidly spreading blanket 4 to 6 inches (10-15 cm) deep.

S. floriferum 'Weihenstephaner Gold' is a rapid spreader with variegated green-and-gold foliage that creates a beautiful solid mat about 6 inches (15 cm) deep.

S. kamtschaticum (Russian stonecrop) is a handsome species identified by its scalloped leaves and bright orange-yellow flowers. It forms a mat about 6 inches (15 cm) deep. 'Variegatum,' which spreads slowly, has green-and-white foliage and golden flowers.

S. oreganum (Oregon stonecrop) is a North American native whose fleshy, shiny green leaves turn bright red in hot, dry weather. The flowers are yellow. It slowly forms a mat 6 inches (15 cm) deep.

S. reflexum (blue stonecrop) has soft bluish stems that resemble spruce cuttings about 6 inches (15 cm) long, topped by bright yellow flowers in summer. It spreads quickly and can be invasive.

S. sexangulare (six-sided stonecrop; watch-chain sedum), zones 5 to 9, has tiny, tightly spiraled bright green leaves that turn copper in full sun and yellow summer flowers. It spreads quickly, forming a mat 4 inches (10 cm) deep.

S. spathulifolium, hardy to zone 5, is one of the most decorative spreaders, with beautiful small rosettes of foliage that create a mat 3 to 6 inches (7.5-15 cm) deep. It has yellow flowers. 'Capa Blanca' has grayish white foliage. 'Purpureum' (purple spoon sedum) has dark purple foliage and spreads slowly.

S. spurium (dragon's blood), hardy to zone 3, has white or pink flowers that may be pale or brilliant, depending on the cultivar. Unlike most others, it tolerates moist ground and shade. 'Ruby Mantle,' with purple foliage and dark pink flowers, is a slower spreader than the others. 'Tricolor' has pink flowers and variegated green, cream and pink foliage. Pinch out any green shoots. 'Bronze Carpet' has pink flowers and green foliage that turns bronze in fall.

S. ternatum, hardy to zone 3 and native to the eastern United States, has white flowers in spring. Give it a spot with some shade. The cultivar 'Larinem Park' has bright green foliage.

SEMPERVIVUM TECTORUM

Sempervivum species; Jovibarba species
Hens-and-chicks, houseleek
Zones 1 to 9

Given time, hens-and-chicks can cover a modest area by the charming practice of creating new offsets on shoots nestled close to the mother plant. The round rosettes of fleshy leaves are shown off best in stone or terra-cotta containers or in the niches in a stone wall. In the garden, they can colonize the spaces between steps or between stones at the front of a sunny flower bed. Leaves may be smooth or hairy, in colors from pale to dark green to bluish, pinkish, maroon and variegated. They look like entirely different plants when in flower — which happens only when they mature — because the stalks, one per rosette, are disproportionately tall and almost as wide as the rosettes themselves, topped by small bright pink or yellow flowers. After a rosette flowers, it dies, but surrounding "chicks" soon fill in. The Latin name *Sempervivum* means "live forever," which these plants will do in ground that is perfectly drained. Planting them in sandy soil on a slope helps ensure good drainage.

The genus names *Sempervivum* and *Jovibarba* are confused and often used for the same plant. There are two additional genera also called hens-and-chicks: *Echeveria*, page 142, are more winter tender. *Orostachys*, whose members are sometimes classed as sempervivums or sedums, wither in fall to leave behind a compact bud of leaves that grow outward in spring.

FAVORITES

All sempervivums are suited to dry gardens. The most widely available are members or hybrids of the species *S. tectorum*, called the houseleek in Europe because it was raised on sod or gravel rooftops, supposedly to fend off lightning and bad spirits. The labeling can be confusing, so choose what you like by its color and size. Like sedums, however, sempervivums may change color with temperature and season.

S. arachnoideum looks quite different. It is called the cobweb, or spiderweb, houseleek because of the fine silvery hairs that form a net over the plant, and is one of the more attractive species in flower because it has slender stems and pink flowers.

S. hirtum (*Jovibarba hirta*), known as false houseleek, is often sold as jovibarba. It has foliage arranged in rosettes and yellow flowers with fringed petals.

STACHYS LANATA

Stachys lanata; S. byzantina
Lamb's ears, betony
Zones 3 to 10

The common name lamb's ears suggests the endearing appearance of this drought-tolerant ground cover. Lamb's ears is a favorite of children, who love to stroke the downy, silvery ear-shaped leaves, which grow in mounded basal rosettes. This plant does best in full or part sun in well-drained soil rich in organic matter. It is usually grown in clumps within a perennial bed, although it will spread fairly quickly to form a ground cover if grown in fertile soil with occasional watering. Small rose-colored flowers bloom on tall woolly spikes that sprout in summer. These are not especially ornamental; it's best to lop them off like lamb's tails unless you want seedlings. After wet winters, remove mushy leaves.

FAVORITES
Best is the shorter 6-to-8-inch (15-20 cm) *S. lanata* cultivar 'Silver Carpet,' which does not flower. 'Primrose Heron' has golden foliage.

Symphoricarpos x chenaultii 'Hancock'
Hancock coralberry
Zones 4 to 7

Taller versions of this hardy shrub are described on page 175. 'Hancock' is a hybrid ground cover about 2 feet (60 cm) tall and 6 feet (2 m) wide with closely massed, almost horizontal twigs. It has small gray-green leaves, pink flowers and, more important, long-lasting lilac-pink fruit. It grows equally well in sun or dense shade. Trim off unwanted branches in early spring. It spreads by suckers.

Taxus species
Yew
Zones vary

Upright-growing yews for the dry garden and general directions for growing yews are described on pages 176-177. There are also fairly drought-tolerant yews that spread into good evergreen ground covers. Some shade will help protect them from sunburn and winter scorching.

FAVORITES
T. baccata (English yew), zones 6 to 9, 'Cavendishii' is a female that forms an almost prostrate mound less than 3 feet (1 m) tall and up to 13 ft (4 m) wide. 'Repandens,' another female, has very dark green foliage and can reach about the same dimensions. It is hardy to zone 5. 'Repens Aurea' is a female whose leaves have yellow margins when young and a cream edge when older. It needs partial sun to develop full color.

T. canadensis (Canada yew), zones 2 to 6, grows about 4 feet (120 cm) tall and almost twice as wide, with red fruit. It is cold-tolerant but not good in sunny, exposed sites. It does best in shade.

T. cuspidata (Japanese yew), zones 4 to 7, has a herringbone branching pattern and red berries. 'Monloo' (Emerald Spreader™) grows 2 to 3 feet (30-60 cm) tall and twice as wide. 'Greenwave' forms a low mounding plant about the same size. 'Nana Aurescens' is a golden form that needs part shade and should be protected with burlap where winters are harsh.

T. x media, zones 4 to 7, is a species mostly represented by broadly pyramidal shrubs, but 'Wardii' grows 6 feet (180 cm) tall and twice as wide, and 'Everlow' grows just 2 feet (60 cm) tall and 5 feet (150 cm) wide.

THYMUS PRAECOX

Thymus species
Thyme
Zones 3 to 10

The cooking thymes (page 52) are joined by several ground-cover types that are less esteemed in the kitchen but are wonderful in open, sunny spots in the garden. They will not win a battle with weeds but will form a solid blanket of foliage and flowers if they are tended. Grown between the paving stones of a patio or pathway, all thymes proffer their distinctive fragrance whenever you step on them or brush by. They are easy to divide in spring or fall or can be propagated by stem cuttings or layering. They can also be grown from seed, although it is a slow process.

FAVORITES
T. praecox (creeping thyme) forms flat mats of narrow green leaves topped in early summer with tiny flowers that may be white, red or lilac, depending on the cultivar.

T. serpyllum (mother of thyme) is the most rambunctious and traffic-resistant choice for a ground cover, forming a tumbling 6-inch-deep (15 cm) mat of slender stems and tiny aromatic leaves. Its small, rosy lilac flowers bloom in midsummer. It does not thrive where summers are hot and humid.

T. serpyllum lanuginosus, T. pseudoserpyllum, T. lanuginosus or *T. praecox pseudolanuginosus* (woolly thyme) is well named for its fuzzy foliage. The leaves are tiny, and the entire plant grows less than 1 inch (2.5 cm) tall. It will stand a bit of foot traffic.

Veronica species
Speedwell
Zones vary

As the common name suggests, these plants are rapid spreaders. Indeed, *V. filiformis* invades lawns, revealing itself amid the grass blades with a burst of blue flowers and demonstrating the persistence of some of the low-growing species. Those listed below also grow low or stay almost flat, and although they spread fairly quickly, they are also easy to remove. While the taller veronicas, best known for their spikes of usually blue but sometimes pink or white flowers, do best in moist soil, some of the speedwells appreciate well-drained soil, especially alkaline, and are favorites in xeric demonstration gardens and in rock gardens. They should be given some shade, especially in places where summers are hot.

VERONICA PECTINATA

FAVORITES
Nurseries specializing in rock garden plants carry several mat-forming species in addition to this listing.

V. filifolia, zones 4 to 9, has green, fernlike foliage and large blue flowers in late spring. It grows about 3 inches

VINCA MINOR

(7.5 cm) tall and 18 inches (45 cm) wide.

V. nummularia (Pyrenean speedwell) is evergreen, forming a 2-inch-thick (5 cm) mat of fleshy leaves with clusters of blue or pink flowers.

V. pectinata (comb speedwell), zones 3 to 9, forms a dense mat 2 to 4 inches (5-10 cm) tall, gradually spreading outward. Bright blue flowers bloom for about a month in spring. Its name comes from the shape of the small, slightly woolly leaves, which are toothed like a comb. The variety rosea, or Rubra, has pink flowers.

V. repens (creeping speedwell), zones 2 to 9, makes a flat carpet of tiny green leaves covered with small white flowers in late spring.

Low, mat-forming hybrids with bright blue flowers and glossy green foliage include 'Blue Reflection' and 'Reavis' (Crystal River™).

Vinca minor
Periwinkle; myrtle
Zones 3 to 9

Invasive and even weedy in rich ground where winters are not harsh, periwinkle can be just the thing for poor, dry soil in shade, where its slender stems of glossy, dark green foliage form a tumbling mat to a depth of 1 foot (30 cm) or more. The stems root as they grow. Starry, periwinkle blue flowers dot the foliage in spring. It will flower in the deep shade under a deciduous canopy, but may scorch in full sun, especially in dry soil. In the coldest zones, it may die back in winter but in the warmest zones it is evergreen. Keep this creeper away from low plants that it might grow over.

FAVORITES
The toughest of the bunch is the green-leaved species. Less hardy but more decorative are the cultivars, which include white-flowered 'Alba' and red-flowered 'Rubra' and 'Atropurpurea.' Variegated versions include green-and-gold 'Aureo-variegata,' white-edged 'Variegata' and silver-edged 'Sterling Silver,' with white flowers.

PERENNIAL ORNAMENTAL GRASSES AND GRASSLIKE PLANTS

Ornamental grasses are fine additions to any garden that may experience drought. Not only are most of them able to withstand dry ground and wind once established, but another bonus is that no other classification of landscape plant includes such a high percentage of North American natives. Perhaps this is because grasses do not have a long history of landscape use in Europe.

Ornamental grasses are not lawn grasses, since they are allowed to grow tall and go to seed. Some are not even ground covers in the traditional sense, because they stay in a neat clump. The best way to use them to cover a large space is by mass planting, a role they fill beautifully. A few ornamental grasses do act as traditional ground covers, however, and some spread so fast that they are too invasive for most gardens. Two examples, both about 2 feet (60 cm) tall, are the blue-gray *Elymus arenarius*; *Leymus arenarius* 'Glauca' (blue lyme grass) and *Phalaris arundinacea* (ribbon grass), a pioneer favorite with green-and-white variegated leaves. The cultivars 'Feesey's Form,' with pink shading, and 'Luteo-Picta,' with yellow variegation, are somewhat less invasive. Both blue lyme grass and ribbon grass have invasive rhizomes, so they should be kept out of perennial beds. They are safest given their own bed in sun or shade, grown around trees and tall shrubs or kept in containers. Other ornamental grasses that have become invasive in certain parts of North America include *Arundo donax*, *Cortaderia jubata*, *Festuca arundinacea*, *Miscanthus sacchariflorus* and *Miscanthus sinensis*.

Most grasses produce their seed heads in summer or fall. These may persist for most or all winter. Plants should be positioned so that their vertical, airy form becomes a focus but doesn't block the view of other plants. In colder areas, the

Tall varieties of Miscanthus *such as 'Silverfeather' make a stately backdrop for the perennial garden.*

most upright grasses can be grown on the windward side of the garden to collect snow and act as wind protection in winter, when, although dry and brown, they are among the most attractive plants in the landscape. Smaller grasses can be used as spacers between other perennials.

Most ornamental grasses need no fertilization or watering once established, unless the soil is very sandy or the drought is prolonged. Most should be given well-drained soil and plenty of sun. Given too much shade or dampness, they bloom less and may fall over, a habit called lodging. Ornamental grasses do not need fertilizing — it will weaken them and reduce their winter hardiness.

Do not cut back the tops until early spring, before new growth begins. Then, cut the dead stems back to 4 to 6 inches (10-15 cm) above the ground. If grasses are evergreen, do not cut them back, but pull out unattractive leaves. Division is best done in spring as soon as growth begins. In places where they are not hardy, these grasses can be grown as annuals.

Andropogon species

Bluestem

Zones 3 to 9

These tall, upright, clump-forming grasses are native to the tallgrass prairies of the U.S. Great Plains and the central Canadian provinces. Leaves turn bronze-red in fall. They are easy from seed.

A. gerardii (big bluestem; turkey foot) grows about 4 to 7 feet (1.2-2 m) tall. The blue-green leaves feel smooth. The flower heads, shaped like turkey feet, are purplish and 2 to 3 inches (5 to 7 cm) long.

Andropogon virginicus (broom sedge) forms a bunch as tall as 3 feet (1 m). It is light green in summer and turns a tan color in fall.

Arrhenatherum elatius

Bulbous oatgrass

Zones 4 to 9

'Variegatum' is the usual selection of this clumping grass, which grows slowly to a height of 8 to 12 inches (20-30 cm). It has green-and-white foliage that stays attractive all season.

Arundo donax

Giant reed grass

Zones 5 or 6 to 10

This reed, which can be invasive and has become naturalized in the southern United States, forms a dramatic, arching clump as tall as 14 feet (4.3m), with blue-green leaves about 3 inches (7.5 cm) wide. It will grow in moist, ordinary or dry soil and is sometimes used on slopes to control erosion. Flowers appear only in warmer zones.

Bouteloua curtipendula

Grama grass

Zones 4 to 9

Both of these North American pasture grasses form low clumps. *B. curtipendula* (sideoats grama) grows about 1 foot (30 cm) tall with leaflets all down one side of the stem — thus the common name — and purplish flower scapes that turn white in fall, when the leaves turn yellow. The flowers are beautiful whether fresh or dried.

B. gracilis (blue grama grass) grows as tall as 20 inches (50 cm).

BOUTELOUA GRACILIS

Calamagrostis x acutifolia

Feather reed grass

Zones 4 to 9

These clumping grasses are strongly vertical, reaching about 30 inches (75 cm) tall in dry ground, twice as tall in wet, with flower scapes that rise a couple of feet (60 cm) above the leaves, giving the plant the look of a sheaf of wheat. The flowers are pinkish, fading to brown. They remain upright in winter.

'Karl Foerster' was chosen Perennial Plant of the Year in 1999. It has green foliage. 'Overdam' is more

CALAMAGROSTIS 'OVERDAM'

attractive, with variegated green-and-white leaves. It is a little less hardy than 'Karl Foerster' and may need a mulch in zone 4.

Carex species

Sedge

Zones vary

Sedges are, botanically speaking, not grasses at all, although they also form clumps of slender leaves with parallel veins. There are many species and cultivars of sedge for the garden, most of which enjoy ordinary to moist soil and are excellent in flower borders and containers. They spread by rhizome. Their foliage remains attractive in winter. Sedges recommended for dry gardens include two evergreen cultivars of *C. morowii*, zones 5 to 9. 'Ice Dance' grows 1 foot (30 cm) tall with green-and-white foliage. It is moderately invasive. 'Variegata' (variegated Japanese sedge) has a thin white leaf margin.

Chasmanthium latifolium
Northern sea oats
Zones 5 to 9

This arching, upright grass, native to the eastern and southeastern states, grows about 35 inches (90 cm) tall, with drooping, oatlike flower scapes that are good for flower arrangements. The foliage is deep green in shade, light green in sun. The fall color is bright yellow and the plant remains attractive all winter.

FESTUCA GLAUCA

Deschampsia cespitosa
Tufted hair grass
Zones 3 to 8

This green clumping grass grows about 16 inches (40 cm) tall with hairlike flower stalks about 40 inches (100 cm) tall. The flowers are beige. It grows in either moist or dry sites.

Festuca species
Fescue
Zones vary

Ornamental selections of fescue are some of the best grasses for dry gardens. They form low clumps of evergreen foliage that varies from green through blue-green to distinctly gray-blue. A spray of slender stems bear beige or tan flowers in summer. Since these grasses form neat low clumps, they are effective as edging plants, in the manner of small hedges.

F. amethystina, zones 5 to 8, is a bluish European species that grows about 1 foot (30 cm) tall. 'April Green' is olive green. 'Bronzeglanz' is blue-green. 'Klose' is light blue. 'Superba' is blue-green.

F. cinerea, zones 4 to 9, is a smaller, short-lived European species, about 8 to 10 inches (20-25 cm) tall. There are many cultivars. 'Solling' does not flower. 'Silberreiher' (silver egret fescue) grows just 6 inches (15 cm) tall.

F. glauca; *F. ovina glauca* (blue fescue), zones 3 to 9, is represented by many cultivars, including 'Elijah Blue,' 'Sea Urchin' and the paler 'Boulder Blue.' Most grow about 1 foot (30 cm) tall.

Helictotrichon sempervirens
Blue oat grass
Zones 4 to 8

This distinctly blue-gray, clump-forming grass grows about 16 inches (40 cm) tall, with flowers that reach twice as high. Give it sun to part shade.

Hystrix patula
Bottlebrush grass
Zones 3 to 8

This green grass is a native of the North American woods. It does best in dry shade, where it forms a clump about 1 foot (30 cm) tall. The greenish flowers, which are good for flower arrangements, bloom on 2-foot (60 cm) stems in early summer. It may self-sow and is easy from seed.

Liriope muscari;
L. platyphylla
Lilyturf, border grass
Zones 6 to 10

Not a grass but a member of the lily family, lilyturf functions as a grass in the landscape. (Also see *Ophiopogon*, page 77). Because of its heat tolerance, this shade-loving Oriental perennial is best known in warmer zones, where it is used as an evergreen ground cover or edging in well-drained soil in shade or part sun. It tolerates drought and salty air. From a low clump of strap-shaped leaves, small muscari-like bells bloom in clusters along the upper half of purple, 12-inch (30 cm) stalks in late summer or early fall. The flowers are good for cutting. The usual flower color is purple, but there are also white and lavender flowers, all followed by tiny black berries. Foliage may be green or variegated. Trim damaged leaves in the spring. Lilyturf can be divided in spring.

There are about 100 varieties of *L. muscari. L. spicata* (creeping lily-turf), zones 5 to 9, is a slightly shorter, creeping version that spreads by underground rhizome. Its flowers are lilac or white. It should be sheared back each spring.

MISCANTHUS 'MALEPARTUS'

Miscanthus sinensis
Maiden grass
Zones vary

This tall, graceful, clump-forming grass, sometimes taller than 7 feet (2 m), has long been a popular landscape plant in the Orient. Its garden longevity is evident in its development into more garden cultivars than any other grass. There are variegated forms, different colors and variations in the shape of the seed head, including highly decorative plumes, feathers and tails,

usually white. Some of these grasses enjoy moist soil, while most do fine in ordinary or dry, although they may not grow as tall. All form a dense clump and are not invasive by rhizome, although in gardens in zones 6 to 10, many spread by seed. Drought-tolerant cultivars hardy to zone 4 include 'Condensatus,' green with a white midrib; 'Gracillimus' with a white midrib; 'Graziella,' with a silver midrib; 'Malepartus,' a weeping form 5 to 6 feet (1.5-1.8 m) tall; 'Puenktchen,' with white dots; 'Purpurascens,' with burgundy foliage in fall; and 'Silverfeather' ('Silberfeder').

Drought-tolerant cultivars hardy to zone 5 include 'Adagio,' 'Arabesque,' 'Berlin,' 6 feet (180 cm) with golden flowers; 'Dixieland,' 'Grosse Fontaine,' 'Kleine Fontaine,' 'Morning Light,' 'November Sunset,' 'Positano,' 'Rotsilber,' 'Sarabande,' 4 to 5 feet (120-150 cm) with silver foliage; 'Silberpfeil,' 5 to 7 feet (150-210 cm) with late-fall flowers; 'Silberspinne,' 'Sirene,' 'Strictus,' 6 to 8 feet (180-240 cm), with upright, horizontally variegated foliage; 'Undine,' 'Variegatus,' 5 to 6 feet (150-180 cm) and variegated; 'Yaku Jima' and 'Zebrinus,' much like 'Strictus.'

Molinia caerulea
Purple moor grass
Zones 4 to 8

This green clump-forming European grass has strong, almost vertical flower stems that form a tight fan shape. 'Skyracer' is one of the tallest at 3 feet (90 cm), with purplish flowers on stems almost twice as tall. 'Heidebraut' and 'Moorhexe' grow 1 foot (30 cm) with flowers reaching 3 feet (90 cm). 'Variegata'

grows 18 inches (45 cm) with green-and-yellow leaves. Golden flowers appear in late summer. All are fine in sun or shade.

Ophiopogon japonicus
Mondo grass, monkey grass
Zones 6/7 to 10

Not really a grass at all, this perennial is often confused with liriope, another member of the lily family grown chiefly for its clumps of slender, grasslike foliage. Compared with liriope, this plant has more slender foliage, smaller flowers that are hidden by the leaves and blue fruit rather than black. It grows about 8 to 12 inches (20-30 cm) tall. The white to lilac-tinted flowers bloom in summer or early fall. Give mondo grass well-drained soil, either moist or dry. Since full sun can turn it brown, give it at least part shade, for instance under deciduous trees where true grasses struggle. It also makes an effective edging and does well in the spaces between flagstones. Trim off any unsightly leaves in spring. There are variegated versions and several smaller cultivars, including 'Kioto,' 'Nippon,' variegated 'Fuiri Gyoku-ryu' and the smallest of all, 'Super Dwarf,' about 3 inches (7.5 cm) tall, the latter two suggested as a ground cover around a potted bonsai.

Panicum virgatum
Switchgrass
Zones 4 to 9

Switchgrass is a North American plains grass that forms an arching clump about 3 feet (90 cm) tall with flowers reaching 4 to 8 feet (120-240 cm). It remains upright all winter. There are many cultivars, some developed in Germany before the plant was discovered on its own turf. 'Heavy Metal' and 'Prairie Sky' have bluish foliage. 'Huron Solstice' is burgundy. 'Shenandoah' is reddish. 'Rehbraun' and 'Warrior' turn red in fall. They spread by underground rhizome, especially rapidly in moist soil, so should be given a spot away from other perennials.

PENNISETUM VILLOSUM

Pennisetum alopecuroides
Fountain grass; Chinese pennisetum
Zones 5 to 9

This green, clump-forming grass grows in poor, even salty soil in full sun or part shade. It forms a graceful fountain shape of slender leaves about 3 feet (1 m) tall and equally wide, with a spray of bottlebrush seed heads in summer. There are several cultivars. Best known,

although a rampant self-seeder, is 'Moudry,' also called *P. viridescens.* Instead of the usual beige, its flower heads, which appear later than other cultivars, are purple-brown to nearly black, giving it the common name black fountain grass. Other cultivars include the dwarf 'Hameln,' 18 inches (36 cm) with whitish flowers reaching just above the foliage in late summer. 'Little Bunny' and 'Little Honey' are just 8 inches (20 cm). The latter is variegated green-and-white.

P. flaccidum has aggressive rhizomes and can self-seed, so is not recommended.

P. villosum (feathertop) is grown as an annual in northern zones and can be an aggressive perennial in zones 8 to 10.

Saccharum ravennae; Erianthus ravennae
Ravenna grass; hardy pampas grass
Zones 7 to 10

This tall, upright, arching European grass related to sugar cane makes a dramatic statement at the back of a perennial bed or in its own spot surrounded by lawn or patio. It grows as tall as 5 feet (1.5 m), with silvery-purple flower spikes that may ascend to 15 feet (4.6 m). It has become naturalized in parts of the U.S. Southwest.

Schizachyrium scoparium; Andropogon scoparius
Little bluestem
Zones 3 to 9

A native North American grass of the plains and prairies, this dependably drought-tolerant species also survives in ground that is quite

moist, but it should be in sun. It forms dense, upright tufts of slender, bluish or greenish blades about 2 feet (60 cm) tall, and turns red to bronze in fall. The showy flower heads are white and feathery. There are several cultivars.

Sorghastrum nutans
Indian grass
Zones 3 to 9

A bluish North American species that grows upright to almost 6 feet (1.8 m) and produces long plumes of flowers, Indian grass is handsome all summer and winter. While the species is easy to grow from seed, the best-known cultivar is 'Sioux Blue' with blue, 3-foot-tall (90 cm) foliage that turns golden in fall. It grows best in rich moist soil in sun but will survive in dry. The flowers are yellow-brown.

Sporobolus heterolepis
Prairie dropseed
Zones 4 to 8

Clumps of green foliage about 1 foot (30 cm) tall produce airy, finely textured fragrant brownish flowers on stems about 2 feet (60 cm) tall in late summer. It is a North American native.

Stipa gigantea
Feathergrass; needlegrass
Zones 6/7 to 10

This Mediterranean species forms a neat clump of narrow, arching evergreen leaves and 6-foot (2 m) stems bearing huge heads of seeds that resemble purplish oats. The seed heads turn yellow in winter.

ANNUAL ORNAMENTAL GRASSES

There are many annual ornamental grasses. These grasses form a clump; they don't spend long enough in the garden to spread by rhizome and become ground covers. Some self-sow to return next year, and most can be sown directly in the garden, although obviously this is a dangerous practice, since all grass seedlings look much alike, and you may end up weeding out your precious ornamentals. Smaller grasses look best in drifts of several plants but should be thinned to at least 6 inches (15 cm) apart.

Annual grasses are grown primarily for their decorative seed heads, which are not only attractive in the garden but also useful in dried arrangements, especially if picked before they are fully open. The foliage of the annuals is generally quite ordinary-looking, so plant them among and behind other plants with more attractive leaves.

Following are some of the best annual grasses for dry places. Their demands are few. Ornamental-grass specialist Peter Loewer writes, "As long as the soil drains and is capable of supporting a good crop of weeds, the annual grasses do quite well."

Agrostis nebulosa (cloud grass)
Avena sterilis (animated oats)
Briza maxima (quaking grass, puffed wheat)
Briza minor (little quaking grass)
Bromus lanceolatus; B. macrostachys (bromegrass)
Bromus madritensis
Lagurus ovatus (hare's-tail grass)
Lamarckia aurea (golden top)
Pennisetum glaucum 'Purple Majesty' (ornamental millet), an All-America winner especially recommended for containers.
Pennisetum setaceum (*P. ruppelii*)
Rhynchelytrum repens; R. roseum; Tricholaena rosea (ruby grass, Natal grass, champagne grass)
Zea mays japonica (japonica, striped maize)

GROUND COVERS FOR DRY SHADE

The following plants will survive in dry shade once established. However, flowering will be reduced: the deeper the shade, the fewer the blooms.

Aegopodium podagraria
Carex species
Cerastium tomentosum
Convallaria majalis
Elymus arenarius
Galium odoratum
Geranium macrorrhizum
Hemerocallis, naturalized orange- or yellow-flowered
Lamiastrum galeobdolon
Lamium 'Pale Peril'
Microbiota decussata
Ophiopogon japonicus
Phalaris arundinacea
Vinca minor

WILDFLOWER MEADOWS

Beautiful vistas of flowers and grasses in places of scant rainfall are not necesarily the result of a gardener's hard work. Meadow and prairie wildflowers grow without any human watering or fertilizing. Unplanted farm fields in the first or second year after the land has been cleared can be breathtaking in bloom. Rugged mountain slopes, cliffs and pockets of gravel host a multitude of plant species. Rock gardeners emulate these conditions to grow native alpine plants, and the same techniques can be used to grow nursery perennials that thrive on gravel or sand.

To create a wildflower meadow in a sunny or partly shaded part of your own garden, you will first need to clear the ground of all plants, including lawn and weeds, although you can leave any shrubs and trees you want to save. Till and prepare the soil as you would for any garden, and rake it

A mixture of annuals and perennials results in a home wildflower meadow with long-lasting color.

flat. Into this prepared ground, you can set plants or you can broadcast seeds, or a combination of both. Water transplants, rake the seeds in, and keep the soil moist till they sprout, removing any unwanted weed seedlings that appear. You may choose to grow a purchased seed mixture, which may or may not be predominantly species of your own area. If you prepare your own seed mixture, choose both annuals and perennials so there will be color the first year and in subsequent years. And choose a mixture of flowers and ornamental grasses, both annual and perennial, for the most natural-looking meadow.

Some examples of seeds to scatter on a wild-flower meadow include annual centaurea and papaver and daisies of all types, both annual and perennial, including aster, callistephus, coreopsis, gaillardia, helianthus and rudbeckia. Also include linum and annual euphorbia.

Meadows are very low-maintenance — they need no fertilizing and, once established, little or no watering — but they are not carefree. In nature, shrubs and trees eventually take root and take over, along with invasive weeds that may be more bully than beauty. You will need to weed out any plants you do not want and may need to add new plants or seeds in later years. In time, all meadows become dominated by a few species or too weedy or too limited in flower color. Then, the best plan is to start again from scratch.

CHAPTER FIVE

BULBS

Plants that grow from bulbs and other plump underground parts such as rhizomes and corms are among the best candidates for dry gardens. A bulb acts something like a camel's hump, storing moisture and nutrients to help the plant survive droughts. Many of the hardy bulbous plants originated in such places as semidesert grasslands that dry out in summer. These plants build strength right after blooming, usually in spring when their foliage is green and the soil is still wet. They ripen their seeds and die back to the ground, weathering the summer, fall and winter invisibly.

Not only can bulbs survive parched summers, but many need a dry period for survival. Their worst enemy is wet ground in summer, which causes them to rot, turning species that should be perennial into annuals that must be replanted every fall. Planting hardy bulbs among herbaceous perennials can be risky for the bulbs if you intend to water the perennials all summer. The same thing can happen at the edge of a watered lawn. The bulbs would rather dry out in a neglected spot on their own, even on a grassy slope left unmowed — or at least not mowed until their leaves have turned brown. After the foliage has died is also the best time to dig them up so that clumps can be separated and the smaller bulbs discarded or used for propagation in another place. Overcrowded bulbs produce fewer, smaller flowers.

White *Anemone blanda* complements *Pulsatilla*, a perennial member of the buttercup family that is sometimes also called anemone.

Grape hyacinths look best in groups, edging a garden bed.

Hardy bulbs, pages 84 to 91, are those that can survive frozen soil in winter and require a period of cold to flower. They are normally planted in fall to bloom the next spring. In warm zones, they can be grown as annuals or given a few weeks in the refrigerator between blooming seasons.

On the other hand, tender bulbs, corms or rhizomes that are perennial in warm zones (zone 7 or warmer), pages 92 to 94, need to be grown as annuals where winters are harsh. Or they can be overwintered indoors and replanted outdoors after spring frosts. Unlike the hardy bulbs, many will put up with moist soil in summer, although it

should not be soggy. If they are grown in containers, the pots can be brought indoors to spend the frosty months in a cool, bright place. If grown in the ground, they should be cut back almost to the base after the first fall frost, then carefully dug up, dried and dusted off before they are brought indoors. These bulbs need to be overwintered in conditions that will prevent them from drying out or rotting. They can be stored in cardboard cartons under layers of newspaper or buried in dry peat moss or vermiculite. The best storage temperature is above freezing but under 50 degrees F (10°C). Plant them in the garden around the last spring frost date, but if you want earlier flowers, start them in pots about a month earlier, and fertilize with houseplant fertilizer.

In addition to the species listed below, there are many lesser-known bulbs that will also succeed in sun and well-drained soil, including *Bessera* (zones 6 to 10), *Brodiae* (both tender and hardy species), *Calochortus* (zones 5 to 10), *Chionodoxa* (zones 3 to 10), *Eranthis* (zones 4 to 9), *Galtonia* (zones 5 to 10), *Hyacinth* (zones 4 to 10), *Ipheion; Triteleia* (zones 6 to 10), *Ixia* (zones 8 to 10), *Ornithogallum* (both tender and hardy species), *Puschkinia* (zones 3 to 10), *Sternbergia* (zones 6 to 10) and *Zephyranthes* (zones 6 to 10). Additional bulbs, corms and rhizomes listed in other chapters are *Iris*, *Convallaria majalis* (lily of the valley) and the edible *Alliums*. *Liriope* and *Ophiopogon* are listed with the perennial grasses on pages 76 and 77.

HARDY BULBS

The following bulbs will take pretty well any soil, but if it is heavy clay, they should be planted on a slope or in another well-drained area.

ALLIUM OSTROWSKIANUM

Allium species
Ornamental onion
Zones 3 to 10, except as noted

This genus presents the dryland gardener with a beautiful selection of umbel flowers from late spring until late fall. They vary from tiny to stately. Blues, pinks, purples and lilacs are most strongly represented, but there are also whites, yellows and more subtle shades. Many attract butterflies. Unlike most bulbs, alliums have remarkably long-lasting flowers, sometimes colored for weeks and then fading to beige or brown stars that have their own beauty and are prized for dry arrangements. Fallen seeds may sprout, so if you allow the flower heads to dry on the stem, be prepared to weed out the grassy seedlings next spring. Stalks cut while the flowers are at the peak of color can be hung upside down in a warm, dry place to dry for seeds or everlasting flower arrangements.

Most alliums grow from bulbs much like their kitchen cousins, the edible onions. Indeed, all the bulbs are edible, although they would be expensive fare. In northern zones, the bulbs are planted in fall anytime before the soil freezes. Most do best in well-drained soil in sun, although they will take some shade. For best appearance, grow them in groups. If clumps become too dense, dig them up and divide them in fall or early spring.

FAVORITES

Almost all of the ornamental onions (many of which are not listed here) are fine in dryland gardens — a notable exception is the tender, moisture-loving species *A. neapolitanum.* The larger-flowered hybrids need watering in spring.

A. caeruleum; A. azureum (blue globe onion, azure onion) has small starry, sky-blue umbels in early summer on 1-to-3-foot (30-90 cm) stalks. The narrow leaves wither by the time the flowers bloom. Zones 2 to 7.

A. cernuum (nodding onion) is a drought-tolerant North American wildflower with white or pink flowers on 18-to-24-inch (45-60 cm) stems.

A. christophii; A. albopilosum (star of Persia) produces impressive umbels of silvery starlike flowers, very eye-catching in early summer and in a vase. The stiff stem is just 1 to 2 feet (30-60 cm) tall, holding a flower as wide as 1 foot (30 cm).

A. flavum (small nodding onion, small yellow onion) has flat, sweetly scented, loose, bright yellow flower heads 2 to 3 inches (5-7.5 cm) across in midsummer. Stems are about 1 foot (30 cm) tall, and the foliage is bluish.

A. giganteum (giant onion) is often pictured in seed catalogs beside and at eye level with a standing child. A single bulb may set you back a couple of dollars, but 4-foot (1.2 m) or taller stems bearing 4-to-5-inch (10-13 cm) flower balls of deep violet in early summer may be worth the investment. 'Globemaster' is the usual violet-colored hybrid, the largest of all the giant alliums.

A. hollandicum; A. aflatunense has stiff stems as tall as 3 feet (1 m) topped with 4-inch (10 cm) pink or lilac-purple flower balls in late spring. Excellent in mid-border or toward the back, it is usually sold as 'Purple Sensation.' Additional large-flowered hybrids are listed on the next page.

A. karataviense is just 6 inches (15 cm) tall, with unusually wide, purplish leaves, sometimes twisted, and a pale pink, rose-colored or dark red flower ball in spring. It is excellent in a rock garden or a border's edge in full sun. 'Ivory Queen' is white.

A. moly (yellow onion, lily leek, golden garlic) has flat, bright yellow early-summer flowers 2 to 3 inches (5-7.5 cm) wide on 6-to-12-inch (15-30 cm) stems. The leaves are narrow and gray-green. In full sun, the leaf tips may scorch, so give it a bit of shade. Zones 4 to 10.

A. ostrowskianum; A. oreophilum (Dutch hyacinth) is 6 inches (15 cm) tall with loose pink or purple umbels in late spring. It needs sun but will tolerate a bit of shade cast by other plants. The cultivar 'Zwanenburg' has carmine flowers.

A. rosenbachianum (Rosenbach onion) has 2-foot (60 cm) ribbed stems bearing loose umbels of starry violet flowers in early June. 'Album' has white flowers. Zone 5.

A. senescens (German garlic) produces a foot-tall (30 cm) clump of strap-shaped foliage and, in late summer or fall, lilac globe flowers about 1 1/2 inches (4 cm) wide, a front of the border alternative to Liriope. 'Glaucum' (curly twist allium) has unusual, attention-getting twisted blue-gray foliage. The pink flowers seem almost an afterthought.

A. sphaerocephalum (roundheaded leek, ballhead or drumstick) has tightly compacted oval purple-red heads, 1 inch (2.5 cm) or wider, on slender 3-to-4-foot (90-120 cm) stems.

Spectacular allium hybrids with thick vertical stems 3 feet (90 cm) or taller supporting globe-shaped flower heads 5 inches (12 cm) or wider are becoming increasingly available. These tend to be short-lived, are hardy to about zone 5 and demand moist soil while in spring, but they become drought-tolerant in bloom. Cultivars include the dark purple 'Globemaster,' dark lilac purple 'Lucille Ball,' rose purple 'Gladiator,' deep purple 'Firmament,' amethyst 'Rien Poortvliet,' creamy white 'Mount Everest' and 'Mars,' with silvery reddish purple globes 6 inches (15 cm) wide.

ANEMONE BLANDA

Anemone blanda
Grecian windflower
Zones 4 to 8

There are hardy anemones and tender ones, described on page 92. The hardy group is the more modest, with small daisylike flowers above bright green, deeply divided foliage. In the early spring garden, they are a surprising contrast with the more usual cup- or bell-shaped spring bulbs. Most common is *A. blanda*, about 5 inches (13 cm) tall, available in shades of white, pink, red and blue, with the color often brightest at the petal tips, blending into a paler shade toward the green or dark center. Anemones grow from corms that look like small black twigs and are best planted in fall. Plant them 5 inches (12.5 cm) deep and 1 to 2 inches (2.5-5 cm) apart in dry or moist soil in part shade. Since they are easily hidden by taller flowers, they look best in a rock garden or at the front of a border.

FAVORITES
'Radar' is deep rose turning paler pink toward the center. 'Rose' and 'Blue Shades' are self-explanatory. 'White Splendor' is white with a dark center.

Colchicum autumnale
Autumn crocus
Zones 5 to 9

A surprise when it emerges from the ground in fall, without foliage — thus one common name, naked ladies — the colchicum flower seems like a giant crocus that has lost its sense of both proportion and time. Since it is a lily, not a crocus, it may have lost its sense of identity as well. On stems about 8 inches (20 cm) or a little taller, 2-inch (5 cm) mauve, lavender or white flowers appear without foliage because the straplike leaves emerge on a different schedule. They sprout in spring, grow about 6 inches (15 cm) tall and die by summer. These leaves must be left undisturbed since they feed the growing bulbs, but you may want to disguise them behind bedding annuals that will finish by the time the colchicum flowers appear. Plant the corms in late summer 4 inches (10 cm) deep and 6 inches (15 cm) apart. Give them full sun or part shade in fertile but light, well-drained soil. Planting in an area of low ornamental grasses such as fescues makes them easy to manage. The corms contain the poisonous alkaloid colchicine, used by geneticists to induce genetic mutations, so handle carefully. In zone 5, mulch the plants with 6 inches (15 cm) of dry leaves for winter protection. Where colchicums are content, they will multiply rapidly, thanks in part to their lack of appeal to squirrels. Divide them any time after the foliage dies back.

FAVORITES
The singles are lovely, but double flowers are longer-lasting. Doubles include the violet 'Roseum Plenum' and lavender pink 'Waterlily.'

CROCOSMIA 'LUCIFER'

Crocosmia hybrids

Montbretia
Zones 6 to 9

Clumps of broad, grassy foliage are decorated with 12-to-36-inch (30-90 cm) arched or straight stems bearing rows of bright orange, copper, pink or red starry trumpet flowers in late summer. These stems are favorites of flower arrangers but equally decorative in the garden. In a cutting garden, they make pretty companions for gladiolus and tigridia, although montbretia will withstand more shade. Plant the bulbs 4 inches (10 cm) deep and the same distance apart in light but humus-rich, well-drained soil. They are best grown in masses. Where they are content, they multiply rapidly. If crocosmia is mulched and the dead foliage is left on the plant, it may overwinter in zone 5.

FAVORITES
Widely available selections and hybrids include the yellow 'Citronella' and 'Norwich Canary' and tall, fiery scarlet 'Lucifer' with arching branches as tall as 36 inches (90 cm). 'Emily McKenzie' is bright orange with a red circle around the golden throat.

Crocus species

Crocus
Zones 3 to 8

Large-flowered hybrid Dutch crocuses in Easter shades of white, yellow and lilac help define the beginning of the gardener's spring, but there are many additional types known as species crocuses, some of which bloom even earlier, especially if they are planted in a south-facing, sunny location. Among the earliest are *C. ancyrensis*, *C. angustifolius* (cloth of gold) and *C. sieberi*. All look best grown in groups. Plant them 2 inches (5 cm) deep and about 3 inches (7 cm) apart in well-drained soil. All produce their cup-shaped flowers over clumps of slender, arching, grasslike, often striped foliage that continues to grow after the bulbs finish. Crocus bulbs are a favorite food of mice and squirrels. Where these rodents are a problem, dip corms in bitter-tasting Ro-pel or another predator repellent before planting. Also, spray the planted area with the same substance, or sprinkle it regularly with cayenne pepper.

FAVORITES
Although there are additional species crocuses, these are some of the most widely available.

C. chrysanthus (golden crocus), a parent of many garden hybrids, is recommended for naturalizing. The best-known cultivars are the pale yellow 'Cream Beauty' and the pale blue 'Blue Pearl,' winner of a Royal Horticultural Society Award of Merit.

C. tommasinianus has been grown in gardens for almost two centuries. Its stems are about 6 inches (15 cm) tall with blue, purple or mauve flowers. Easiest to find is the dark purple 'Ruby Giant.' The grassy foliage looks untidy for weeks after blooming, so situate them carefully. They naturalize well.

C. vernus, another garden heirloom, has 3-inch (7.5 cm) flowers that may be white or purple, striped or feathered. The most popular cultivar, 'Joan of Arc' ('Jeanne d'Arc') is all white. This species naturalizes well and can succeed in a lawn.

There are also hardy fall-blooming crocuses, notably *C. speciosus*, with blue or white flowers on 6-inch (15 cm) stems.

CROCUS ANCYRENSIS

FRITILLARIA IMPERIALIS

Fritillaria species
Fritillaria, fritillary
Zones 3 to 9

The standard-bearer of this genus is the tall, showy crown imperial (*F. imperialis*), as tall as 4 feet (120 cm) with a topknot of green foliage above a circle of orange, red or yellow bells, but it is fussy, and experimenting can be expensive — a single grapefruit-sized bulb can cost more than $20. Many of the charming but smaller fritillarias are far easier, and you can buy a bedful of bulbs for the same price. Flower colors tend to be purplish, brownish or greenish, often with yellow accents. Plant only fresh bulbs, since they do not store well. Give them well-drained, even sandy soil with some sun. The bulbs resent moving.

FAVORITES

All of these are hardy and bloom in spring. Additional species can be found in specialist catalogs.

F. acmopetala flowers are olive green with purplish markings on stems as tall as 20 inches (50 cm).

F. assyriaca (purple fritillary) has 12-inch (30 cm) multi-branched stems of nodding bell flowers that are purple outside, yellow inside.

F. meleagris (purple snake's-head fritillary, checker lily) has nodding bells with interesting checkered petals atop 10-inch-tall (25 cm) stems. There is a white version.

F. michailovskyi (Michael's flower) grows 8 inches (20 cm) tall with small maroon-purple, yellow-edged bells.

F. pallidiflora has 1-foot-tall (30 cm) stems bearing clusters of bright greenish yellow bells that brighten dark garden corners.

F. persica is a good and easy substitute for the crown imperial. It can grow as tall as 2 feet (60 cm) and has narrow grayish foliage and fragrant, dark purple flowers. "I let mine lean against euphorbia," writes English gardener Beth Chatto.

Lilium species
Lily
Zones 3 to 10

Among the classiest of flowers for arrangements, lilies of many species, sizes and colors, especially the Asian lilies, tiger lilies, Turk's cap lilies and several other species will survive and bloom in very dry soil. They bloom in all colors except blue — red, pink, yellow, white, orange, sometimes speckled or striped. In general, the whites, reds and pinks predominate early in the season, while the yellows and oranges bloom later. Given some water, they will grow bigger and more lush.

Plant the bulbs in early spring or fall in well-drained, organic soil. Plant them three times as deep as the height of the bulb or as deep as 1 foot (30 cm), because roots grow from the stem as well as the bulb. The Madonna lily (*L. candidum*) is an exception. It must be planted very shallowly in August or September, with just 1 inch (2.5 cm) of soil over the bulb. It prefers alkaline soil. Full sun suits all lilies, but partial shade is a better choice in sunny southern gardens, where full sun will fade the colors. In zones 9 and 10, the bulbs should be dug up in fall and refrigerated for two months before replanting. A surrounding ground cover such as periwinkle or perennial oregano will help keep the bulbs cool, which they prefer. Give them plenty of space when planting — about 2 feet (60 cm) apart. They will soon create

LILIUM 'BRENDA WATTS'

a clump that fills the spaces between. Deadhead flowers as they fade; otherwise, they set seed, which draws energy from the bulb. Pull out or cut off dead lily stems when they start to look unsightly.

Lilies are easy to divide almost anytime. Dig out entire sections of a clump, or plant stem bulblets or bulbils (the aerial beads along the stems of some varieties) or scales (healthy outer sections of a bulb, similar to cloves of garlic). Scales can be rooted in plastic bags filled with damp peat moss or vermiculite, tied and kept in a warm place. Bulblets will grow on the scales and can be detached and planted.

Lilies are vulnerable to the lily leaf beetle, a pest whose larvae emerge in spring and eat the foliage from the base of the stem upwards. Handpicking may take care of small infestations, or dust infected parts of plants with Rotenone.

FAVORITES
There are hundreds of lilies, all beautiful. The Orientals and their hybrids are moisture lovers, but if you choose from other offerings in local nurseries or from nursery catalogs or online sources in your own climatic zone, you should be able to obtain varieties suited to the dry places in your garden. Choose what you like by color, height and the shape, size and attitude of the flower. Some point upward, some downward and some sideways. Turk's cap and Martagon lilies have downward-facing flowers with recurved petals and protruding stamens. Other lilies have trumpet flowers. Nursery catalogs identify the bloom time of their offerings, so select accordingly for flowers from June through late summer.

MUSCARI BOTRYOIDES

Muscari species
Grape hyacinth
Zones 2 to 8

There are about 40 species of muscari. The best known resemble tiny bunches of grapes held upright on the tip of each stem. At 4 to 6 inches (10-15 cm) tall, they make excellent edgings. They also make a good ground cover under deciduous trees or shrubs. Muscari blooms in early spring and multiplies dependably by division and by seed, creating a sea of early color wherever it is planted, preferably in sun or light shade and preferably in masses. Plant the bulbs 3 (7 cm) inches deep and 3 inches (7 cm) apart. Most loved are the blues, from sky to purplish, although there are also whites and pinks. Clumps of grassy foliage appear after the flowers, last through winter and then die back.

FAVORITES
M. botryoides (common grape hyacinth), the most common species, has 1-inch-tall (2.5 cm) flower clusters, usually purple, on 6-inch (15 cm) stems. 'Album' is white, 'Carneum' is pink, 'Caeruleum' is bright blue.

M. armeniacum (Armenian grape hyacinth) is a littler taller than *M. botryoides*, about 8 inches (20 cm) with bigger flowers. 'Blue Spike' is a double blue, 'Sapphire' is an especially long-lasting blue, 'Early Giant' is a single blue, 'Heavenly Blue' has a musky fragrance.

M. comosum (tassel grape hyacinth) looks very different, with purple topknots on stems as tall as 12 inches (30 cm).

M. latifolium (bicolor grape hyacinth) is showy, a bicolor whose flower clusters are purple on the lower half, sky blue on top. It grows about 12 inches (30 cm) tall.

Muscari hybrids include 'Dark Eyes,' 6 to 8 inches (15-20 cm) tall with white-rimmed blue flowers, zones 4 to 8.

Narcissus species

Daffodil, narcissus, jonquil
Zones 2 to 10

These spring bulbs are loved for their trumpet flowers in shades of yellow and orange. There are also pinks and whites, doubles, fragrant jonquils and tiny species for border edges and rock gardens. A few, such as *N. tazetta*, naturalized along the Gulf Coast but best known in northern zones as the paper-whites purchased for forcing indoors, are not winter-hardy, but most are — although they will not survive in soggy ground.

All are technically known as narcissus. The word daffodil usually describes a flower with a long, flaring trumpet, technically a corona; the circle of petals around the corona is called the perianth. Jonquil was a term once applied only to the species *N. jonquilus*, but is now used for fragrant narcissus in general. Where daffodils, or narcissus, are content, especially in slightly acidic soil, they will form gradually widening clumps that can be easily divided after the foliage fades. They can even be coaxed to naturalize in grassy areas, provided the grass is not cut until the foliage fades, around mid-June. The best survival approach is to grow several types in different spots to find out what suits your own garden.

Plant narcissus bulbs soon after they become available in fall, since they need some time to become established. Plant them three times as deep as their diameter, in very well-drained soil, perhaps on a slope. They will grow in full sun or light shade.

The narcissus bulb fly infests bulbs in some areas. The fly lays its eggs at the base of the foliage. When the eggs hatch, the grubs move into the soil and burrow into the bulbs to feed. In spring, the grubs emerge as flies. Covering the plants after they bloom with a fabric cover such as Reemay excludes the flies. Also, bulbs growing through a ground cover are less likely to be attacked; the flies prefer bare soil. The biological control BioSafe is also effective.

FAVORITES

Choosing narcissus (or daffodils, if you prefer) is mostly a matter of taste. There are hundreds of varieties tall and short, yellow, orange, white, pink or bicolored, single or double. Bulb catalogs present pages of temptations. The monarch of daffodils for more than a century has been 'King Alfred,' a term now used to market any of a number of excellent large golden yellow narcissus, especially 'Golden Harvest,' 'Yellow Sun,' 'Dutch Master' or 'Standard Value.' 'Carlton' is similar but lighter yellow. For naturalizing in grass, look for special mixes sold for that purpose — some of the older cultivars, especially, are more resilient and apt to multiply than newer hybrids. For rock gardens and border edges, consider some of the smaller species such as the 8-inch (20 cm) *N. bulbocodium* (petticoat daffodil), the 4-inch (10 cm) *N. cyclamineus*, especially yellow 'February Gold,' white 'February Silver,' white-and-lemon yellow 'Jack Snipe,' white-and-pink 'Foundling' and gold 'Peeping Tom,' and the 8-inch (20 cm), multi-flowering *N. triandrus* (angel's tears) such as yellow 'Liberty Bells' and white 'Thalia.'

N. tazetta (paper-white), zones 8 to 10, flowers are mostly white with a white, cream or yellow corona. An exception is the all-yellow 'Soleil d'Or.'

NARCISSUS 'WHITE PLUME'

Tulipa species

Tulip

Zones 2 to 7

There are tulips large and small for the dry garden. Some of the smaller species begin blooming soon after the snow melts, while better-known tulips such as the tall hybrids, especially the doubles, continue into early summer. They bloom in all colors except blue. The cup flowers may be pointed, fringed, flaring or flat.

Earliest to bloom are the species, or botanical, tulips. Some of these are only about the height of crocuses and bloom not long after. The blooming of later species tulips overlaps with the first of the hybrids, tulips labeled early, mid-season and late. Early cultivars include the fragrant yellow 'Bellona.' Mid-season tulips, which bloom around mid-May in zone 4, include the Mendels and Triumphs. Later come the most popular tulips, the Darwins, some as tall as 2 feet (60 cm). Also late are the Rembrandts, with their "broken" colors, the feathery Parrot tulips and, finally, the Double Late, or Peony-Flowered, tulips, which have so many petals that they scarcely look like tulips at all. Another late group are the Viridiflora tulips, whose petals are striped with green. Consider varieties with variegated foliage for interest past blooming time. 'Garant,' for instance, is a Darwin hybrid whose leaves have a yellow edge. *T. greigii* and its cultivars have striped or mottled leaves. *T. pulchella* has leaves edged in red.

Where squirrels are a problem, dip bulbs in bitter-tasting Ro-pel or another predator repellent before planting. Also, spray the planted area with the same substance, or sprinkle the ground regularly with cayenne. Grow bulbs through a low ground cover, which helps fool predators and also enhances the appearance of the bulbs. Tulips should have full sun or a little shade and must be planted where they can dry out thoroughly in summer, or they may not survive. Although the foliage becomes unsightly, it must not be removed until it has begun to fade, since it feeds the bulbs. Grow tulips behind low ornamental grasses to disguise the foliage or dig the bulbs, complete with foliage, and heel into a sunny, hidden spot. Replant after the foliage dies. Tulip bulbs multiply and become smaller and less floriferous each year. They should be dug up in late summer or fall and re-spaced, with only the largest bulbs preserved.

The large-flowered tulips need a cold winter. In zones 8 to 10, refrigerate the bulbs for about 8 weeks ending in November or December, then plant. The smaller-flowered species are more successful where winters are warm.

The butterfly tulip (*Calochortus* spp.) is more tender, to about zone 6. It does best in part shade in well-drained sandy or gravelly soil and must dry out in summer.

TULIPA KAUFMANNIANA

FAVORITES

Some gardeners grow tulips as annuals, discarding the bulbs when flowering is done. If you want perennials, but your tulips don't bloom a second or third year despite a dry summer and a cold period, it may not be your fault. In trials at North Carolina State University, only about one-quarter of more than 100 cultivars tested proved to be perennial. Among species and cultivars with a proven record as perennials are a host of species and several hybrids, including the following:

T. fosteriana grows about 1 foot (30 cm) tall, with gray-green foliage and wide-open flowers. Dependable hybrids include 'Candela,' 'Red Emperor,' 'Princeps' and 'Purissima.'

T. greigii is 10 to 12 inches (25-30 cm) tall, with large flowers and gray-green striped or mottled foliage. Dependable cultivars include 'Plaisir' and 'Red Riding Hood,' both more than a century old.

T. kaufmanniana (water-lily tulip), one of the first species to bloom, has starry flowers that resemble water lilies and open flat. Most are bicolored. Dependable cultivars include 'Giuseppe Verdi,' 'Heart's Delight,' 'Shakespeare,' 'Showwinner' and 'Stresa.'

T. praestans has been cultivated in Holland since the 1600s. It is tall, to 16 inches (40 cm), with abundant foliage and as many as four red cup-shaped flowers per stem.

T. turkestanica has 8-inch (20 cm) stems bearing creamy white star-shaped flowers with bright yellow centers.

Among perennial hybrids are the red 'Apeldoorn,' yellow 'Golden Appeldoorn,' 'China Pink,' cream-and-green 'Spring Green,' deep purple 'Queen of the Night,' 'White Triumphator,' 'Red Shine' and the double pink 'Angelique.'

TENDER BULBS

The following bulbs can be grown year-round in the warmest zones but must be grown as annuals or overwintered indoors where winters are cold. Many tender bulbs, such as begonias, callas and dahlias, need steady moisture, but the following list includes some of the better choices for dry places. They should be given full sun and well-drained soil. See also *Narcissus tazetta*, page 90.

Acidanthera bicolor; Gladiolus callianthus
Peacock orchid, sword lily
Zones 7 to 10

This gladiolus relative has about 10 sweetly fragrant flowers on each stem. The stems, usually 24 to 36 inches tall (60-90 cm) are self-supporting, although they can reach 4 feet (120 cm) in rich ground and may need staking. The orchidlike flowers, white with a contrasting purple or brown triangular blotch at the base of each petal, open from the bottom of the spike upward. Like glads, they are excellent cut flowers. Plant the corms 5 inches (7 cm) deep and 8 inches (20 cm) apart in dry or well-drained moist soil, sun or part shade. Mulch for the winter in zones 7 and 8. In zones 9 to 11, they may naturalize.

FAVORITES
Murielae, sometimes listed as a cultivar, is a synonym for the species *Acidanthera bicolor*, also known as *Acidanthera bicolor* subspecies murielae or simply *A. murielae*.

ALSTROEMERIA AURANTIACA

Alstroemeria aurantiaca
Peruvian lily; Inca lily
Zones 7 to 10

Tropical alstroemerias are favorites of the florist industry, with their clusters of bright trumpet flowers, pink, red, brown, orange and yellow, often spotted, that last well when cut. *A. aurantiaca* is a hardier yellow- or orange-flowered cousin that may overwinter in zone 7 and even zone 6 if heavily mulched. Often grown in pots, not only where it is tender but also where it is hardy, it grows from a thick tuber that must be handled carefully, since it resents transplanting. Set the roots about 10 inches (25 cm) deep in soil with excellent drainage. Each plant grows about 3 feet (90 cm) tall and equally wide. Alstroemeria should be planted in full sun except in the hottest gardens, where it needs some shade. Where winters are frosty, move potted plants indoors in fall to a cool window where the temperature is just above freezing.

FAVORITES
The Ligtu Hybrids, as tall as 4 feet (120 cm), have yellow, orange or red flowers. Look for bright red 'Redcoat,' yellow-veined, orange 'Moerheim

Orange,' 'Sweet Laura,' with fragrant yellow flowers striped red, and 'Freedom,' in various shades of pink.

Anemone species
Anemone
Zones 7 to 10

Unlike the hardy anemones, page 86, which resemble small daisies, there are tender anemones that mimic low-growing poppies. I once saw fields of glorious, brightly colored poppy-flowered anemones (*A. coronaria*) blooming wild on the dry, grassy hills of the Middle East. Red, blue, pink, white or lavender 3-inch (7 cm) bowl-shaped flowers with black centers bloom on 6-to-9-inch-tall (15-22.5 cm) stems. The flowers open in sunlight and close at night and on overcast days. They do best where the spring weather is cool and moist and summers are hot and dry, in well-drained soil in sun or part shade. Soak the tubers in water overnight before planting 2 inches (5 cm) deep and 4 inches (10 cm) apart. Staggered plantings produce a long season of bloom. Where they are hardy, planting in November gives flowers in February and planting in April gives flowers in October. Apply winter mulch in zones 7 and 8.

FAVORITES
A. coronaria is the best known of the tender anemones. The de Caen group are the usual singles. The St. Brigids are the usual semidouble or double flowers, with a zinnia-like frill of petals around a black or green center.

A. x *fulgens* hybrids are usually represented by the St. Bavo strain, which grow about 1 foot (30 cm) tall with 2-inch (5 cm) flowers in lavender and red.

Gladiolus hybridus
Gladiolus
Zones 8 to 10

A supreme vase flower, the gladiolus, with its towers of trumpet blooms opening from the base up, can be difficult to place in the garden, so it is often grown in rows in a vegetable garden or massed in its own plot, ready for cutting. Or it can be mingled with other tall flowers such as tall zinnias, marigolds and white daisies. The stiff stems, one per corm, tend to lean at slightly different angles, giving a gladiolus-only plot a dizzy look unless each stem is staked. All colors are available except blue. The corms will grow in any soil from rich to sandy, moist to dry. Sandy loam and full sun suits them best. They do best with regular watering for the first month, but even with minimal water all season will bloom, although stems will be shorter and flowers smaller. Mulch around them as soon as they are tall enough. Where they are hardy, they are planted from October to December. In northern zones, plant them around the last spring frost date. Pick the spikes when a couple of flowers have opened; the others will open in the vase.

FAVORITES
The largest-flowered glads, with individual blooms wider than 4 inches (10 cm) on stems as tall as 5 feet (150 cm) are the least able to deal with growing conditions other than perfect. The usual bagged mixtures of corms sold for home gardens have more modest flowers. For the dry garden, choose these or other smaller-flowered types such as the miniatures, those with flowers no larger than 2½ inches (7 cm).
   G. nanus (butterfly gladiolus; winter hardy gladiolus) is a lower-growing 2-foot (60 cm) species that never needs staking. It has flaring starry flowers, often white with contrasting red or pink markings that resemble butterfly wings. There are also reds and pinks, such as 'Nathalie.' This species is hardy in zone 5 with a winter mulch.
   The hybrid 'The Bride' has grasslike foliage and slender 18-inch (45 cm) stems topped with clusters of pure white 2-inch (5 cm) flowers.

Nerine species
Nerine lily
Zones 9 to 11

N. bowdenii, the species that represents virtually all the nerine bulbs sold, produces clusters of 3-inch (7 cm) trumpet-shaped flowers with petals curled backwards, usually magenta pink and seemingly dusted with silver. After the large, strap-shaped leaves appear, this species blooms on 2-foot (60 cm) stems in fall. Plant the bulbs 4 inches (10 cm) deep and about 6 inches (15 cm) apart in summer or early fall in rich, well-drained soil. Give them full sun in cloudy areas, part shade in bright areas. In zone 8, they should be mulched for the winter. Clumps can be divided in spring and replanted. Nerine lilies are often grown in containers since they flower best when rootbound. Overwinter containers in a cool, bright place.

FAVORITES
The usual *N. bowdenii* offering is 'Pink Triumph' with especially large, 3-inch (7.5 cm) flowers. The species *N. sarniensis* produces its flowers before the foliage appears. *N. undulata* has pink flowers with unusual twisted petals.

Ranunculus
Persian buttercup
Zones 8 to 10

The cultivated and cossetted ranunculus is related to the roadside buttercup, evidence of its inherent tenacity. But the two plants both act and look entirely different. Unlike the buttercup with its waxy single yellow flowers, the cultivated species is generally grown in its double form, an almost solid globe of petals in every color but green or blue. The flower globes may be 2 to 5 inches (5-12 cm) wide, produced for several months and prized for cutting. They grow from corms that have thick, easily broken roots called claws. Plant them 1 or 2 inches (2.5-5 cm) deep and 3 inches (7.5 cm) apart. Plants grow about 18 inches (45 cm) tall, excellent massed in mid-border or grown in a container. Give them full sun in well-drained soil. Where they are hardy, they are planted in late fall to flower in spring. In zone 8, give them a winter mulch. From zone 7 north, they are planted in spring like other tender bulbs. Even where they are hardy, they are generally dug up after flowering and stored for the winter.

FAVORITES
Ranunculus is generally sold as a mixture of colors, although there are occasional offerings such as 'Pink with Red Picotee' and 'Yellow with Red Picotee.'

Sparaxis tricolor
Harlequin flower, wandflower
Zones 9 and 10

Harlequins, clowns that wear brightly patterned clothing, inspired the merry name of these bright, starry flowers that may be red, yellow, blue, purple, lilac or white, often with a contrasting yellow throat and a black spot at the base of each petal. The waxy-looking 2-inch (5 cm) flowers, excellent for cutting, bloom from the bottom to the top of spikes 12 to 18 inches (30-45 cm) tall. The sword-shaped foliage appears in late fall and dies the following summer. Give harlequin flowers full sun at the front of a border or in a rock garden, anywhere with very well-drained soil. Where they are hardy, plant the corms in fall about 2 inches (5 cm) apart and deep. In cooler zones, they are grown in pots that are brought indoors for winter so the foliage can mature.

FAVORITES
Cultivars and hybrids include the red 'Fire King,' purple 'Horning,' white 'Alba Maxima' and red-striped, white 'Robert Schuman.'

Tigridia
Mexican tiger flower;
Mexican shell flower
Zones 7 to 10

Like the gladiolus to which it is related, this corm also produces a straight spire as tall as 30 inches (75 cm) with few leaves. The flowers are generally larger, however, as wide as 6 inches (15 cm). They are red, orange, pink, yellow or buff, usually with a spotted cup. Although each bloom lasts just a day, the extravagance of each flower makes a lasting impression, and since there are numerous buds, flowering may be extended over several weeks in summer. Plant the corms 4 inches (10 cm) deep and the same distance apart in sandy soil in sun or a little shade. They should be mulched for the winter in zones 7 and 8.

CHAPTER SIX

PERENNIALS AND VINES

The theater metaphor has often been used to describe a perennial garden. Various players have their "hour upon the stage," then retreat to the wings. Whenever you look at a garden, you can pick out the stars from the supporting cast that may well be front and center next week. The dry garden may have a somewhat lesser-known cast of perennials than you're used to. Call it Off Broadway, if you like. But these, too, are long-term players that will keep the garden colorful and blooming season after season, provided you choose plants suitable for your climatic zone (see map, page 179). Note that although some perennials are listed as suitable for zones 9 and 10, they may not do well in southern Florida and the Gulf Coast because of the combination of high humidity and warm winters.

If these plants are not available locally, they can be purchased by mail order (see Sources, page 180). In addition, most perennials, especially the species rather than named varieties, can be grown from seeds.

Chrysanthemums are among the most colorful daisies in the fall garden.

Acanthus species

Acanthus, bear's breeches
Zones vary

Acanthus is a dramatic plant known mostly for its glossy green, deeply lobed or spiny leaves as long as 2 feet (60 cm) and half as wide that grow straight from the ground. Some gardeners snip off the flower stems, which otherwise rise far above the foliage for weeks in summer, bearing small, tubular, lipped pink, lilac or white flowers, excellent for cutting and good for drying. Acanthus does best in very well-drained soil and full sun except in the hottest gardens, where it should have some shade. Set plants about 3 feet (1 m) away from other perennials or shrubs, since the roots are wide-ranging. Plants that have been flowering for three or four years can be divided in spring or fall. Acanthus takes a season or two to become established but is then difficult to relocate or eradicate. In the warmer zones, such as coastal California, acanthus can become weedy and should be planted with caution.

FAVORITES
A. mollis latifolius is the hardiest, to zone 6, with beautiful, shiny green soft leaves that are evergreen except where winters are severe. Flower spikes can grow more than 5 feet (1.5 m) tall, with white flowers with pink bracts. Mulch for the winter in the coolest gardens.

A. spinosus, zones 8 to 10, has more finely divided, leathery dark green foliage with soft spines. The flower stems are not quite as tall, but flowering may last longer in sunny gardens.

ACHILLEA MILLEFOLIUM

Achillea species

Yarrow, milfoil, sneezeweed
Zones 2 to 9

Yarrows ranging from aggressive to unassuming deserve places in almost any garden, but it is where the soil is poor and dry and winters are harsh that they take on star status, whether in full sun or partial shade. All have aromatic foliage, and most produce vertical stems holding long-lasting flat umbels of tiny flowers whose color fades as they age, so a single plant may have several colors at once. There are whites as well as yellows, oranges, pinks, roses and reds. When they turn brown or black, the flower stems should be removed.

Common yarrow (*A. millefolium*) grows on prairie roadsides and into the mountains where little else will survive. It is one of the white-flowered types, with flower stems as tall as 3 feet (1 m), and may be the toughest and pushiest of the lot, although its cultivars are somewhat less hardy. *A. ptarmica* is extremely hardy, white-flowered and inclined to spread. There is also a ground-covering species, *A. tomentosa*. Most yarrows are extremely winter hardy but *A. ageratum* is less so, to zone 7.

Set plants 18 to 24 inches (45-60 cm) apart, preferably in full sun and well-drained soil. By the second season, most should fill in the empty spaces. After three or four years, established clumps should be divided. Stems of achillea can be cut in full flower for drying; hang them upside down in an airy place.

Fungal disease may strike achilleas, especially if plants are watered or fertilized. *A. ageratum* and *A. ptarmica* are the species most likely to suffer from powdery mildew.

FAVORITES
A five-year study of yarrows took place at the Chicago Botanic Garden, where 42 species and cultivars were tested for ornamental value, ease of cultivation and distinctiveness. Another characteristic that was noted was the habit of flopping. Some cultivars flopped so badly that all the fallen stems had to be removed, leaving nothing but a patch of brown stubs and bits of leaves. Of the 42 types tested, here are the best:

A. 'Citronella' has creamy flowers that fade to grayish brown and last a full month on stems which usually stay upright. There is some repeat blooming.

A. 'Coronation Gold' bears dense clusters of large, long-lasting golden flowers on relaxed 3-foot (1 m) stems. It has silvery green foliage and a non-spreading habit. There is no repeat bloom.

A. 'Hoffnung' produces a solid mass of yellow flowers on spreading upright plants. Repeat bloom is good.

A. millefolium 'Lilac Beauty' and the similar 'Sawa Sawa' are the only two cultivars given the Chicago trial's top rating of "excellent." Both have upright stems and lavender flowers that fade to pink or white.

A. millefolium 'Rosea' has large, loose clusters of reddish flowers and a better growing habit than the similar 'Nakuru' and 'Rosy Red.' The stems usually remain upright, and repeat blooming is good. In a different trial, the similar cultivar 'Fire King' was found to be one of the best perennials for long bloom, about 15 weeks from July to October.

A. 'Parker's Yellow' is similar to 'Coronation Gold,' although it differs in its greener foliage and greater height, about 4 feet (1.2 m).

A. 'Peach Blossom' produced the clearest pink flowers in the trial. It reblooms well, and the stems are mostly erect.

A. *ptarmica* 'The Pearl' was the best of the whites in the trial. This species is quite different from the others, with dark green foliage, relaxed stems and double pure white button flowers that are not borne in flat heads. The stems grow as tall as 3 feet (1 m). 'The Pearl' can be invasive, but it blooms for a full six weeks in July and August and puts up with almost anything, even wet ground — although that encourages floppiness. It is easy from seed. Similar cultivars are 'Ballerina,' 'Perry's White' and 'Snowball' ('Boule de Neige' or 'Schneeball').

A. 'Snow Taler' produces bright white flowers for a full two months on stems that usually remain upright. There is little reblooming, but deadheading is not needed until late in the season.

Although a popular choice among gardeners because of its luminous pale yellow flowers, A. 'Moonshine' did not make the top-10 list because of occasional flopping.

All these achilleas, except for 'The Pearl,' must be purchased or grown from divisions or cuttings. Other species and cultivars can be grown easily from seed, but they did not rate as high and may be invasive or variable. In the Chicago trial, dead-heading had little effect on encouraging repeat blooming.

It is important to note that since this trial concluded, additional excellent cultivars have appeared. One is 'Fireland,' whose red flowers fade to gold. 'Marmalade' is dark orange. There are also additional species which may take some searching, but offer additional features to the dryland garden. A. *grandiflora*, hardy to zone 4, grows 6 feet (2 m) tall with flat heads of white flowers. A. x *kellereri* is just 8 inches (20 cm) tall with silver foliage and yellow-centered white flowers.

Agave
Century plant
Zones 8 to 10, except as noted

Fabulous and distinctive, agave resembles nothing else in the garden save their smaller kin the yucca and their Old World cousin, the aloe, all of which form rosettes of upward-pointing foliage. Agave has fleshy triangular leaves, usually 2 to 4 feet (60-120 cm) tall that may be green or striped with yellow or white. Leaf edges may be spiky, hairy or thorned. Agave is a slow-growing plant that takes its common name, century plant, from the belief that some species native to hot, dry regions of the Americas live that long before producing a towering flower stalk. Smaller agaves produce flowers in 10 years or more but in any case, once the flowers mature, the plant dies. Give it full sun and perfectly drained soil. Dry soil is especially important in cooler or moister areas, where it may be necessary to amend the soil with gravel and plant it on a hill. Some species survive in zone 7, especially if planted near large, sheltering rocks.

AGAVE PALMERI

The smaller types of agave are excellent for a container, and in cool areas can be wintered indoors. If you are growing agave in a container, use sand, soil and gravel but no peat moss.

FAVORITES
While gardeners with relatively warm and dry winters can grow any agave, the smaller agaves are more versatile in terms of climatic zone and garden position. They are especially good in containers. Among the choicest of the smaller agaves are:

A. *bracteosa*, 1 to 2 feet (30-60 cm) tall.

A. *colorata*, which grows less than 1 foot (30 cm) tall with gray-blue leaves.

A. *lechuguilla*, 12 to 18 inches (30 to 45 cm) tall with yellow-green leaves, hardy to zone 7.

A. *parryi*, 2 feet (60 cm) tall and wide, with blue-gray leaves, hardy to zone 7.

A. *utahensis*, hardy to zone 5.

A. *victoria-reginae*, 23 inches (30 cm) tall and hardy to zone 7.

Anthemis tinctoria
Golden marguerite, chamomile
Zones 2 to 10

This vigorous plant, related to culinary chamomile, is not itself used for tea or medicine but has been used as a source of yellow dye. Relaxed stems, usually about 2 feet (60 cm) tall, bear attractive, ferny foliage and a crop of 2-inch (5 cm) yellow daisies for several weeks in summer. They are excellent for cutting. The plant tolerates dry ground, even excessively alkaline, and spreads well to fill empty areas while slower plants are gathering steam. Golden marguerite is easy from seed and will self-sow where it is content, so it is an excellent choice for a wildflower meadow. Give it full sun and well-drained soil. After two years of flowering, clumps can be divided in spring.

FAVORITES
'Kelwayi,' the usual cultivar offered, grows 2 to 3 feet (60-90 cm) tall with yellow flowers.

The species *A. sancti-johannis* (orange marguerite), zones 3 to 8, forms a bush of hairy gray foliage topped with yellow-centered orange flowers.

ARMERIA MARITIMA

Armeria species
Thrift, sea pink
Zones 4 to 10

The common name, thrift, for the species *A. maritima*, attests to the ease with which pieces of this low-growing perennial will root. From a cushion of thin, bluish green grassy leaves (often weeded out by mistake) grows slender 6-inch (15 cm) stems bearing 1-inch-wide (2.5 cm) pompoms of pink, red, lilac or white petals in early summer. Armerias form neat, round cushions of foliage in well-drained soil in sun. They are unhappy in shade or if crowded by other plants, but do well in poor, dry soil in sunny rock gardens, border edges or along paths. They are easily grown from seed. In temperate climates, they are evergreen and may bloom all year. Since clumps eventually die out in the middle, they should be divided every three years.

FAVORITES
A. maritima is the usual species offered. Its cultivars include the white 'Alba,' bright pink 'Laucheana,' which spreads well to form a good ground cover, and bright red 'Splendens' with taller 1-foot (30 cm) stems.

A. juncea is smaller, with its pink flower balls held on 1-inch (2.5 cm) stems.

A. juniperifolia (Spanish thrift) is a 3-inch-tall (7.5 cm) version that is perfect for the spaces between patio stones or for other spots where it will be displayed well.

A. pseudoarmeria (*A. pseudameria*) is equally drought-tolerant but much taller, up to 16 inches (40 cm), and a little less hardy, to zone 5. Most frequently offered is the Joystick series.

ANTHEMIS TINCTORIA

Aster species

Aster, Michaelmas daisy
Zones 4 to 9

Probably best known as the little purple daisies growing wild along rural roadsides in late summer, more refined asters add welcome color to the garden as other flowers fade in late summer. While the large-flowered show asters need moisture, staking and coddling, the smaller-flowered types are drought-tolerant and easy care. Typical flower colors are blue, pink, purple or lilac, with yellow centers. There are also whites. Depending upon species and cultivar, flowers may be single or double, and stems vary from a few inches to 5 feet (150 cm) or taller. The taller types may be less tender, to zone 5. Asters need well-drained soil and prefer full sun, although they will also bloom in part shade. The species can be grown from seeds; others must be purchased or propagated vegetatively.

FAVORITES

A. alpinus (alpine aster) is just 6 to 9 inches (15-22 cm) tall with blue, pink or white flowers, recommended for rock gardens or the front of a dry border.

A. divaricatus (white wood aster) is shade-tolerant, with dark purple 2-to-3-foot (45-90 cm) stems and white flowers.

A. ericoides (heath aster) forms a bushy mound as tall as 3 feet (90 cm) with tiny leaves and small, starry white flowers. 'Blue Cloud' and 'Pink Cloud' are colored accordingly.

A. novae-angliae (New England aster) is a common wildflower throughout the Northeast and one of the most dependable species where winters are cold. It tolerates both wet and dry soils. There are many cultivars. The

ASTER NOVAE-ANGLIAE

larger the flowers, the more it will appreciate watering. Those with taller stems tend to flop over, which may be fine at the edge of a bed, or you may want to stake plants or surround them with a low cage. There are many good varieties, including the 40-inch (100 cm) salmon pink 'Alma Potschke,' violet-blue 'Hella Lacy,' 36-inch (90 cm) 'Pink Winner' and 18-inch (45 cm) 'Purple Dome.' Deep red 'September Ruby' ('September-rubin') grows 4 feet (120 cm) tall.

A. novae-belgii (New York aster) has smooth, dark green, shiny foliage and flowers usually less than 2 inches (5 cm) wide. There are scores of cultivars, and again, those with larger blooms appreciate more watering. New England and New York asters spread rapidly and so can be divided in spring or fall every year.

A. sedifolius 'Nanus' (Rhone aster), hardy to zone 2, produces clouds of small blue flowers on 18-to-24-inch (45-60 cm) stems.

A. tongolensis (East Indies aster), zones 4 to 8, grows 16 inches (40 cm) tall with lilac-colored flowers, recommended for containers. 'Wartburg Star' is the usual cultivar sold.

Boltonia asteroides

Boltonia
Zones 4 to 10

On thread-thin but upright branching stems as tall as 3 to 4 feet (1-1.2 m), *Boltonia asteroides* bears starry white daisy flowers that are disproportionately small, only 1 inch (2.5 cm) wide but produced in great numbers, giving the plant a little of the airy quality of baby's-breath, although boltonia is more substantial. It will grow in ordinary to poor soil in full sun or light shade. The stems can be staked or surrounded by a cage. The leaves are narrow and grayish. The daisy flowers, white or pinkish with a yellow center, make excellent cut flowers. Blooming begins in July and continues until fall. Boltonia clumps widen rapidly so should be divided every second year in spring or fall.

FAVORITES

'Snowbank' is the usual choice, an excellent, mildew-resistant, bushy cultivar about 4 feet (120 cm) tall. The pink-flowered 'Pink Beauty' has a looser form.

CAMPANULA PERSICIFOLIA

Campanula species

Bellflower, harebell, bluebell
Zones 3 to 7

Bellflowers are well named for the shape of the single flowers, usually in shades of blue and purple, although there are also pinks and whites. Flowers are produced in large numbers over several weeks in summer. Certain bellflowers have a pampered English-cottage-garden appearance, and others look wild, but most are tough and can be given full sun or light shade in decent, well-drained soil. When well established and given some shade and cool weather, they will survive considerable drought. The lowest of the ground covers are described on pages 62-63. Deadhead to encourage continued flowering. Watch out for the aggressive species *C. portenschlagiana* and *C. poscharskyana* except in containers, since any bit of root left in the ground will produce a new plant. There are many small species suitable for rock gardens, available from specialist nurseries.

FAVORITES
C. cochleariifolia grows 4 to 5 inches (5 to 7.5 cm) tall with drooping blue or white flowers. It is suited to a rock

garden or a niche in a rock wall.

C. medium (Canterbury bell) is a biennial. It forms a rosette of foliage in its first year from seed and the second, flower stalks bearing showy 2-inch (5 cm) blue, pink, rose or white flowers, some double cultivars resembling a bell within a bell or a cup and saucer.

C. persicifolia (peach-leaved bellflower) is one of the most durable species in dry ground. This citizen of the traditional English cottage garden grows masses of wiry 2-to-4-foot (60-120 cm) stems that are strong and wind-resistant unless they are grown in rich soil. Blue or white flowers bloom on the upper half of the stalks. The plants form a clump of basal foliage that widens quickly and is easily divided. They also spread by seed if not deadheaded.

C. takesimana (Korean bellflower) is hardy to zone 4. Tolerant of dry shade, it forms a mass of dangling, pale lavender flowers on 18-to 24-inch (45-60 cm) stems.

Centaurea species

Cornflower, bachelor's button, basketflower
Zones 2 to 9, except as noted

Basketflower, the common name for some centaureas, indicates a method of identifying all centaureas by the basketlike arrangement of sepals just below the ring of petals. Blue shades may be the most prized, but there are also good centaureas in red, yellow, purple, lilac, pink and white. *C. macrocephala* and *C. rupestris* are bright yellow. There are annual, (page 140) biennial and perennial members of this sometimes weedy genus. The weediest, called knapweeds, are notorious invaders of pastureland, which suggests that almost any cornflower is an ideal candidate for a wildflower meadow. The perennials that are not commonly available from plant nurseries are easy from seed sown in pots indoors or directly in the garden in spring. All are excellent, long-lasting cut flowers, and all should have their flower stems sheared back after blooming.

FAVORITES
C. dealbata (Persian cornflower), hardy to zone 3, has 2-inch (5 cm) feathery, lilac to purplish red flowers on 2-foot (60 cm) stems with grayish, fernlike foliage. It blooms from summer through fall.

C. hypoleuca 'John Coutts,' hardy to zone 3, has finely divided grayish foliage and clear pink flowers on 2-foot (60 cm) stems.

C. macrocephala (globe centaurea) has arresting golden yellow flowers as wide as 4 inches (10 cm) on strong stems 3 to 4 feet (1-1.2 m) tall. English dryland gardener Beth Chatto says that this beauty can be planted

CENTAUREA MONTANA

near trees and shrubs, as it is strong enough to compete with their roots.

C. montana (mountain bluet, perennial bachelor's button) is one of the most drought-tolerant species. It looks like a larger version of the common annual bachelor's button (*C. cyanus*), with 2-to-3-foot stems (60-90 cm) supporting 3-inch (7.5 cm) summer flowers that are usually bright blue or violet blue, although there are also whites and pinks. It may need staking. Once established, *C. montana* will survive in little more than dry sand. It can spread rapidly. After a couple of years, it can be divided in spring — and every two years thereafter.

C. rupestris, zones 6 to 8, grows 6 to 12 inches (15-30 cm) with prickly, gray foliage and yellow flowers all summer.

C. scabiosa, zones 3 to 8, forms multiple branches 3 to 4 feet (1-1.2 m) tall, with large, purple flowers that resemble scabiosa.

Chrysanthemum (Dendranthema) species

Chrysanthemum, Shasta daisy, pyrethrum, marguerite
Zones 4 to 10, except as noted

There are chrysanthemums and chrysanthemums. Flowers may be modest or flamboyant, stems tall or short, plants weedy or as finely bred as racehorses. The roadside oxeye daisies are at the opposite end of the plant spectrum from the fussy potted plants sold for Mother's Day, yet both are chrysanthemums. The latter need careful tending and are not recommended for the dry garden. No wonder taxonomists sometimes group the garden species under a different genus name, *Dendranthema*. (Labeling confusion reigns throughout the genus *Chrysanthemum*.) During the 1990s, however, *Chrysanthemum* was officially approved as the genus name for all the mums. All have a couple of qualities in common; they have daisy flowers, and they are excellent for cutting.

The fall-blooming hybrid chrysanthemums called garden mums may survive winters to about zone 5. They are valued for their late-fall bloom in sun or a little shade but are not especially drought-tolerant. The plants build their strength during the hot, dry weather of summer, when they need an occasional watering. There are dwarf, medium and tall types, as well as different flower shapes, from the simple daisies that recall their wild forebears to complex pompoms, some with threadlike or spoon-shaped petals.

If you have any doubts about the hardiness of your garden chrysanthemums, mulch them heavily after the soil freezes. A safer way to overwinter marginally hardy chrysanthemums is to dig them up after the leaves and flowers have been killed by frost, taking a good-sized root ball, and store them in boxes in a garage or other unheated building. Water the soil about once a month. As the weather warms in spring, growth will begin and plants can be divided and planted out. Discard the older middle of the plant, and retain the new shoots emerging around the edges. Water thoroughly after planting, and continue to water until new growth is evident. Plants can also be multiplied from rooted cuttings.

CHRYSANTHEMUM LEUCANTHEMUM

When you order garden chrysanthemums by mail, you will receive rooted cuttings in spring. After the last spring frost date, plant them in fairly rich soil, and water them until growth resumes. Pinch the plants back at least once, starting when they are about 6 inches (15 cm) tall, to encourage bushiness. Stop pinching back in early July.

FAVORITES
The following species are easier to grow and more drought-tolerant than garden mums.

C. coccineum; *Tanacetum coccineum* (painted daisy or pyrethrum) has wide early-summer red, pink or white daisies on 18-to-24-inch stems (45-60 cm) with ferny foliage. Although this is called the pyrethrum daisy, the type of chrysanthemum used to make the insecticide pyrethrum is *C. cinerariifolium*.

C. nipponicum; *Nipponanthemum nipponicum* (Nippon daisy, Montauk daisy), hardy to zone 5, forms a shrubby mound 3 feet (1 m) tall, with succulent foliage and large white daisies in fall. In spring, cut plants back to 4 inches (10 cm) tall.

C. x superbum; *C. maximum*; *Leucanthemum maximum* (Shasta daisy) looks like a larger version of the common oxeye (*C. leucanthemum*), with white-petaled yellow-centered daisies on stems that may be tall and floppy or short and stiff, depending on the cultivar and strain. Some bloom in June, while others don't begin until August. The larger the flowers, the more likely this species is to fade in dry weather and suffer in cold winters, especially if the soil is not sufficiently well drained. There are many good cultivars, from the 8-inch 'Tinkerbelle' and 10-inch (25 cm) 'Snow Lady' to 3-foot (90 cm) 'Polaris.'

COREOPSIS GRANDIFLORA

Coreopsis species
Coreopsis, tickseed
Zones 4/5 to 9

The perennial types of coreopsis recommended below for the dry garden — and almost any garden — are all North American wildflowers, some more domesticated than others. They are known for a long season of bloom on self-supporting stems, tall or short. Flowers are yellow or orange daisies, some bicolored, some double. They appreciate poor soil provided it is well drained and not soggy in winter or spring. They do well in wildflower gardens, are easy, drought-resistant and bloom for an extended period, especially if deadheaded. All are easy from seeds, except as noted. Divide clumps in spring.

FAVORITES
C. grandiflora is a North American wildflower that forms an upright, multibranching plant about 2 feet (60 cm) tall, with flowers that are bright yellow or orange with yellow centers. Award-winning cultivars include 'Early Sunrise,' noted for excellent heat-tolerance as well as masses of bright yellow semi-double flowers, and 'Rising Sun,' with double flowers wider than 2 inches (5.5 cm) that are golden

with a mahogany center. 'Mayfield Giant' is similar in color, but the flowers are single and as wide as 3 inches (7.5 cm) on stems that may grow as tall as 3 feet (90 cm). Dwarfs 12 to 16 inches (30-40 cm) tall include 'Sunray,' with a profusion of double golden flowers, 'Baby Sun,' a single version, and 'Heliot,' whose single yellow flowers have brown centers.

C. palmata (prairie coreopsis) is a midwestern wildflower that thrives in poor, sandy soil in sun. It is a common sight in the Ozarks in summer. The first coreopsis to bloom, starting around May and continuing for most of the summer, it grows about 2 feet (60 cm) tall with slender stems and leaves and 2-inch (5 cm) single yellow or orange daisies.

C. tripteris (tall coreopsis) is a wildflower of eastern North America that can grow 6 to 7 feet (2 m) but is strongly self-supporting. It has grayish foliage and in late summer, small, pale yellow daisies. It tolerates sun or part shade and is is easy from seed.

C. verticillata (thread-leaved coreopsis) 'Moonbeam' was celebrated as Perennial Plant of the Year for 1992. The pale yellow of its 1-inch (2.5 cm) daisies combines well with most other colors in the garden. A cluster of wiry stems grows only about 1 foot (30 cm) tall, best at the front of a sunny border. 'Creme Brulee' is an improved version with larger flowers that are slightly deeper yellow. Other well-known cultivars are the orange-flowered 'Zagreb' and 'Golden Shower.' Because *C. verticillata* is slow to appear in spring, you should mark its spot to avoid damage. It cannot be grown from seeds, but tip cuttings are easy to root and are best taken before the plant begins blooming.

DIANTHUS GRATIANOPOLITANUS

Dianthus species

Pink, carnation
Zones 2 to 9, except as noted

Unlike the long-stemmed greenhouse or florist's carnations that require staking in rich, moist soil, some dianthus species and hybrids are among the best, most carefree perennials for parched alkaline ground, whether in sun or light shade. Stems are generally under 2 feet (60 cm) tall, with foliage that is a dense tuft of grasslike leaves. The dominant flower color is pink, from light to shocking, but flowers can also be rose to dark purple, some bicolored, some white. Flowers usually bloom in late spring or early summer. Many are very fragrant. The mat-forming ground cover types are described on page 65. Plants resent mulching and should be planted so the roots are just covered in soil, since they need good air circulation at the base. Dianthus is easy from seed. Most of the perennials tend to be short-lived, so they should be renewed periodically. Plants can be multiplied by layering

stems and keeping the buried stems moist until they root. Clump-formers can be divided after about three years. Since dianthus resents very hot summers, it is best grown in zones 8 to 10 as a biennial.

FAVORITES

D. allwoodii (Allwood's pink) grows 12 to 18 inches (30-45 cm) with 2-inch (5 cm) carnations in late spring.

D. 'Allwoodii Alpinus,' (alpine pink) also called *D. alpinus* and *D.* x *allwoodii* grows about 6 inches (15 cm) tall, with broad silver foliage.

D. amurensis (Amur pink), zones 3 to 8, grows 6 to 12 inches (15-30 cm) tall, has unusually large 2-inch (5 cm) pink flowers that bloom for weeks in late summer.

D. barbatus (sweet William) is a showy, somewhat demanding biennial whose selections and cultivars grow as tall as 2 feet (60 cm). They have given rise to much smaller, more drought-resistant hybrids (*D. barbatus* x *chinensis*) such as the Telstar and Ideal series. The Festival series resembles the Ideals, but all are bicolors or picotees (petal edges are white).

Floral Lace, with lacy-edged petals, has better heat-tolerance than most.

The hybrid *D.* 'Berry Burst' was chosen in 1996 as the best modern cultivar by The American Dianthus Society of Santa Fe. It grows 1 foot (30 cm) tall, with fragrant purplish pink flowers splashed with red. It is drought-resistant and hardy to zone 4.

D. carthusianorum (clusterhead pink), zones 3 to 8, grows 2 to 3 feet (60-90 cm) tall, with grasslike foliage and clusters of small magenta flowers. It is recommended for wildflower meadows.

D. gratianopolitanus (Cheddar pink) is an old-fashioned garden favorite that forms a cushion of grayish or bluish grassy foliage with sweetly scented flowers on stems 8 to 12 inches (20-30 cm) tall, excellent for edging and rock gardens. There are many cultivars.

D. knappii has unusual yellow flowers and an open habit as tall as 18 inches (45 cm).

D. plumarius (cottage pink), hardy to zone 4, grows 6 to 18 inches (15-45 cm) high and has narrow gray foliage and fragrant flowers. There are many cultivars. 'Ursula Le Grove,' which has maroon-eyed white petals on 10-inch (25 cm) stems, was chosen as the best antique cultivar of 1996 by The American Dianthus Society. Another award winner was 'Rose de Mai.'

DICTAMNUS ALBUS

Dictamnus albus

Gas plant, fraxinella, dittany,
burning bush
Zones 3 to 8

Two of the common names for this
perennial come from the flammable,
lemon-scented oil exuded from the
leaves and a flammable gas given off
by its roots when cut. Curious but
classy and dependable, gas plant
forms a shrubby mound, eventually
2 feet (60 cm) high and wide, of
shiny, leathery, deep green foliage. In
late spring or early summer, around
the same time as peonies, stalks
that ascend about a foot (30 cm)
above the foliage bear 2-inch (5 cm)
flowers for two or three weeks, pure
white on the species, pink on the
variety *purpureus* (*D. fraxinella*). After
blooming, cut the stalks of seed pods
to add to dried arrangements.

Gas plant should be confined to a
protected area out of strong winds
and left in place since it does not
transplant well. Position it carefully
in full sun and well-drained soil. It
will take a year or so to become
established, but once settled in, it
is long-lived.

Echinacea species

Purple coneflower
Zones 3 to 10

Coneflowers are native North
American wildflowers whose roots
have long been used medicinally by
indigenous peoples. The roots and
aboveground parts of all four species
listed below are still used to make
teas, medicinal extracts and tinctures
especially valued for strengthening
the immune system. *Echinacea purpurea* is also a beauty in the garden,
especially appreciated for its height,
sometimes 3 feet (1 m), and its con-
tribution of the color magenta to the
daisy spectrum, although there are
also pinks and whites and, most
recently, oranges. All are excellent
cut flowers. On the species, petals
curve back and the dark center pro-
trudes. The foliage is long and rough-
textured. The most common and
tallest form, *E. purpurea*, is not especially drought-resistant. It survives
high temperatures and full sun but
wilts when the ground is parched, so
it needs occasional watering during
dry periods. However, it will not tolerate soggy ground. Divide clumps in
fall. Echinacea is easy from seed and
often self-sows, although it generally
does not bloom until the second year.

FAVORITES
For gardeners who want something
different from the usual tall, magenta-
flowered species, the choices are
increasing. 'Magnus' (also called
'Bravado' and 'Ovation'), Perennial
Plant of the Year for 1998, has petals
that lie flat. 'White Swan,' 'White
Luster' and 'Alba' are shorter, with
white petals. 'Leuchtstern' ('Bright
Star') is rose-pink. 'Art's Pride,' also
known as Orange Meadowbrite™, is
terra-cotta-colored. 'Kim's Knee High'
has rosy-pink flowers on 18 to 24-inch
(45-60 cm). stems. 'Doppelganger' is
an oddity with flowers that develop
in layers.

The following wildflowers are best
grown from seeds, since plants are
seldom available:

E. angustifolia (western coneflower) is more drought-tolerant than
E. purpurea and is smaller, about
2 feet (60 cm), with slender foliage
and narrow white, pink or rose-purple
petals.

E. pallida (pale coneflower) is a
taller pink-flowered form, to 40
inches (100 cm).

E. paradoxa (yellow coneflower)
has yellow flowers on 2-to-3-foot
(60-90 cm) stems.

ECHINACEA PURPUREA

ECHINOPS RITRO

Echinops ritro
Globe thistle
Zones 3 to 9

Dramatic and aggressive-looking, with its 3-foot (1 m) clump of thorny grayish foliage and above it, spiny, slate-blue, metallic-looking flower heads, globe thistle should be represented in almost any sunny or partly shaded garden that has well-drained soil, whether dry or moist. The flowers hold their color into September and are excellent for cutting. Echinops spreads by seed or underground rhizome, so situate it carefully. Divide clumps every three or four years to prevent overcrowding.

FAVORITES
E. ritro 'Taplow Blue' is bluer than the species, with larger, 2- to 3-inch (5-7.5 cm) flower heads.

E. bannaticus grows about 4 feet (1.2 m) tall with blue globe flowers. 'Blue Glow' is the usual cultivar.

E. exaltatus grows 6 feet (2 m) tall with white to grayish flower heads.

E. sphaerocephalus grows 6 feet (2 m) tall with white to silvery-gray flowers. 'Arctic Glow' is even more spectacular, with red stems and green foliage.

Erigeron species
Fleabane, Spanish daisy, blue-fringed daisy
Zones vary

Fleabanes are a group of mostly North American wildflowers that colonize roadsides, open fields and other sunny, dry places. Most of America's roadside weeds originated in Europe, but fleabane has done the reverse and taken to the roadsides of Europe. Much like asters though generally smaller, the flowers are pink or lilac daisies with yellow centers. Erigeron blooms in summer, while the asters bloom later. The species and cultivars listed below, all more desirable than the roadside species, also tolerate poor, dry soil and make excellent cut flowers. Divide clumps after they have flowered for two or three years.

ERIGERON SPECIOSUS

FAVORITES
E. compositus (alpine fleabane), suitable for rock gardens or gravel beds in zones 3 to 9, grows just 4 inches (10 cm) tall with a tuft of silvery foliage and white to lavender flowers.

E. glaucus (beach aster), zones 5 to 9, is a California native with pale, succulent foliage and violet-colored flowers. It grows about 6 inches (15 cm) tall and 18 inches (45 cm) wide.

E. karvinskianus, zones 5 to 7, is a spreading, 6-inch-tall (15 cm) type popular for pots and hanging baskets and so generally grown as an annual. 'Profusion' has white flowers. The flowers of 'Bleutenmeer' open white and fade to purple.

E. speciosus is the most common garden species, much taller than the others, with single or double flowers in white or shades of lilac, purple and pink. There are many cultivars, most about 2 feet (60 cm) tall, such as the Jewel series, 'Blue Beauty' and violet-blue 'Darkest of All.' They may need staking, especially if the soil is rich. Cut the flower stems back after blooming to promote a second flowering. They are hardy to zone 2.

ERYNGIUM X TRIPARTITUM

Eryngium species
Sea holly
Zones vary

Sea holly, a European native named for its love of salty sand dunes and its prickly, waxy, holly-like leaves, has a thick taproot that enables it to survive drought. Although this bushy perennial can also tolerate heavy soil, it needs good drainage and looks best in full sun. A damp winter or spring can kill it. The unique flowers, which have a central dome rising above a spiny collar in almost metallic-looking colors of white to silvery blue and purple, bloom from summer to early fall and are excellent for cutting and drying. The most common garden choices, *E. alpinum* (alpine sea holly), with its steely blue flowers, and *E. giganteum* (Miss Willmott's Ghost) with its white bracts are not the most drought-tolerant. They need watering in dry weather. The former is a perennial to zone 4, the latter a self-seeding biennial or short-lived perennial for zones 3 to 8. Sea holly need never be disturbed, but large clumps can be divided in spring. All are excellent cut flowers.

FAVORITES

E. agavifolium has long, toothed, narrow leaves reminiscent of agave. The flowers, on stalks about 30 inches (75 cm) tall, are green. It grows in zones 4 to 10 but requires very well-drained soil to survive.

E. amethystinum (amethyst sea holly), zones 4 to 10, is armed with spikes and grows as tall as 3 feet (1 m). It bears big crops of metallic-blue flowers loved by bees. 'Blue Diamond' is a dwarf about 18 inches (45 cm) tall.

E. caucasicum, zones 3 to 8, is about 18 inches (45 cm) tall and spiny with bluish gray flowers, excellent in the rock garden.

E. planum (blue sea holly) is the hardiest, zones 2 to 8. It bears steel-blue flowers on 3-foot (1m) stems. Unlike most others, it tolerates damp soil as well as dry.

E. x tripartitum, zones 3 to 9, is similar to *E. planum*. It grows 2 feet (60 cm) tall with toothed, shiny leaves and small blue flowers.

E. yuccifolium, with the memorable common name of rattlesnake master, is a North American wildflower 3½ feet (1 m) or taller with yucca-like foliage and greenish flower heads into fall. Zones 3 to 8.

Euphorbia species
Spurge
Zones vary

Many gardeners unfamiliar with euphorbias come to love these diverse plants for the dryland garden. Their flowers are often a distinctive, bright yellow-green, and their foliage is attractive all season. There are literally hundreds of species from tree size to prostrate, from hardy to tropical, including the houseplants poinsettia and crown of thorns. The "flowers" of all of them are long-lasting, brightly colored modified leaves called bracts. Many bloom in early spring, and all have foliage that is attractive all season. Some euphorbias will grow in little but sand and so are among the best and most self-reliant members of the dry garden, although they can also put up with well-drained, moist soil, especially in sun. Some can be invasive, either by underground roots, such as the perennial *E. cyparissias* (cypress spurge), or seeds, such as the annual *E. helioscopia*. Many garden-worthy species are easy from seed sown indoors in spring, blooming in their second year. Divide clumps in spring. Be careful when pruning euphorbia, because its milky sap can blister skin. *E. griffithii*, although widely available (especially the cultivars 'Fireglow' and 'Dixter') does not do well in dry soil.

FAVORITES

E. amygdaloides (purple wood spurge), zones 6 to 9, forms a mound of maroon stems and dark green, ever-green foliage 12 to 18 inches (30-45 cm) tall. The spring flowers, produced on the previous year's growth, are green-ish yellow. It does best in part shade and spreads to make a good ground cover under trees. The usual cultivar

EUPHORBIA POLYCHROMA

Gaillardia species
Blanket flower
Zones 2 to 9

G. aristata grows wild along road-sides in the dry hills of the prairies, flaunting its Mexican-skirt flowers decorated with a central circle of dark orange and tips of yellow. Centers are raised brown domes. This is one of the most cheerful flowers for the dry, sunny garden and the wildflower meadow, blooming from early summer until frost. Its ping-pong-sized seed heads are also appealing. Gaillardia flowers are excellent for cutting. The plant does not divide well, but it is easy from seeds sown indoors or directly in the garden in early spring.

FAVORITES

New cultivars appear every year, especially under the umbrella of *G. x grandiflora* — hybrids of *G. aristata* and the annual *G. pulchella* — the usual garden choices, hardy to zone 2 if the soil is perfectly drained. They may grow as hardy annuals or as short-lived perennials that sometimes self-sow. Stems of taller cultivars, such as 'Bremen' and 'Torchlight' are 2 to 3 feet (60-90 cm) tall, with 3-inch-wide flowers.

is 'Rubra,' which turns reddish in fall.

E. characias (evergreen spurge) is a tall, 4-to-5-foot (120-150 cm) evergreen for warmer gardens, zones 7 to 10. It is available in several subspecies and cultivars and may be interbred with or confused with the species *E. wulfenii*. The blue-green leaves are leathery. Greenish yellow flowers open in early spring. Cut flower stalks at the base when finished. It is a short-lived perennial but often self-sows.

E. corollata (flowering spurge), hardy to zone 4, has an unusual cloud of white flowers on a mound of foliage as tall as 3 feet (1 m). It is an easy, more drought-tolerant alternative to baby's-breath. The fall foliage is wine red.

E. dulcis 'Chameleon,' hardy to zone 5, forms a clump of rich bronze-purple foliage about 2 feet (60 cm) tall. The flowers are yellow-green touched with purple. The fall color is bright red.

E. myrsinites (donkey-tail spurge) forms a mound of reclining 6-inch (15 cm) stems of waxy bluish succulent leaves topped with greenish yellow flowers in spring. In zones 5 to 9, it can be weedy, spreading by seeds, but its trailing stems are ideal for unwatered containers of sandy soil or trailing over the edge of a rock wall.

E. polychroma; E. epithymoides (cushion spurge), zones 3 to 9, is probably the most widely available species. It makes a neat, 1-foot-tall (30 cm) dome covered with brilliant golden-green bracts in late spring. The green foliage turns reddish in fall.

E. marginata (snow-on-the-mountain) is an annual that makes a good foliage filler between brighter flowers. It looks unremarkable until, in midsummer, it produces beautifully variegated bracts at the tips, green with white edges, which are topped by small white flowers. It may self-sow and, at about 2 feet (60 cm) tall, looks good almost anywhere. It is most easily sown directly in the garden anytime in spring.

E. rigida, for zones 7 to 10, is 1 to 2 feet (30-60 cm) tall with stiff, narrow, fleshy, gray evergreen leaves, sometimes flushed purple. It has large, bright yellow flowers.

GAILLARDIA ARISTATA

Gaura lindheimeri
Whirling butterflies, butterfly gaura
Zones 5 to 9

This wildflower of the southern United States needs well-drained soil, thrives in sunny, droughty situations and suffers in damp ground. The common name comes from the freely moving delicate pink-tinged white flowers that suggest butterflies. The flowers are modest but are produced in great enough numbers for a cloudy effect. If gaura is dead-headed, it has an unusually long season of bloom, from early summer to fall. The leaves are gray-green, as are the self-supporting wiry stems, which grow about 3 feet (1 m) tall. It is hardy to about zone 5 but should be mulched in marginal winter areas. If it does not survive the winter, self-sown seedlings often keep it going. It is quite easy from seed sown indoors in spring. 'Corrie's Gold,' a form with gold-and-green variegated foliage, may be less hardy, to about zone 6.

GERANIUM 'JOHNSON'S BLUE'

Geranium species
Cranesbill
Zones vary

Cranesbills, or hardy geraniums (not to be confused with the frost-tender pelargoniums also called geraniums), are proving such reliable producers of long-lasting flowers and foliage that new varieties are appearing on the marketplace every year. Many spread fast enough to be classified as ground covers, listed on page 66. Many others, listed here, spread slowly and so may have to be left several years before they can be divided. Deadhead to encourage more flowering. Some do best in moist ground.

FAVORITES
G. cinereum, hardy to zone 5, forms a 4-to-6-inch (10-15 cm) mound of grayish foliage and large flowers on trailing stems. It needs well-drained soil and prefers full sun. Cultivars include 'Ballerina,' 'Lawrence Flatman' and 'Giuseppi.'

G. dalmaticum (Dalmatian cranesbill), hardy to zone 3, has glossy green leaves that form a 4-inch (10 cm) mound topped by beautiful pink flowers in late spring. The fall foliage is bright red.

G. 'Johnson's Blue' has long-blooming purplish blue flowers held about 1 foot (30 cm) above a mound of green, deeply divided leaves. *G. endressii* 'Wargrave Pink' looks similar but has dark pink flowers. Both are hardy to zone 2.

G. maculatum is a North American native that grows about 18 inches (45 cm) tall, with slightly hairy leaves and 1-inch-wide (2.5 cm) rosy-to-pink flowers. It is hardy to about zone 4.

G. phaeum (mourning widow) grows 3 feet (1 m) tall, with reflexed maroon to purple flowers. 'Album' is a white version. Hardy to zone 3, they tolerate shady ground, whether moist or dry.

G. renardii has unusual nubbly, grayish foliage. The flowers, which are white striped with purple, bloom in clusters. It is hardy to zone 4.

GYPSOPHILA PANICULATA

Gypsophila paniculata

Baby's-breath; chalk plant
Zones 2 to 8

Fragile though it may appear, with its thread-thin stems, small bluish leaves and sprays of tiny white or pink flowers, this florist's favorite can put up with dry soil so well that it is a pest in parts of the prairies and on the dunes around the Great Lakes. Since the cultivated doubles form little or no seed, they are not invasive. As the genus name *Gypsophila* suggests, baby's breath is a lover of gypsum — in other words, alkaline soil. It also likes cool summers. It is less tolerant of acidic ground and soggy winters and springs. In the garden, baby's-breath looks best either given plenty of room to create a cloud of color or squeezed between other plants as an airy filler, much the way it's used in bridal bouquets. Pick fresh stems for flower arrangements or dry by hanging in bunches upside down in an airy, shaded place. Shear it back after the first blooming to encourage more flowers. The clump does not widen quickly and resents being moved or divided. In zones 2 and 3, mulch it for winter protection.

FAVORITES
The single-flowered types such as the species *G. paniculata*, which has white flowers on 3-foot (90 cm) stems, have a much more delicate presence in the garden than the doubles, and can be grown from seed. The doubles, with the exception of the partially-double 'Snowflake' ('Schneeflocke') and 'Festival,' must be grown from cuttings or transplants. 'Bristol Fairy' is a fully double version, 24 inches (60 cm) tall, hardy to zone 4 and apt to bloom twice in a season, although often short-lived. 'Perfecta' is taller, about 4 feet (1.2 m) with larger white flowers. Pinks include the double pale pink 'Flamingo,' 18-inch (45 cm) 'Viette's Dwarf' and the double pink 'Pink Fairy,' the same height but hardy to zone 2 and often blooming till frost. 'Red Sea' is a double dark pink.

The creeping form is *G. repens*. 'Rosy Veil' ('Rosenschlier') is a hybrid of *G. paniculata* and *G. repens* that forms a trailing mound with double white flowers which fade to pink.

G. oldhamiana (Manchurian baby's-breath), zones 3 to 8, grows about 1 to 3 feet (30-90 cm) tall with single pink flowers.

Helianthemum nummularium; H. mutabile

Rock rose, sun rose
Zones 4 to 9

Helianthemum can be considered a perennial, an annual, a modestly spreading ground cover or a shrub, depending on where and how you garden and what species you choose. No matter how long-lived it is, this is one of the loveliest and most distinctive small flowers for the moderately dry garden. *H. nummularium* is most dependable in places colder than zones 5 and 6, although even there, it demands well-drained soil, preferably alkaline, for survival and does best in full sun. It forms a shrubby mound about 6 inches (15 cm) tall, upon which bloom flowers that resemble small single or double roses in shades of white, yellow, orange, pink or red. The flowers begin blooming in late spring and continue sporadically through summer, especially if deadheaded. Helianthemum forms a gradually spreading mat as the stems root where they touch the ground. It is evergreen, so it needs protection in and beyond zone 4, but does well where there is a good snow cover. Otherwise, a winter mulch such as a cover of evergreen boughs may bring plants through the winter. If all else fails, they can be grown as annuals.

The species is easy to grow from seeds started eight weeks early indoors. Set the plants outdoors while they are still small, as large plants do not transplant easily. Cultivars must be grown from cuttings or divisions.

FAVORITES
There are many cultivars with different flower colors and foliage that may be green or grayish. Among the doubles with green foliage are 'Annabel,' pink; 'Double Apricot,' as described; and 'Fireball,' red. Single cultivars with contrasting grayish foliage include the bright orange 'Firedragon,' orange-red 'Henfield Brilliant,' yellow 'Wisley Primrose' and pink 'Wisley Pink.' 'Raspberry Ripple' has upright grayish-green foliage and single deep pink flowers streaked with white. 'St. Mary's' is taller than most, about 10 inches (25 cm), with green foliage and large single white flowers.

HELIOPSIS HELIANTHOIDES

Heliopsis helianthoides

Sunflower heliopsis, false sunflower, rough heliopsis
Zones 2 to 9

Heliopsis is a North American wild-flower that resembles a sunflower but is shrubbier, with 2-to 4-inch (5-10 cm) golden, orange- or green-centered daisies that bloom steadily throughout summer and into fall. Clusters of strong stems up to 6 feet (2 m) tall with bright green leaves are excellent at the back of a border. Plants are moderately drought-tolerant once established. The species has single flowers, while the variety 'scabra' and its cultivars are semi-double or double, all excellent for cutting. Heliopsis seeds can be sown directly in the spring garden. Choose a sunny spot with well-drained soil. Divide plants every two or three years. The variegated 'Loraine Sunshine' is not drought-tolerant but needs moist soil and part shade.

FAVORITES
The most common garden cultivar is the golden semidouble 'Summer Sun.' 'Asahi' is a compact version, about 3 feet (90 cm) tall. The singles are more graceful than the doubles and worth a search. One is 'Prairie Sunset,' 6 feet (180 cm) tall with purple stems, dark green foliage with purple veins and an attractive orange ring in the center of each yellow flower.

Hemerocallis hybrids

Daylily
Zones 3 to 10

Visit a daylily farm sometime, if you can, to see with your own eyes how varied these lovely but sturdy lilies can be. Height varies from a few inches to almost 5 feet (1.5 m). Petals may be ruffled or plain, bicol-ored or single-toned. Colors range from cream through pale and bright yellow to orange, pink, burgundy and plum, all with undertones of yellow, with flowers tiny to large, some fragrant, some double. Each flower blooms just a day, but plants can produce as many as 50 buds, so that the average plant blooms for three weeks and some new cultivars carry on for six to eight weeks or even longer.

Daylilies do best in full sun but will also flower in partial shade, even the shade under deciduous trees, although extended cloudiness and dampness reduce flowering. In the hottest climates, they do best with some shade. Their chief demand is well-drained soil. So tol-erant of neglect are daylilies that they escaped pioneer gardens and colonized roadsides as far north as zone 3. Given plenty of water in sum-mer, they grow tall and bloom more profusely, but they will survive drought. Most do best where sum-mer nights are warm. Daylilies that are evergreen in zone 5 or milder gardens need a heavy mulch where winters are colder.

Daylilies grow not from bulbs, like true lilies, but from fleshy tuberous roots. Clumps gradually expand, so certain daylilies are excellent tall, grassy ground covers. Fast spread is now a breeding prior-ity, so check with the catalog or nursery if this is something you want. Most daylilies are best divided every four or five years to keep them blooming well and to increase plantings. Push a spade into a clump to break it into sections, or pull the roots apart. The only pests are slugs and snails, especially on young plants in damp areas.

HEMEROCALLIS CULTIVAR

FAVORITES
There are hundreds of daylily cultivars, all of which will survive some drought, although flowering may be compromised. For best wind- and drought-resistance, stay away from the largest-flowered beauties, choosing instead varieties with smaller flowers. Best-known of the long bloomers in trying conditions is 'Stella d'Oro,' which "did for daylilies what Olga Korbut did for gymnastics," says Angelo Cerchione, executive director of the All-America Daylily Selection Council. 'Stella d'Oro,' although smaller in height and flower size than many cultivars, produces its clear yellow-orange flowers almost nonstop from early summer until frost. Any variety with the word 'Stella' or 'Siloam' in its name can be assumed to bloom a long time. Additional drought-resistant cultivars include the red 'Baltimore Oriole,' gold 'Bertie

Ferris' and pink 'Catherine Woodberry.' Also, look for 'Dr. Regel,' 'Red Hot Returns,' 'Strawberry Candy,' 'Summer Wine,' and, for the warmer zones, the Starburst® series of evergreen daylilies.

H. fulva, zones 2 to 9, is the wild orange daylily of the roadside, a tall, aggressive spreader as tall as 4 feet (120 cm). It is as capable of growing in the shade under trees as in a dry meadow or on a rocky hillside. 'Kwanso,' a double-flowered form, is somewhat less aggressive.

H. lilio-asphodelus (lemon lily), zones 2 to 9, has lemon-yellow flowers that bloom in late spring, earlier than the others. It grows about 3 feet (90 cm) tall and spreads gradually.

Hesperis matronalis
Dame's rocket, sweet rocket
Zones 2 to 9

This wild form of phlox is a European wildflower that has become naturalized in the northeastern states and eastern Canada, where it is a common sight along field edges and roadsides in late spring. It has 3-foot (1 m) spires of fragrant flowers that bloom white through light to dark pink and lilac. A lover of moist, well-drained soil, it also survives dry, alkaline conditions and is invasive in some areas, spreading gradually by seed, acting like a biennial or short-lived perennial. Best grown in masses, it suits wild gardens and grows well at the edges of woods or under a deciduous canopy. It is easy to grow from seed.

HESPERIS MATRONALIS

Iris species

Iris, flag

Zones vary

Old-fashioned bearded irises (*I. germanica*) will survive for many years in neglected farmyard gardens, a testament to their toughness. Their flowers are only about half the size of some of the modern hybrids, but they don't need staking, fertilizing or watering. The usual colors are yellow, cream, brown and blue, sometimes bicolored. Newer selections — there are hundreds — may have flowers as big as an outstretched hand, in shades of pink, rose, burgundy and brown, bicolored and plain, ruffled and lacy. Stems may reach 3 feet (1 m), making them vulnerable to toppling in heavy rains or strong winds unless they are staked. Dwarf varieties 10 to 15 inches (25-38 cm) tall and the even smaller miniatures do not require staking. For all of them, blooming may last little more than a week if the weather is hot, but the fanlike foliage persists until late summer, gradually turning browner and more ragged. Grow bearded irises behind something that will camouflage the foliage late in the season, as it should not be cut back until it has yellowed.

Plant bearded irises in late summer or early fall in loamy or sandy soil in full sun or a little shade. Dig a shallow hole wide enough to accommodate the roots, then arrange the roots so that they extend outward. Fill in the hole with soil so that the tops of the rhizomes are slightly exposed. Water thoroughly after planting, and continue to water whenever the soil is dry until growth commences. When dividing irises, which should be done about every three years to keep clumps from becoming over-crowded, discard any unproductive or damaged rhizomes, and make sure each piece of planted rhizome has an eye, the spot from which leaves emerge.

If you are growing large-flowered hybrids or if you garden in a place with harsh winters, cover the rhizomes with a 4-inch (10 cm) mulch as soon as the ground freezes. Deadhead spent flowers, and remove the flower stems when blooming has finished. Louisiana iris, suited to zones 7 to 10, is a lover of moist, acidic soil.

IRIS GERMANICA

FAVORITES

I. germanica irises with smallish flowers, such as any of the dwarf varieties, are best able to withstand wind and drought.

Not troubled by a common pest, the iris borer, and tougher in many other ways are irises with grassy foliage that stays attractive all season, especially *I. sibirica* (Siberian iris). The blooming period may be even briefer than that of bearded irises, but the flowers are delicate and lovely. Siberian irises thrive in damp sites, where they may grow taller than 4 feet (1.2 m), but they will survive in dry places too, although they will not grow as tall. The flowers are purple, blue, white, yellow, pink and bicolors. All bloom in late spring or early summer, about the same time as the bearded types, and are very hardy. Elaine Peek of Peek's Perennials in Edson, Alberta (zone 2), says that not all Siberian irises do well for her, but she recommends the Sino-Siberian hybrid 'Puget Polka,' "dainty but drought-tolerant," and the Siberian cultivars 'Augury,' with pink-lavender flowers, and 'Sparkling Rose,' red-violet.

Plant Siberian irises in fall in full sun or some shade. Divide them every three or four years, because the crown gradually widens, leaving an empty spot in the center of the plant. Dig down with a spade and remove sections in spring when the leaves appear.

I. pallida 'Variegata' has eye-catching variegated green foliage, banded with either white or gold. The flowers are medium blue.

Lewisia cotyledon

Lewisia
Zones 3 to 9

Lewisia cotyledon, a native of the Pacific Northwest, is one member of a group of North American wildflowers related to portulaca. It develops a rosette of fleshy evergreen foliage decorated with disproportionately large, somewhat daisylike flowers on 6-inch (15 cm) stems. *Lewisia* hybrids, mostly based on *L. cotyledon*, have brightly colored flowers, especially pink or salmon, either striped or solid. They can be short-lived since they are even more demanding of the conditions that suit portulaca: perfectly drained, somewhat acidic soil and no winter sogginess, although they appreciate some moisture when their foliage and buds are developing in spring. They do best in part shade and take well to wall crevices, rock gardens, stone or concrete trough gardens and gravelly or sandy slopes. 'Fransi' is taller than most, with 10-inch (25 cm) stems of orange flowers.

Liatris species

Gayfeather, blazing star
Zones vary

Like goldenrod and rudbeckia, liatris is a North American wildflower that was accepted into European gardens before it was considered worth growing at home. From clumps of grassy foliage, stiff bottle-brush spikes of fluffy magenta pink, purple or white flowers bloom from the tip down in late summer when many other perennials have finished. They attract butterflies and bees. Remove faded flower spikes to encourage more flowering. There are about 40 species varying in height from a few inches to 6 feet (2 m), although most are not yet available to gardeners. The garden selections are excellent for cutting and widely used in the florist industry, fresh or dried. To dry, pick when about half of the flowers are open, strip off the foliage and hang them upside down in a dry, dark place. Give all of them full sun or light shade and soil with plenty of humus. Most will also survive in moist ground provided it is well drained; too much winter wetness can kill them. All varieties are susceptible to powdery mildew. Divide clumps every three or four years.

FAVORITES
The following species are drought-resistant once established.

L. scariosa (tall gayfeather), zones 6 to 9, is the tallest garden type, up to 6 feet (180 cm). 'September Glory' has 3-foot (90 cm) spikes of purple button flowers. 'White Spires' and 'Alba' have large white flowers.

L. spicata, zones 3 to 9, about 2 feet (60 cm) tall, is native to moist meadows but also tolerates drought.

In a four-year comparison of 21 liatris species and cultivars at the Chicago Botanic Garden, zone 5, the top rating of "excellent" went to only two varieties: the mauve-purple *L. spicata* cultivars 'Floristan Violet' and 'Kobold,' a dwarf. Both received the top rating because of their uniformity, erect stems, robustness, floral quality and length of time in bloom. The next highest rating went to the white-flowered *L. spicata* cultivars 'Alba' and creamy 'Floristan White.' Both grow 3 to 4 feet (1-1.2 m) tall. *L. spicata* is easy from seed.

L. punctata (snakeroot), zones 3 to 8, grows about 2 feet (60 cm) tall. It is less widely available since it is a wildflower. It is a native of grasslands and the most drought-tolerant species, requiring sun or light shade and well-drained soil. It produces many spikes densely covered with pink or purple flowers in summer.

Limonium latifolium

Sea lavender; hardy statice
Zones 3 to 9

This unusual plant, able to grow on sandy beaches and in salty soil, produces a rosette of leathery, dark green leaves out of which emerge slender 2-foot-tall (60 cm) stems holding clouds of delicate violet-blue or pink flowers resembling baby's-breath. It flowers throughout late summer. The perennial types of limonium are seldom available from plant nurseries, since they develop a long taproot, resent being moved and are difficult to divide.

Fortunately, they are easily grown from seeds. Choose their position carefully, in well-drained soil in full sun, and then leave them undisturbed. Limonium makes an excellent cut flower, either fresh or dried. To dry, cut stems when the flowers are open and hang them in bunches in an airy, shaded place.

FAVORITES
L. latifolium is the most widely available species.

L. otolepis grows 3 to 4 feet (90-120 cm) with white-and-blue flowers in sprays in late summer. 'Lavender Lace' is the usual selection.

L. tataricum (German statice) grows 2 feet (60 cm) tall, with masses of silvery-white flowers.

LINUM FLAVUM

Linum species

Flowering flax
Zones vary

Sky-blue, five-petaled flowers on graceful stems that move with every breeze are the hallmark of the most popular of the flowering flaxes, *Linum perenne*. All are short-lived perennials, especially if winters are wet, but tend to drop their seed and reappear if you do not weed out the grassy-looking seedlings; they are easy to start from seeds scattered in the garden in spring. All do fine in sun or part shade and look best in masses, whether in the company of annuals, perennials, shrubs or all three in a wildflower meadow. They are among the best perennials to fill the spaces between other plants in the manner of baby's-breath, although these flowers are much larger.

FAVORITES
L. flavum (golden flax), zones 5 to 9, has bell-shaped bright yellow flowers and dark green foliage. It generally grows about 1 foot (30 cm) tall and can be floppy in shade. 'Compactum' is half as tall, good for rock gardens.

L. lewisii (Lewis flax), zones 3 to 9, bears pale blue, striped flowers 2 inches (5 cm) wide on stems as tall as 3 feet (90 cm).

L. narbonense, zones 6 to 9, grows about 16 inches (40 cm) tall with blue flowers a little larger than those of *L. perenne*. It spreads somewhat. 'Heavenly Blue' is bright blue.

L. perenne, zones 2 to 9, grows stems about 18 inches (45 cm) tall, covered base to tip with gray-green needle leaves and topped with flat, pale blue 1-inch (2.5 cm) flowers that continue to open for weeks through the summer even though each blossom lasts just a day. 'Saphir' ('Nanum Sapphire,' 'Sapphire') is shorter, about 10 inches (25 cm), with large, bright blue flowers. 'Diamant' ('White Diamond') has white flowers.

Lupinus hybrids

Lupin
Zones 4 to 9

Lupins sometimes establish colonies sustained by self-sowing where they are happy — that is, where springs are cool and the soil is acidic and well-drained, even if it is mostly sand. They have become naturalized along roadsides along the Pacific Northwest, the Atlantic coast and north of the Great Lakes. Lupins bloom in late spring to early summer, then should be camouflaged behind showier plants while they fade. The palmate foliage is attractive and distinctive. Since they resent moving, they should be left in place once planted.

The best-known garden lupins are hybrids such as the Russell and Gallery series, with dramatic spires of flowers in a wide range of colors, but like one of their parents, the West Coast wildflower *L. polyphyllus*, they are flowers for moist, preferably acidic soils. *L. arboreus*, the drought-hardy, winter-tender tree lilac of California, is such a rampant seeder that it is not recommended for the garden.

LUPINUS RUSSELL HYBRID

FAVORITES

Gather seeds from naturalized plants if you can. Scratching the seed coat with sandpaper speeds germination. Sow directly in the garden in early spring. Also, the following species are drought-tolerant, short-lived perennials that can be easily renewed by seeds sown directly in the garden.

L. argenteus, zones 4 to 9, grows 15 to 20 inches (40-50 cm) tall, with flowers that are usually lilac or blue, less often white or pink.

L. perennis, zones 2 to 8, grows about 2 feet (60 cm) tall with flowers that are generally blue.

Lychnis species

Campion, catchfly, Maltese cross
Zones vary

The campions are a showy group of usually short-lived perennials that have downy grayish foliage and bright contrasting flowers, usually scarlet or magenta. Most require well-drained soil and prefer sun. An exception is *Lychnis flos-cuculi* (cuckoo flower, ragged robin), a 3-foot (90 cm) European species that has become naturalized in wetlands in the northeastern states and Quebec. They often self-sow, showing up somewhere other than where you planted them. All are easy and best grown in groups. Divide clumps in early spring.

FAVORITES

L. coronaria (rose campion), zones 2 to 8, has rigid, gray 2-foot (60 cm) stems holding bright magenta flowers about 1 1/2 inches (4 cm) wide. Before it flowers, the plant forms a clump of downy green leaves something like lamb's ears (*Stachys*). It can be started from seeds sown indoors or directly in the garden and may act as a bien-

LYCHNIS FLOS-CUCULI

nial, flowering in its second year but dropping enough seeds each year to keep itself going. The magenta form is sometimes called 'Atrosanguinea.' 'Blood Red' is darker red. 'Angel Blush' is pink. There are also white and bicolored forms.

L. flos-jovi (flower of Jove) grows 10 inches to 2 feet (25-60 cm) tall with dense tufts of white-haired leaves and terminal clusters of rose-pink flowers.

L. viscaria (German catchfly), zones 3 to 8, is named for stems that are sticky enough to trap small insects. It is not quite as drought-tolerant as the two species above, has narrow grasslike leaves and 18-inch (45 cm) spikes holding massed purple or magenta flowers. There are also white, double and dwarf forms.

Oenothera species

Evening primrose, sundrop
Zones vary

This group of North American wild-flowers for the dry garden can be divided into two groups: sundrops and evening primroses. Sundrops open in the morning and generally close in the afternoon or on cloudy days. Evening primroses open in the afternoon or evening and may stay open till morning, attracting polli-nating moths. The best-known and most widely available species, although not the most drought-tolerant, is a sundrop, *O. tetragona* (*O. fruticosa*), hardy to zone 4 and usually misnamed evening prim-rose. Its brilliant yellow flowers bloom for about six weeks through summer on red stems that are 1-foot (30 cm) or taller. It will wilt if dry weather lasts for more than a week or so but, even if left unwatered, will generally recover when the rains return. It forms a gradually spread-ing ground cover with new rosettes that can be removed for propaga-tion. 'Sonnewende' ('Summer Solstice') has bronze-colored foliage

and large bright yellow flowers. The remaining species listed below, except *O. kunthiana, O. missouriensis* and *O. speciosa*, are evening bloomers. You may want to grow them near a deck or pathway where their late flowers can be enjoyed. All are easy from seed, which should be lightly covered to ensure darkness. They need sun and excellent drainage, especially in winter when soggy soil can kill them. Clumps should be divided about every three years.

FAVORITES

O. berlandieri 'Siskiyou' (Mexican evening primrose), zones 5 to 9, has 2-inch (5 cm) fragrant, cup-shaped pink flowers all summer on a mat of green foliage. It is somewhat invasive so should be kept away from neigh-bors it could overwhelm.

O. biennis (common evening prim-rose), zones 4 to 8, can grow as tall as 6 feet (1.8 m) with hairy foliage and fragrant, pale yellow flowers that bloom in the evening. This species is a biennial that often self-sows and can become weedy.

O. caespitosa (tufted evening prim-rose), zones 4 to 8, is a native of the

southwestern United States. with white flowers.

O. howardii (bronze evening prim-rose), zones 4 to 9, is a biennial 3 to 4 feet (90-120 cm) tall with hairy green foliage and large pale yellow flowers all summer.

O. kunthiana (Kunch sundrop), zones 6 to 9, grows 7 to 15 inches (18-38 cm) tall with dark green foliage and morning-blooming pink or occasionally white flowers.

O. lamarckiana, zones 4 to 8, grows 36 inches (90 cm) tall with 4-inch (10 cm) yellow flowers.

O. missouriensis; *O. macrocarpa* (Ozark sundrop), zones 3 to 8, is a sprawling plant with 3-to-5-inch (7.5 to 12.5 cm) bright yellow flowers all summer, perfect for the front of a border. It is very drought-tolerant. 'Silver Blade' is just 5 inches (12.5 cm) tall with silvery foliage.

O. pallida (pale evening primrose), zones 4 to 7, has 1-to-1½-inch (2.5-3.5 cm) white flowers tinted pink, on 20-inch (50 cm) stems. There is a lilac-colored selection. Give this plant sandy soil. It blooms spring to fall and spreads by runners to make a good ground cover.

O. speciosa (showy primrose), zones 5 to 9, has 2-foot (60 cm) stems topped with day-blooming white or pink flowers as wide as 2½ inches (7 cm). It blooms for about six weeks in May and June. It spreads by seeds and underground runners, so it is invasive and should be given a spot on its own or grown in a container.

O. 'Sunset Boulevard,' is hardy in zones 8 to 10 and otherwise grown as an annual, since it blooms the first year from seed. Stems 20 to 28 inches (50-70 cm) tall bear orange flowers that fade to red.

OENOTHERA SPECIOSA

OPUNTIA ENGELMANNII

Opuntia species
Cactus, prickly pear
Zones vary

The direction "do not water" in a package of mail-order opuntias is the gardener's first indication that cacti are not like other plants. My shipment also brought the typed warning: "We suggest using barbecue tongs to unpack and handle *Opuntia*." True enough; the merest brush against these long spines is painful. *Opuntia* must be given perfectly drained soil in sun in a place where they are out of touch.

The genus *Opuntia*, the prickly pears — also called bunny ears, beaver tails, cactus pears and Indian figs — are probably the best-known cacti and certainly the best hardy ones, since some will survive in zone 2. There are around 150 species, and in addition many cultivars, from ground-huggers to 100-foot (30 m) trees. They grow wild from the dry plains of northern Canada to the mountains and deserts of Chile and Argentina. Their stems are flattened into large pads with smooth skin and prickles that can be formidable. Deceptively soft-looking fuzzy patches are covered with stickers called glochids, which easily pene-

trate the skin but can be scraped off with a sharp knife. Pads can produce several large, showy flowers apiece, generally in spring. The flower colors can be variable within a species, generally in the range from white to yellow to pink, so some cacti are not sold until they have bloomed. Each flower yields a fruit called a prickly pear. The fruit of all species is edible and high in ascorbic acid, but only a few are tasty and sweet. If you want to try them, scrape off the glochids, then, using tongs, twist the fruit from the pad to avoid tearing the plant. It can be eaten either raw or cooked. The pads are also edible. They can be skinned and the inner fruit eaten like cucumber. The sap from the pads can be applied topically to sooth burns and cuts, much like aloe vera.

Cacti gradually spread by growing new pads from the edges of the old, making them appear like cartoon mouse ears. *O. engelmannii*, a strongly upright-growing species native to the Southwest and Mexico, is best known as the Mickey Mouse cactus. It is easy to multiply plants from pads that are at least six months old. Using tongs and a knife, slice off a pad where it joins the parent and lie the pad flat on the soil. It's not necessary to water it. Space plants 6 to 12 inches (15-30 cm) apart on sandy soil.

In the colder zones, opuntias often wither or turn limp in winter, looking as though they are at death's door. This happens because they eliminate water from their cells to prevent damage from freezing. Some varieties also lie close to the ground to escape winter winds. In spring, pads lying on the soil may root.

FAVORITES
Cactus specialists sell an enormous variety of species and cultivars (see Sources). Following are some of the most widely available winter-hardy species. All grow to zone 10.

O. basilaris, zone 4, has grayish pads and flowers that open pale yellow and fade to white.

O. compressa (*O. humifusa*) is a native of eastern North America with almost spine-free pads that are slightly purple. Flowers are usually yellow.

O. fragilis, zone 2, is small with long thin pads that make it resemble a cholla.

O. humisifa, native to the eastern United States, has yellow flowers and dark green pads that are often spineless.

O. macrorhiza, zone 4, has yellow flowers and pads as long as 10 inches (25 cm). 'Black Mesa Pink' has magenta pink flowers.

O. phaecantha, zone 4, is a spreading species whose large pads, about 1 foot (30 cm) long and half as wide, have long spines. Flowers are yellow or salmon-colored and bloom later than most others. The fruits are bright red.

O. polyacantha, zone 2, has a sprawling habit, 4-to-6-inch (10-15 cm) pads, white spines and 3-inch (7 cm) yellow or pink flowers. There are many cultivars, including 'Crystal Tide,' with large whitish or yellowish flowers, 'Claude Arno,' dark red, and 'Wasash Pink,' bright pink.

Paeonia lactiflora

Peony

Zones 3 to 7

Peonies look far too lush for dry gardens, yet the herbaceous peony (*P. lactiflora*), the type that dies back to the ground in winter, is among the toughest of plants, capable of surviving considerable neglect. Tree peonies are more demanding. *P. lactiflora* flowers bloom for a couple of weeks in spring, and the dark green foliage remains attractive until late fall, when it turns rusty red before it blackens and can be cut back.

A week or so after the buds appear, surround the young stems with a tomato cage or a circle of sticks and twine — the support will be camouflaged as the plant grows. Peony flowers, especially the doubles, are so heavy that they may bow to the ground after a rain. All are excellent cut flowers. Cut just before the buds open, and they will last for weeks in a cool room. Cut flower stems back after blooming.

Peonies are often grown as specimen plants, but they look best in midborder surrounded by other plants. Give them full sun or a little shade in well-drained soil. The most common reason herbaceous peonies fail to bloom is too much water at their roots. The growing point, or eye, should be no more than 2 inches (5 cm) below the surface. Once established, they resent dividing or moving and may take a couple of years to revive. They spread very slowly and can be left in place indefinitely. If you do want to divide a herbaceous peony, take a piece with at least three eyes from a well-established plant soon after it sprouts in spring.

PAEONIA LACTIFLORA 'LOTUS QUEEN'

FAVORITES

Fortunately, limiting yourself to herbaceous peonies is not a hardship. From heirlooms to hybrids, fragrant doubles — some with flowers as big as cabbages — to graceful singles, in shades from white and pink through red and purple, there is a herbaceous peony for almost every garden. Because the doubles are so vulnerable to drooping after a rain, the singles are becoming increasingly popular even though their blooming time is shorter.

Papaver species

Poppy

Zones vary

There are both annual (page 148) and perennial poppies for the dry garden. All have short-lived flowers with silky petals in the crystal colors of a stained-glass window, from cream and yellow through pink, orange and red. The stems are slender but do not need staking. Grow in a sunny spot of well-drained soil. Deadhead flowers to prolong blooming. The seed heads are attractive and self-seeding often occurs. If you must transplant seedlings, do so

with as much soil as possible, and then water thoroughly, since most transplant poorly. Growing from seed is the best way to obtain most species except *P. orientale*. All except *P. orientale* tend to be short-lived perennials.

FAVORITES

P. atlanticum, zones 5 to 9, forms a low clump of silver-green hairy leaves and 12-to-18-inch (30-45 cm) stems holding copper-colored flowers. There is a double form.

P. bracteatum, zones 3 to 8, is the largest of all poppies, one of the ancestors of *P. orientale* but larger and sturdier. It grows 3 feet (90 cm) or taller with 18-inch (45 cm) fernlike foliage

PAPAVER ORIENTALE

and small leaves directly under the dark red, black-eyed flowers as wide as 7 inches (18 cm). It does poorly where summers are hot and humid.

P. lateritium, zones 7 to 9, grows best in cool, dry, rocky places, where it spreads by underground stolons. Stems grow 20 inches (45 cm) tall, with bright orange, semi-double flowers as wide as 2 inches (5 cm).

P. orientale (Oriental poppy), zones 2 to 7, is the most widely cultivated of the perennial poppies and also one of the toughest and longest-lived. It may grow taller than 3 feet (1 m) and is fabulous during its brief late-spring season of bloom, although its dark-throated flowers often fall victim to heavy spring rains and gusty winds. The foliage dies back by midsummer, leaving a gap in the garden that should be camouflaged with bedding annuals or more durable perennials. Division or moving is best done during dormancy in late summer. If you dig close to the crown and leave some lateral roots in the soil, both the crown and the remaining roots may develop into flowering plants. A compact version is 'Baby Kiss,' just 20 inches (50 cm) tall with dark orange, white-edged petals.

P. pilosum (Turkish poppy), zones 4 to 7, grows 2 feet (60 cm) tall with hairy foliage and 4-inch (10 cm) light orange flowers for several weeks.

P. rupifragum (Spanish poppy) grows evergreen rosettes of smooth, blue-gray toothed leaves and many 18-inch (45 cm) stems of 3-inch (7 cm) pale orange flowers in summer. There is a double-flowered version.

Many small species, known collectively as alpine poppies, are suitable for a rock garden or the front of a dry border.

Penstemon species
Penstemon, beardtongue
Zones vary

Just a decade ago, penstemons were known only by garden connoisseurs, but after 'Husker Red,' with its bronze foliage and spires of white trumpet flowers, was named Perennial Plant of the Year in 1996, the genus hit the garden mainstream in a big way. Now, the beauty and variability of penstemons have brought them to the forefront of home gardening, especially in areas subjected to droughts. There are hundreds of species native to rocky slopes and semidesert regions of North and Central America, and it has been estimated that 75 percent of them will do fine in unimproved clay soil with little water, summer temperatures as hot as 100 degrees F (38°C) and winters as cold as minus 40 degrees F (−40°C) with no snow cover. Most penstemons do best in full sun in well-drained, generally acidic soil, even sand or gravel. On the other hand, they are extremely sensitive to winter moisture. Raised beds will help them survive wet weather. There are evergreen species, but the hardiest types die back to the ground in winter.

Penstemons are related to foxgloves and snapdragons, a kinship evident in the vertical flower spikes and the tubular shape of the flower, which often has a hairy throat or lip; hence the common name beardtongue. Most bloom in shades of blue, lilac, pink and scarlet, but there are also whites and yellows. Hummingbirds are drawn to them, especially the red-flowered types. Heights vary from creepers to 6 feet (1.8 m) tall. They may bloom in spring or summer. They are short-lived perennials, generally lasting two or three years, but can be renewed every few years if the gardener takes cuttings. Hybrids such as 'Garnet,' 'King George' and 'Sour Grapes' and the Mexicali hybrids tend to be showier but less drought-tolerant. Wild types can be grown from seed.

FAVORITES
There are so many good penstemons, with new ones coming onto the marketplace every year, that the best plan is to look through the offerings of good nurseries or seed houses. Everywhere in North America, it is possible to grow at least one penstemon native to your area. These are some of the best and most widely available choices:

P. angustifolius (pagoda penstemon), zones 3 to 8, and recommended for containers, is an evergreen whose 1-foot-tall (30 cm) stems bear bright blue flowers all summer.

P. barbatus (common beardtongue), zones 4 to 9, forms a low mound of evergreen foliage with 2-to-4-foot (30-60 cm) spikes of trumpet flowers in early summer. It is not as drought-tolerant as the others but is very showy. 'Coccineus' has red flowers. 'Elfin Pink' grows 1 foot (30 cm) tall with pink flowers. The hybrid 'Prairie Dusk' has a flat rosette of foliage and 2-foot (60 cm) spikes of rose-purple flowers.

P. caespitosa (mat penstemon) 'Claude Barr,' zones 4 to 9, has bright purple flowers on a matt of foliage just 3 to 6 inches (4.5-15 cm) high.

P. cobaea (foxglove penstemon), zones 3 to 9, has unusually large white or lilac flowers on 2-foot (30 cm) stems over a clump of downy foliage.

P. cyananthus (Wasatch penstemon), zones 4 to 8, is native to the high country of Utah, Wyoming and Idaho. It grows as tall as 3 feet (90 cm) with bright blue flowers in late spring.

P. digitalis, zones 2 to 8, named for its resemblance to the flowers of foxglove (*Digitalis*), is a 4-to-5-foot (1.2 m-1.5 m) native of the northeastern states. The much shorter 'Husker Red,' released from the University of Nebraska, grows 30 inches (75 cm) tall, with green foliage burnished with bronze and masses of white flowers in July and August. 'Albus' is a taller form. Both will flower in light shade. This species is more tolerant of high humidity and moist soil and less drought-tolerant than those of western origin.

P. eatonii (firecracker penstemon), zones 4 to 8, is a southwestern and California native with brilliant red hummingbird-magnet flowers on 1-to-3-foot (30-90 cm) stems. It has large, leathery evergreen leaves.

P. fruticosus, zones 4 to 9, is a shrubby plant whose leathery evergreen foliage makes a good, drought-resistant ground cover and turns bronze in winter. The flowers are lilac-purple.

P. grandiflorus, zones 3 to 9, a native of the prairies and Great Plains, has large, 2-inch (5 cm) pink or lavender-blue flowers and blue-gray, waxy foliage.

P. heterophyllus, zones 5 to 8, a native of California, grows 18 inches (45 cm) with silvery green, glossy leaves and blue flowers. It is very drought-tolerant. Cultivars include 'Blue Springs' and 'Züriblau' ('True Blue')

P. x mexicali (Mexicali hybrids), zones 5 to 8, include cherry pink Red Rocks™ and violet purple Pikes Peak Purple™. They have narrow, dark green leaves and 15-inch (38 cm) stems and bloom in late summer and fall. They require some watering.

P. nitidus (shining or smooth penstemon), zones 2 to 8, is a Canadian prairie wildflower with blue, lavender

PENSTEMON OVATUS

or purple flowers in early spring on 10-inch (25 cm) stalks above a rosette of fleshy leaves. It is drought-tolerant.

P. ovatus (broad-leaved penstemon), zones 4 to 8, is a 3-foot (90 cm) native of the Pacific Northwest, with wide leaves and purple flowers. 'Albus' is white.

P. palmeri (pink snapdragon), zones 5 to 8, is unusual in that its flowers are fragrant. It grows as tall as 7 feet (2 m), with a 1-foot-wide (30 cm) clump of leaves and pinkish or white flowers in late spring.

P. pinifolius (pineleaf penstemon), zones 4 to 9, from the southern United States and Mexico, is a small, bushy evergreen about 1 foot (30 cm) tall that does well in a niche in a stone wall or another protected place in sun. It has needlelike foliage and tubular, bright orange-red flowers. 'Mersea Yellow' has yellow flowers.

P. pseudospectabilis (canyon penstemon), zones 5 to 10, is a native of southern New Mexico with hot pink flowers that bloom almost all year on 36-inch (90 cm) stems over large gray leaves. It is very drought-tolerant.

P. strictus (Rocky Mountain penstemon), zones 4 to 9, grows 2 feet (60 cm) tall, has evergreen, purplish foliage and spikes of purple-blue flowers. A hybrid is 'Midnight Blue.'

Perovskia atriplicifolia

Russian sage
Zones 4 to 8

Russian sage takes its name from its slender spikes of small bluish to purple summer flowers reminiscent of the flowers of its cousins the sages (*Salvia*). The aromatic leaves are gray-green like those of kitchen sage. *Perovskia* grows into a loose clump about 3 feet (90 cm) tall and almost as wide, and blooms in late summer and fall, looking most effective when mass planted or used as a cloudy filler near the back of a flower bed. Prune stems back to 6 inches (15 cm) in late fall or spring to encourage the growth of new shoots. Perovskia needs occasional watering to reach its full size but can die if the soil is too wet, especially in winter or early spring. Give it well-drained soil in sun.

FAVORITES

P. atriplicifolia was chosen Perennial Plant of the Year in 1995. The bluish-flowered species, or purple-flowered 'Blue Spire' or lavender 'Filigran,' are the best choices if you have plenty of space, but if not, grow 'Little Spire,' a Dutch release that grows about 25 inches (60 cm) tall.

Platycodon grandiflorus
Balloon flower
Zones 3 to 8

The buds of this remarkable perennial swell into spherical balloons. Suddenly, they pop open to reveal single 2-inch (5 cm) starlike, five-petaled flowers that may be white, pale pink or purple. Beautiful in every way, this elegant perennial forms a 2-foot (60 cm) or taller clump of shiny gray-green leaves and graceful stems that support flowers from early until late summer. Give balloon flower well-drained soil in full or part sun. Mark the plant's spot, as it is late to emerge in spring and thus can be easily damaged with early cultivating. Balloon flower is difficult to divide and may resent transplanting. It does not spread and should not be disturbed. Plants grown from seed will take two or three years to flower. It makes an excellent cut flower, but before placing in water, sear the bottom of the stem with a flame.

FAVORITES
Good cultivars include 'Double Blue,' 'Fuji White,' 'Fuji Pink' and dark blue 'Mariesii.'

POLYGONATUM ODORATUM 'VARIEGATUM'

Polygonatum species
Solomon's seal
Zones 2/3 to 9

Solomon's seal grows naturally in moist woodlands, yet it looks splendid all summer in a sunny, dry border, where it persists while other plants wilt around it. It is grown mainly for its ladder of foliage, born on attractively arching stems. Small white, dangling bells are replaced with black berries. Both species described below spread slowly by underground rhizome and are easy to divide and move but can be difficult to get rid of, so situate them carefully. Give them partial or total shade if they grow in dry ground.

FAVORITES
P. commutatum, zones 3 to 9, is a North American native plant. It grows 3 to 4 feet tall (90-120 cm) in moist soil, about half that height in dry ground.

P. odoratum; P. officinale, zones 2 to 9, is a British native once esteemed in Europe as a medicinal plant, used to bleach freckles and clear up a black eye. It is a woodland plant but is amenable to shady spots elsewhere, whether moist or dry. The most decorative choice is the variegated version 'Variegatum,' whose white-edged green leaves are excellent in flower arrangements.

PLATYCODON GRANDIFLORUS

PULSATILLA VULGARIS

Pulsatilla species; Anemone species

Pasqueflower, prairie crocus
Zones 2 to 7

Two members of this genus, once gathered under the umbrella of the anemones, are described here, one a naturalized wildflower of the North American plains, the other a cultivated garden plant. Both are natives of Europe. Pulsatillas are often the first perennials to bloom in early spring and are often purple with bright yellow stamens — thus the common name prairie crocus — although there are also other colors, and their ferny foliage is not at all like crocus leaves. These species produce their flowers before the foliage —unlike the bulbous anemones, which yield their foliage first. Silky down covers the leaves and stems. Whether in sun or part shade, they light up the spring garden with a burst of unusual texture and color. They grow only 6 to 12 inches (15-30 cm) tall, so need a spot at the front of the border or in a rock garden where they can be appreciated. The soil for Pulsatilla must be well drained, preferably sandy or gravelly and alkaline. They will naturalize where they are content.

FAVORITES
P. patens; Anemone patens (prairie crocus; pasqueflower) is seldom sold, so you may have to grow it from seed, a fairly difficult process as the seed must be fresh and may need a winter to germinate. Dark lavender to white flowers bloom in early spring on 6-inch (15 cm) stems.

The common name pasqueflower is usually applied to a close relative that is widely available, *Pulsatilla vulgaris; Anemone pulsatilla*, a 6-to-12-inch (15-30 cm) perennial with feathery foliage and large 2-to-3-inch (5-7.5 cm) upfacing bell-shaped flowers that are usually blue to violet-purple, although there are also white, bluish white, pink and red forms. Graceful, airy seed heads follow.

Rudbeckia species

Black-eyed Susan
Zones vary

There are annual, biennial and perennial types of rudbeckia suitable for the no-care garden. All have daisy flowers with green to black centers and yellow to orange rays. Flowering takes place from midsummer until fall. Some rudbeckias like moist soil, such as *R. nitida* (usually 'Herbstonne,' 'Autumn Glory' and 'Viette's Little Suzy'). Another somewhat thirsty species is *R. laciniata*. One variety, the sterile double heirloom 'Golden Glow,' or 'Hortensia,' grows 6 feet (1.8 m) tall and can be invasive. The knee-high *R. fulgida sullivantii* 'Goldsturm' is an excellent cultivar but it, too, requires regular watering.

FAVORITES
There are rudbeckias that are superlative for dry places.
R. hirta (gloriosa daisy), zones 3 to 9, generally acts as a self-seeding annual or biennial but may also be perennial. It is easy from seed, which can be scattered directly in the spring

RUDBECKIA HIRTA

SALVIA 'EAST FRIESLAND'

garden. It grows about 2 to 3 feet (60-90 cm) tall and needs watering only after a week or so of hot, dry weather. While there are many beautiful black- or brown-eyed singles in shades of reddish brown, gold, yellow and bicolors, unusual cultivars include the double 'Goldilocks' and the green-centered 'Irish Eyes.'

R. maxima (giant coneflower), zones 4 to 9, is given a high rating by Kristl Walek of Gardens North, near Ottawa, Ontario. It forms a clump of bluish foliage, then grows flower stems about 8 feet (2.4 m) tall topped with drooping black-eyed Susan flowers that are "fabulous with ornamental grasses. I have planted it in spots where no other tall plant would remain standing because of strong winds. Prefers full sun and tolerates a wide range of wet or dry soils. Easy from seed."

R. triloba (three-lobed coneflower; brown-eyed Susan), zones 3 to 10, has bright yellow flowers from summer to late fall. The winner of the 1997 Georgia gold medal for herbaceous perennials, it is tolerant of drought, heat, pests and a considerable amount of shade. It grows about 3 feet (1 m) tall.

Salvia species
Salvia, sage
Zones vary

There are both annual and perennial forms of salvia in great number. A few of the annuals are described on pages 149 and some of the kitchen or medicinal sages are described on page 50. A couple of species, *S. aethiopis* and *S. virgata*, have become invasive in rangelands. Most salvias have grayish foliage and flowers in the spectrum of lilac and blue to pink and rose, light or dark. They are favorites of hummingbirds. If deadheaded after blooming, they may flower again in late summer. Salvias can be grown in full sun or light shade but do best out of strong wind. Perennials are generally short-lived; a wet spring often spells their demise. While named varieties must be purchased or divided, the species often self-sow, ensuring a crop of flowers even if the plants do not survive the winter. Leave some flower spikes for seeds, but otherwise, trim them off after flowering to encourage more flowers. Divide plants in spring.

FAVORITES
S. argentea (silver sage), zones 3 to 9, is grown chiefly for its felted silver leaves up to 8 inches (20 cm) long. The second year, a spire of spotted white or yellowish flowers grows as tall as 3 feet (90 cm).

S. azurea (blue sage), zones 5 to 9, is a wildflower of the southeastern United States that grows 1 to 5 feet (30-150 cm) tall with slender stems of deep blue or purplish flowers from summer till hard frost. Pinch this back in spring to make it more bushy. The selection 'Grandiflora' (*S. pitcheri* 'Grandiflora;' *S. grandiflora*) has larger, showy flowers.

S. forskaohlei, zones 5 to 9, forms a flat rosette of large hairy leaves followed by 3-foot (90 cm) spires of vivid blue flowers with white tongues.

S. roemericana (cedar sage), zones 7 to 10, forms a basal rosette of foliage with red stems and bright tubular flowers in summer and fall. This Texan native grows about 1 foot (30 cm) tall.

The largest group of perennial garden salvias are the *S.* x *superba* hybrids, zones 3 to 9, a combination of the hybrid *S.* x *sylvestris* and *S. villicaulis*. The *S.* x *superba* hybrids have deep blue, purple or pink flowers on 18-to-30-inch (45-75 cm) spikes that do not need staking and may retain their color for as long as 12 weeks. Cultivars include dark purple 'Lubeca,' violet-purple 'East Friesland' ('Ostfriesland'), rosy-violet 'Rose Queen' ('Rosakonig'), pale blue 'Blue Hill' ('Blauhugel') and white 'Snow Hill' ('Schneehugel'). 'East Friesland' was one of the most outstanding survivors of the 1995 drought at the Xeriscape Demonstration Garden in Plainview, New York.

S. x *sylvestris* is a hybrid of *S. nemorosa* x *S. pratensis*. The best-known of the *S.* x *sylvestris* hybrids is 'May Night' ('Mainacht'), which has dark blue flower spikes $2^1/2$ feet (75 cm) tall and blooms almost steadily from June until September. It was Perennial Plant of the Year for 1997.

S. verticillata (lilac sage), zones 5 to 8, is a European wildflower with 18-to-24-inch (45-60 cm) arching spires of smoky purple flowers over a rosette of fuzzy green foliage. 'Purple Rain' and 'White Rain' are the usual cultivars.

Santolina species
Santolina; lavender cotton
Zones 7 to 10

This tender perennial is known for its foliage, an airy mound of fragrant, deeply indented leaves. While the white-leaved types are most often grown, those with green leaves make a good contrast. Since santolina is usually kept sheared into a neat mound, its summer crop of yellow button flowers are seldom seen. Santolina may survive mild winters in zones 5 and 6 if the soil is well drained but is usually grown as an annual.

FAVORITES
All three of the following species make excellent low hedges or borders, and where hardy, can be pruned back in spring to encourage more foliage
   S. chamaecyparissus (lavender cotton) is the best-known of the santolinas. Around 12 to 18 inches (30-45 cm) tall, it is traditionally clipped to edge a herb garden, a perennial border or a pathway. 'Lemon Queen' has silvery-green foliage. A shorter sea-green version, 'Small-Ness,' can be especially effective grown next to any of the other colors. 'Pretty Carol' has two-tone gray foliage.
   S. pinnata neapolitana; S. neapolitana is similar to *S. chamaecyparissus,* but its form is more open and the foliage is lacier, creating a ghostly effect. Cultivars include 'Edward Bowles' with greenish foliage and creamy flowers, and 'Sulphurea' with gray-green leaves and yellow flowers.
   S. rosmarinifolia; S. virens; S. viridis has bright yellow flowers and green needle leaves that resemble rosemary. 'Primrose Gem' has flowers of paler yellow.

Sedum species
Stonecrop
Zones 2 to 9

Garden sedums are succulents divided into two fairly distinct groups, the creeping stonecrops — these are listed as ground covers on pages 69-70 — and the upright and reclining forms for the perennial border or for containers. These grow about 12 to 18 inches (30-43 cm), with thick stems holding roundish, fleshy leaves. They can take full sun but do fine in some shade, especially in very hot, dry places. Well-drained, poor soil suits them. All have an extended bloom time, starting in late summer. The large, flattish heads of tiny pink to rose flowers, which attract bees and butterflies, continue for about two months. When they turn brown they can be snipped off or left in place for winter. Cut stems for a vase just as the flowers begin to open, and they will bloom indoors for weeks, sometimes putting down roots in the vase water. Clumps eventually die out in the center but are easy to renew with divisions taken from the edge.

FAVORITES
The botany of the upright sedums is confusing, with some genetic input from a Chinese species, *S. spectabile* and some from *S. hylotelephium* (*S. telephium; S. purpureum*), which hails from Eastern Europe and Japan. However, since all are treated similarly in the garden, their botanical names are not as important as their appearance. The usual garden plant is labelled *S. spectabile* or 'Autumn Joy' ('Herbstfreude'), with grayish green leaves and rose or dark pink flowers. 'Brilliant' and 'Neon' are versions with brighter flowers. 'Variegatum' has white-and-green foliage that con-

SEDUM SPECTABILE

tributes to the plant's interest all season and makes it a perfect candidate for a large container. It forms a clump about 1 foot (30 cm) tall and has pale pink flowers. Pull out at the base any green shoots that appear. Give it some shade.
   Hybrids with showy purple or pinkish foliage and pink flowers are becoming increasingly available. 'Atropurpureum' has dark purple foliage on stems about 2 feet (60 cm) tall. 'Hester' has especially large, shiny purple-and-green leaves. 'Bertram Anderson' has 8-inch (20 cm) stems of deep purple foliage and bright red flowers. 'Mohrchen' is dark bronze-red, with pink flowers on stems 18 to 24 inches (45-60 cm) tall. 'Vera Jameson' forms a neat 1-foot-high (30 cm) clump of maroon-and-green leaves. 'Ruby Glow' is only 6 inches (15 cm) tall with greenish foliage and bright red flowers. 'Sunset Clouds' is recumbent, with pink stems, bluish green foliage and bright pink flowers.

SOLIDAGO ALTISSIMA

Solidago species
Goldenrod
Zones 3 to 9

Hardiness, drought-tolerance and imposing vertical stems holding fleecy-looking plumes of tiny daisy flowers, usually yellow, from late summer to fall are the gifts of the goldenrods, wildflowers of the northern hemisphere. There are scores of wild species, such as *S. altissima*, all of which can be seeded or transplanted into the garden. Nevertheless, goldenrods were considered little more than weeds on this continent and burdened with an unwarranted reputation for triggering allergies — the culprit is often ragweed — until they were first developed as garden perennials in Europe. Some species grow in woods or near wetlands, but most are tolerant of considerable drought, putting up with any soil that is not too wet. Goldenrods were among the most impressive plants during the 1995 drought at the Xeriscape Demonstration Garden in Plainview, New York. Wild goldenrods can be invasive by rhizome or seed and so are best suited to natural gardens or wildflower meadows, but most cultivars are clump-forming and

drop little or no seed, so are fine in perennial borders. Goldenrod is an excellent cut flower.

FAVORITES

A five-year evaluation of goldenrods at the Chicago Botanic Garden gave the highest rating to the following drought-tolerant species and cultivars, all suited to zones 3 to 9 unless noted:

S. 'Baby Sun,' just 2 feet (60 cm) tall, with yellow flowers in summer on stems that never need staking.

S. 'Goldkind' ('Golden Baby'), similar to 'Baby Sun' but slightly later blooming. It has good disease-resistance.

S. rigida, over 5 feet (150 cm) tall, with stiff stems that allow it to remain upright. It looks quite different from the others, with gray-green foliage and throughout fall, flat clusters of yellow flowers that resemble yarrow. It attracts butterflies.

S. rugosa 'Fireworks,' zones 4 to 8, was the top choice, thanks to fine-textured foliage and arching stems of yellow flowers through late fall. It spreads slowly and stays under 5 feet (150 cm).

S. sphecelata 'Golden Fleece,' a Delaware release for zones 4 to 9, grows just 12 to 18 inches (30-45 cm) with heart-shaped leaves and branching wands of small golden flowers.

New cultivars and hybrids appear every year.

Stokesia laevis
Stokes aster
Zones 5 to 9

Stokesia is a pioneer favorite of the southern United States, where it is a native wildflower. Double, lavender-blue flowers as wide as 4 inches (10 cm) wide bloom on 1-to 2-foot (30-60 cm) stems in late summer. It is evergreen in warmer zones but should be given a winter mulch in zones 4 and 5. Moderately drought-tolerant once established, it grows best in good, well-drained garden soil in sun or part shade. It is an excellent cut flower.

FAVORITES

Tallest of the cultivars is the 5-foot (150 cm) 'Blue Danube.' Whites include 'Alba' and 'Silver Morn.'

TRADESCANTIA X ANDERSONIANA

Tradescantia x andersoniana
Spiderwort
Zones 3 to 9

A real trouper, the garden spider-wort is a hybrid of several North American wildflowers, including *T. virginiana*, which hails from the eastern United States. This perennial is an old-fashioned favorite that hangs in there when other plants fail — in wet ground or dry. In this way, it is similar to many other monocots, such as lilies and day-lilies, all plants with grasslike foliage and weather-resistant root systems. In the driest weather, tradescantia stops blooming, but its foliage remains decent-looking, and the blooming that stopped in early summer may resume with the cooler fall weather. In the sunniest gardens, it should be given part shade. The three-petaled triangular flowers, about 1-inch (2.5 cm) wide, are distinctive and may be purple, blue, red, pink or white. Stems grow 18 to 36 inches (45-90 cm), all slightly shorter in drier soil. If it grows tall, it may need staking. Where it is content, tradescantia spreads quickly enough to need dividing every two years. It is too invasive to grow alongside modest plants.

FAVORITES
If you want plants that spread quickly, stay away from the beautiful golden-leaved form 'Sweet Kate,' which is much slower spreading, less drought-tolerant and should be given winter protection in zone 4. Instead, depend upon the taller green-leaved forms.

Verbascum species
Mullein
Zones vary

Mulleins have recently been elevated from the status of roadside weeds to garden stars. Strong vertical stems that need no staking, some more than 3 to 4 feet (1 m) tall, are perfect at the back of a border of well-drained soil in sun or part shade. Flowers, which bloom up the stem from late summer until fall, are typically an inch (2.5 cm) wide and may be white, pink, yellow or lavender. The basal rosette of foliage may be green or gray with leaves longer than 1 foot (30 cm). Mullein is best known for the weedy *V. thapsus* of country roadsides, but many species and cultivars are appearing on the North American garden scene. Most are biennial, forming a low rosette in their first year and shooting up flower spikes from summer to early fall in the second. Some self-sow. Others are short-lived perennials. All tolerate poor, dry conditions, some even sand or gravel and extreme drought and wind. Verbascums are excellent at the back of a sunny border or along a fence.

FAVORITES
Rather than transplanting *V. thapsus* from the wild, choose the best garden species and the cultivated varieties, which have more impressive flowers and stay in flower longer.

V. blattaria (moth mullein), zones 4 to 8, is a biennial 3 to 4 feet (90-120 cm) tall, with green foliage and white, pink or yellow flower spikes.

V. bombyciferum (giant silver mullein, Turkish mullein), zones 4 to 9, is one of the most spectacular, a biennial as tall as 6 feet (1.8 m), with whitish, felted leaves, such as 'Silver Lining.'

VERBASCUM 'SILVER LINING'

V. chaixii, zones 4 to 9, has green foliage and slender 3-foot-tall (1 m) spikes of small yellow or white flowers. It often self-sows.

V. nigrum, zones 3 to 8, is one of the most winter hardy. It grows 3 to 4 feet (90-120 cm) tall and has dark green leaves and branching spikes of yellow flowers with brown centers.

V. olympicum (Olympic mullein), zones 5 to 8, has grayish foliage and bright yellow flowers. It often forms a cluster of flower spikes that grow taller than 6 feet (1.8 m).

V. phoeniceum (purple mullein) zones 3 to 9, is a short-lived perennial with purple, red, pink or white flower spikes 2 to 4 feet (60-120 cm) tall in late spring and early summer. 'Violetta' is dark violet-purple.

V. pyramidatum, zones 4 to 9, is a short-lived perennial named for the pyramidal shape (resting on the apex) of its stems of yellow flowers. It blooms in early summer.

Hybrids, most best in zones 5 to 9 and all with green foliage, include 'Cotswold Queen' with multiple slender spires of orange, purple or light brown flowers. 'Wega' is similar but yellow. 'Pink Domino' has large pink flowers.

Veronicastrum virginicum; Veronica virginica
Culver's root
Zones 3 to 9

This back-of-the-border perennial is a North American wildflower that grows upright to about 5 feet (1.5 m) tall in moist or dry ground. Large leaves grow in circles around the fuzzy stems, like umbrella spokes. Racemes of blue, white or pink flowers open at the tips of the stems in late summer. It grows in either sun or part shade.

Yucca species
Adam's needle
Zones vary

About 30 species of yucca, most frost-tender, are native to North and South America. Something like the agaves of the New World and the aloes of the Old, they form rosettes of distinctive upward-pointing sword-shaped leaves, lending the dry garden the look of the Wild West. Depending upon species, the leaves may grow as tall as 6 feet (1.8 m). Yuccas are easy from seed, but it may be several years before they form a sizable clump. When plants mature in two or more years, a long flower stalk topped by white or violet-tinted bell flowers emerges from the center of the rosette. Suckers that emerge from the base can be snipped off and planted elsewhere. Yuccas enjoy heat and perfectly drained soil, do well as easy-care plants in large pots and should be mulched in winter where they are marginally hardy. The young plants and the flowers are edible.

FAVORITES
These are some of the hardiest species:

Y. filamentosa; *Y. smalliana* (Adam's needle), zones 4 to 10, is a native of the Atlantic seashore. The slender leaves, which may be as long as 6 feet (180 cm), are edged with long, curly threads. 'Bright Edge' has leaves striped blue-green down the center and creamy white on each edge. 'Golden Sword' has deep green leaves edged with gold.

Y. glauca; *Y. angustifolia* (Spanish bayonet) is the best choice for cooler gardens, zones 3 to 9. It has shorter, narrower 2-foot (60 cm) leaves, with pale margins and fine filaments along the edge.

Y. gloriosa (Spanish dagger), zones 7 to 10, grows 6 to 8 feet (180-240 cm) tall and wide, with flowers as long as 4 inches (10 cm). It is a native of the southeastern United States.

Y. recurvifolia (softleaf yucca) zones 6 to 9, has foliage that curves downward. It grows about 4 feet (120 cm) tall and just as wide. Banana Split® ('Monca'), zones 7 to 9, is striped with yellow centers and green edges.

YUCCA GLAUCA

VINES

What gardeners want in a perennial vine is a plant that covers the desired space beautifully and fairly quickly but doesn't take over the garden. The worst example of a vine that is far too rampant is kudzu, an Asian import that can grow as much as 60 feet (18 m) a year and has become a menace throughout the southern United States.

In gardens that dry out in summer, vines are apt to be less domineering. In the driest and windiest places, they won't grow at all. Since they need something to climb on, vines are native to vertical environments, not plains and deserts. Most vines appreciate plenty of soil moisture, especially in partially sunlit forests, whether tropical or temperate. In the garden, they need walls, fences, archways and other supports, and they need protection from the harshest weather.

All vines can be tattered by strong winds, so grow them in a sheltered place, preferably with the root run shaded by rocks or perennials and the tops in sunshine. Perennial vines that can be considered for the dry garden include the following, as well as certain varieties of euonymus (page 160) and pyracantha (page 170).

To flourish, all vines — but especially those with large flowers such as certain types of clematis — depend upon some shade and shelter from winds.

Akebia quinata
Five-leaf akebia
Zones 4 to 10

Five-leaf akebia is a fast-growing twiner with green oval leaves that grow in circles of five on separate male and female plants. On females, the small spring flowers are brownish purple; on the males, light purple. Prune soon after flowering. It grows to at least 30 feet (10 m) and may reach half that height the first year. Give it full sun or partial shade in almost any soil. It is evergreen in zone 7 and warmer gardens. Plants can be cut back to the ground if overgrown and will quickly regrow.

Ampelopsis brevipedunculata
Porcelain ampelopsis
Zones 5 to 10

This plant shows its kinship to the related grapes with its lobed, grape-like foliage, tendrils and clusters of berries. Ampelopsis fruit is only 1/4-inch (1 cm) wide, however, and changes from pale green to turquoise to purple and pale blue as it ripens. All colors may be present at the same time. Give it well-drained, even dry, rocky soil in sun or part shade. In early spring, it can be cut back close to the ground to control its growth. It can grow 15 to 20 feet (5-6 m) in its first year.

Celastrus scandens
American bittersweet
Zones 4 to 8

Bittersweet is a North American native with shiny, waxy, green leaves on shoots that rapidly grow to a height of 10 feet (3 m) or so. Stems quickly grow straight up, twining

their way through a support, so if you want this plant to cover a trellis, it must be coaxed to grow more horizontally. The trellis or fence must be strong, since the stems become thick and woody. Give the vine plenty of space or prune it heavily every spring, since it can overwhelm nearby plants. The females produce decorative crimson berries, provided a male is close by for pollination — a male of another species will suffice. Bittersweet will grow in either wet or dry ground.

CLEMATIS TANGUTICA

Clematis species
Clematis; virgin's bower
Zones 4 to 9

The large-flowered species and hybrids need regular watering, but there are smaller-flowered species, such as *C. alpina, C. macropetala, C. paniculata, C. serratifolia* and *C. tangutica* and the hybrid 'Prairie Traveller's Joy' that survive in dry soil, although all need occasional watering in spring. *C. serratifolia* and *C. tangutica* spread by rhizomes and can thus be weedy. Many of the species sometimes self-sow. All like to have their heads in sun and roots

in shade. Position a couple of rocks or perennials within shading distance of the base to create ideal growing conditions. Since most of the above-mentioned species bloom on new wood, they should be cut back very early in the spring to just above the lowest pair of strong, healthy buds. A year later, cut back the main shoots to half their height. Every summer thereafter, cut back all stems that flowered that year to nearly their base. If the vines become too tangled, the entire plant can be cut back almost to the ground, but if possible, prune back to just above a pair of healthy buds. All clematises need training as the vines begin to grow. After the flowers fade, lovely silky seedheads remain decorative until winter. The species often look best clambering through trees or shrubs, or allowed to tumble over rocks.

HUMULUS LUPULUS

Humulus species
Hops
Zones vary

Hops are aggressive, fast-growing twiners with rough green leaves and, on the females, papery green fruits that resemble small artichokes. They grow in either moist or dry soils. Among the hardiest cultivars of *H. lupulus* — the plant that gives characteristic flavor to lagers and ales and grows 12 to 20 feet (3.7-6 m) — are 'Cascade,' bred at Oregon State University and hardy to zone 4, and the even hardier 'Old Early Cluster,' or 'Old Cluster,' brought to North America by European settlers and capable of surviving in zone 2. 'Tettnang,' a German type favored for lagers, is hardy to about zone 5. The ornamental cultivar 'Aureus,' (golden hops) the most beautiful choice for the garden, should be kept out of full sun to prevent scorching but is dependable and hardy to zone 3, with beautiful golden foliage on 10-foot (3 m) stems. Hops spread underground and can be invasive. Cut stems back to the ground in fall. The stems quickly grow vertically, so you must train them sideways if you want them to cover a trellis. *H. japonicus*; *H. scandens* (Japanese hops), zones 5 to 9, is an ornamental species with bright green foliage that can grow more than 20 feet (6 m) in a season and is grown as an annual in zones 3 and 4. 'Variegatus' has green leaves splashed and spotted with white. It is neither as hardy nor as tall as the species.

Lonicera species
Honeysuckle vine
Zones vary

The two most drought-tolerant honeysuckle vines can be too weedy for garden use; *L. japonica* 'Halliana' (Hall's honeysuckle) and *L. sempervirens* (trumpet honeysuckle), both hardy to zone 4. More refined but requiring some watering is *L.* x *brownii* 'Dropmore Scarlet,' a vining

**LONICERA
'DROPMORE SCARLET'**

honeysuckle hardy to zone 2b. It bears orange-scarlet flowers from June to November. A selection from Dropmore, Manitoba, it was one of the varieties found to be aphid-resistant at North Dakota State University.

**PARTHENOCISSUS
QUINQUEFOLIA**

Parthenocissus species
Boston ivy; Virginia creeper
Zones 3 to 10

These green-leaved clinging plants are ivy substitutes for climates too severe for the real thing. Both

quickly create a dense cover and have beautiful red or gold fall color. They can grow on bare walls, since they cling with adhesive discs. They grow in sun or partial shade and will tolerate moist or dry soil. Especially hardy is *P. quinquefolia* (Virginia creeper), which was judged one of the best perennial climbing plants by the Devonian Botanic Garden, near Edmonton, Alberta. It is distinguished by five-lobed leaves, in contrast with the three-lobed leaves of *P. tricuspidata* (Boston ivy), which is a little less rampant and a bit more demanding of good soil. It is a favorite for covering building walls, where it can ascend 60 feet (20 m). There are several cultivars.

Polygonum aubertii
Silver fleece vine
Zones 4 to 8

Where it is content, silver fleece is fast-growing, to about 20 feet (6 m), and will overwhelm neighboring plants. The jointed stems, reminiscent of bamboo, twine around any support. The foliage is bright green. Fragrant, lacy white flowers appear in large masses in summer. This vine should be pruned severely at the end of the season. In zones 4 and 5, it may die back to the ground after severe winters but generally reappears in spring. It can be cut back in fall, as it blooms on the new wood produced in spring.

CHAPTER SEVEN

ANNUAL FLOWERS

Of all the flowers in the garden, annuals are the group most vulnerable to weather extremes, since they have only a single growing season to put down their roots and flower. Best suited to drought survival are the annuals that self-sow. Provided you don't pick all the flowers, they'll drop their seeds around them in summer or fall. The seeds remain dormant in the winter garden, awaiting their favored germination temperature, then sprout while the soil is still damp. The roots are already deep in the soil by the time it begins to dry out. This is the survival strategy of annual weeds. Sowing the seeds of annuals anytime between fall and early spring has the same effect as self-sowing.

Among the flowers apt to self-sow, some of which are described in other chapters, are annual species and varieties of Anthemis, Antirrhinum, Argemone, Calendula, Centaurea, Cleome, Consolida, Coreopsis, Cynoglossum, Dianthus, Eschscholzia, Gaillardia, Helianthus, Iberis, Linaria, Lobularia, Nigella, Papaver, Petunia, Portulaca, Rudbeckia and Salvia. *A color-coordinated mixture of these sown in early spring in moist, sunny soil can create a lovely annual "wildflower meadow" that will bloom all summer and self-sow for flowers next year.*

As their name suggests, sunflowers love plenty of sun, but as seedlings, the multi-branching types need moisture to bloom profusely.

Celosia 'Apricot Brandy' is one of many esteemed cultivars that have bloomed well across the continent.

Other drought-tolerant annuals can be grown from seed started indoors, or they can be purchased as transplants. Water them in their pots, and once they're in the garden, you'll have to water them until they have sprouted and are well rooted. A few tender perennials treated as annuals are sterile hybrids that can be grown only from cuttings; some of the verbenas are like this.

If you have favorite annuals that are not drought-tolerant, consider growing them in a container close to a water source so that you can give them a drink as often as they need it — in many cases, once a day. Partial shade and shelter from the wind will reduce water requirements.

There are two award-granting institutions fre-quently mentioned in this chapter. All-America Selections (AAS) conducts trials of new vegetables and flowers throughout the United States and Canada, then rewards and promotes the best ones every year. Fleuroselect, based in Holland, per-forms the same role in Europe, although it tests and rewards only flowers. New cultivars given an All-America or Fleuroselect award are deemed to have made some kind of advance, usually in color, uniformity, duration of flowering or disease-resist-ance. A nod from either of these organizations probably signifies a variety that will do well in your garden, but it doesn't mean it will be one of your favorites. In fact, you might prefer something older and wilder.

ARGEMONE GRANDIFLORA

Argemone species
Prickly poppy

These beautiful but well-armed poppies thrive in dry places and often self-sow to reappear next year. Most have white flowers. Because of their prickly foliage, they are best grown in a spot on their own. Weed the area well at planting time to avoid having to handle them later. Like other poppies, they resent transplanting but all are easy from seeds sown directly in the spring garden. Thin seedlings to about 6 inches (15 cm) apart, then leave them alone if possible.

FAVORITES
There are about a dozen species, all native to North and South America and all worth searching out in specialist seed catalogs such as Chiltern.
   A. grandiflora has 4-inch (10 cm) white flowers on 14-inch (35 cm) stems of prickly bluish foliage. 'Yellow Luster' is a bright yellow version. The Devonian Botanic Garden near Edmonton, Alberta, displays *A. grandiflora* and the similar *A. platyceras* as well as *A. ochroleuca* and *A. subfusiformis*, both with yellow flowers above more slender, greener foliage.

A. squarrosa 'Purity' has been selected for especially white flowers.
   A. hunemannii has the usual spiny blue foliage and dramatic yellow-centered white flowers as wide as 6 inches (15 cm). It grows 2 feet (60 cm) or taller.

Begonia semperflorens-cultorum hybrids
Wax begonia

Unlike the big, blowsy, thirsty tuberous begonias, the wax begonias, a species with fibrous roots, are suited to borders that dry out occasionally. Like the tuberous begonias, however, these small plants also prefer shade. Their common name comes from the waxy appearance of the roundish leaves. Plants grow 8 to 10 inches (20-25 cm) tall, with 1-inch (2.5 cm) flowers all summer in shades of pink, rose, red, white and bicolors. Although they are frost-tender, they can move indoors to do double duty as excellent house plants. They will continue to bloom all winter in a bright, cool window with little attention. Plants can be hardened off and move outdoors again in spring.

FAVORITES
While it is possible to grow wax begonias from seeds, they are a little tricky in their demands. It is far easier to purchase plants in spring, since most nurseries carry a selection. Foliage may be green or bronze, so choose your favorites by foliage and flower color.

Brachycome iberidifolia
Swan River daisy

A popular container and window-box annual for sun and also appropriate to edge a border or pathway, brachycome has flat daisy flowers with contrasting centers. It is most appreciated for its unusual daisy shades of blue and purple, but there are also whites. The delicately scented flowers open in sun, so this plant requires a sunny site and does best in rich soil. The daisies are only about 1 inch (2.5 cm) wide but are produced in great numbers on slim 10-inch (25 cm) stems of handsome, ferny foliage. Stems tend to flop, so position them accordingly or tie them to a stake. Pinching the stem tips once or twice during growth helps promote bushiness. Spring transplants are fairly easy to find, or you can start seeds indoors six weeks early.

FAVORITES
'Brachy Blue' is a shorter, sturdier, 9-inch (23 cm) cultivar that forms a self-supporting clump with a profusion of deep lavender-blue flowers all season.

BRACHYCOME IBERIDIFOLIA

Calandrinia grandiflora
Rock purslane

This tender perennial member of the portulaca family, hardy in zone 7, has silky, magenta, 1-inch-wide (2.5 cm) primroselike flowers that bloom one day apiece, and long, gray-green, hairy, somewhat succulent-looking foliage. The species has trailing stems as long as 3 feet (1 m), but a couple of dwarf forms and a few additional species, also smaller, are available from specialist catalogs. Calandrinia blooms in about 15 weeks from seed, so it is best started indoors about six weeks before the last spring frost date. It can also be propagated from cuttings. Give it well-drained soil in full sun to part shade. It appreciates occasional moisture but does best if it dries completely between waterings.

CALLISTEPHUS CHINENSIS

Callistephus chinensis
Chinese aster

The annual asters are now grouped under the genus *Callistephus*. Although not lovers of parched soil, they do well in full sun and respond quickly to an occasional evening watering. Resembling large centau-

reas in their double form, yellow-centered daisies in their single form, they bloom in a bluish palette from lilac to purple, as well as in pink, magenta and white. They suit wildflower meadows or can be allowed to grow in a border among other annuals and perennials of a similar height. They make excellent cut flowers. They often self-sow.

Like its relatives the asters, callistephus is vulnerable to the fungal disease aster yellows, which causes plants to become yellow and die in midsummer. Pull out infected plants, and where the disease is a problem, rotate asters from one area to another each year.

FAVORITES
More beautiful and graceful than the doubles, I think, are the tall singles such as the Single California Mix and the earlier-blooming Astoria Mix, both about 28 inches (70 cm) tall. They self-seed faithfully and seedlings are easy to transplant. The result is drifts of color beginning in late summer, when many other flowers are finished. If you prefer doubles, consider the drought-tolerant Compliment Mix, with 4-inch (10 cm) fully double flowers in the usual shades, including yellow. Stiff stems are 30 inches (75 cm) tall.

CATHARANTHUS VINCA

Catharanthus hybrids
Vinca, Madagascar periwinkle

Once labeled *Vinca rosea*, this tender perennial (zone 9) relative of hardy trailing periwinkle (page 73) has similar attractive, glossy, dark green foliage and flat, five-petaled single flowers. Now called catharanthus, it is a newcomer on the horticultural scene. The wildflower, about 1 1/2 inches (3.8 cm) wide, is pale pink with a purple eye. Only since 1991 have other colors been available, pink and lilac through magenta to red, often with a contrasting eye. Flowers are usually about 2 inches (5 cm). They sell best where summers are hot, since they tolerate heat, grow slowly in cool weather and will die if the ground is too wet. They are best planted in dry, sunny places, especially where the soil is slightly acidic and not too rich, at the border front, in hanging baskets or other containers — situations where impatiens and fibrous begonias, additional long-blooming plants of similar height and flower size, do not thrive. No pinching or deadheading is required. Plants grow about 1 foot (30 cm) tall and wide. Leaves may curl in the daytime during a drought but should unfurl in the evening. Many cultivars are now popularly available as transplants, but if you want to grow your own, the seeds should be sown indoors 10 to 12 weeks before the last spring frost date and kept warm. Do not overfeed or overwater. Plant outdoors when temperatures are consistently above 65 degrees F (18°C). Where catharanthus has a long growing season, it may self-sow.

FAVORITES

Catharanthus is best purchased locally, where you can see flower colors for yourself. Outstanding cultivars include the Pacifica series, 14 inches (35 cm) tall with large, 2-inch (5 cm) flowers, including the first red. The Stardust series is named for star-shaped white centers. One of these, 'Stardust Orchid,' with lilac flowers, was chosen an All-America Selection. The Cooler series, including 'Peppermint Cooler,' which is white with a red eye, tolerates cool, moist conditions better than most. The 'Heatwave' series is especially heat-tolerant and dwarf, with 'Heatwave Pink' the smallest. The Mediterranean series and 'Cascade Appleblossom' are somewhat different, since they have stems that trail as long as 30 inches (75 cm), suiting them to hanging baskets, window boxes and other containers.

CELOSIA ARGENTEA PLUMOSA

Celosia argentea plumosa
Plumed celosia, prince's feather

Tolerant of almost any soil in sun, this annual produces vertical flower plumes so bright you can spot them on the other side of a city park, which is their usual setting. Mass plantings or edgings are the norm. The usual colors are red, yellow, purple and orange, all erupting about 2 feet tall (60 cm) from a base of pointed green foliage. Seeds can be started indoors a month before the last frost, or sown directly in the garden once the soil is warm. All do best with occasional watering.

FAVORITES

The brightest colors can be difficult to situate in a home garden, since they take the attention away from everything else. Consider instead paler flowers such as the aptly named All-America winner 'Apricot Brandy.' The Castle series includes one winner, 'Castle Pink,' which is also less intrusive than some of the others.

Celosia argentea spicata (wheat celosia) is better yet, with narrow pink, red or purple plumes as tall as 3 feet (90 cm), excellent in containers and massed in mid-border, although the colors fade quickly. 'Flamingo Feather' is a pink/white bicolor.

CENTAUREA CYANUS

Centaurea species
Cornflower, bachelor's button

Certain centaureas known as knap-weed are pests of the midwestern plains, demonstrating the ability of the genus to endure neglect and dry soil. Perennial species are described on page 102. One of the annual forms, *C. cyanus* can also be too much of a good thing in some places. One common name, corn-flower, comes from its infestation of farm fields in its native Europe.

FAVORITES
C. cyanus (cornflower; bachelor's button) thrives on sandy soil, pro-duces its single or double flowers in summer and drops its seeds to reappear the next year. Blooming is most prolonged where the weather is not too hot. The typical blue color is a perfect complement to the many white, yellow and orange daisies that grow in similar conditions, but there are also lovely pinks, reds, lavenders and mauves, as well as white. The usual height is 2 feet (60 cm) or taller on stems that are slender but seldom need staking. There are also dwarf varieties such as the 1-foot to 16-inch-tall (30-40 cm) Midget series, Florence series and Polka Dot series,

all in cornflower blue as well as white, pink, red, lavender and mauve. The Frosty series has petals frosted with white tips. 'Black Ball' has deep purple flowers.

C. cineraria (*C. maritima, Senecio cineraria*), known as dusty miller, is grown for its finely divided silver foliage rather than the rather unap-pealing purple flowers. It is a tender perennial (zone 9) but is grown almost everywhere as an annual since it doesn't overwinter well. This and two other annuals called dusty miller — *Senecio viravira* and *Chrysanthemum ptarmiciflorum* (*Cineraria candicans, Pyrethrum ptarmiciflorum, Tanacetum ptarmiciflorum*) — are sold as spring transplants to fill out window boxes, containers and hanging baskets in sun, although they are also good for border edges. The species differ chiefly in the shape of the foliage, whether feathery, deeply divided or with scalloped edges. There are several cultivars, including the 12-inch-tall (30 cm), almost pure white 'Cirrus' and Silverdust™.

C. moschata (sweet sultan) has fra-grant, fuzzy-looking flowers 2 inches (5 cm) or wider on erect stems about 2 feet (60 cm) tall. As well as the usual cornflower colors, there is also a bright yellow.

Cleome hasslerana; C. spinosa
Spider flower

With its self-supporting stems 3 feet (1 m) or taller topped in summer by delicate flowers with prominent threadlike stamens that resemble insect legs, cleome looks like noth-ing else in the garden. The foliage is deeply divided and decorative. Gardeners either love this plant's airy presence or dislike its spidery

quality. The usual flower colors are pink, lavender and white. Sow seeds directly in the garden in early spring, and thin to 6 inches (15 cm) apart. It is a good specimen plant grown in a bed on its own, or it can fill the back of a sunny border where the soil is fertile but not wet. If the flowers are left to mature, cleome will self-sow.

CLEOME 'WHITE QUEEN'

FAVORITES
Cleome is not always available as a bedding plant, so you may have to grow it from seed. You'll be able to choose whatever color you like from a good seed house. There are now semi-dwarf hybrids on the market, such as the Sparkler series, but thankfully, they are more bushy than stubby. They grow about 3 feet (90 cm) tall, stately enough for the back of the border. The regular open-pollinated cleomes such as the Queen series grow 4 to 6 feet (120-180 cm) tall. 'White Queen' is also known as 'Helen Campbell.'

COREOPSIS TINCTORIA

Coreopsis species

Tickseed, calliopsis

Sometimes called calliopsis to distinguish it from the perennial types of coreopsis described on pages 104, the annual versions are apt to reappear every year too, because they often self-sow. Sunny-colored daisy flowers bloom all summer, no matter how dry or hot the weather; unlike many drought-tolerant plants, coreopsis is not averse to high temperatures. It can thus be a good companion for plants such as California poppy, whose blooming declines in hot weather. Calliopsis is a bushy plant whose tolerance of pollution makes it a good choice for roadside plantings. It also looks at home in wildflower meadows and in mid-border. Sow the seeds outdoors in early spring directly where they will grow.

FAVORITES

The usual species offered is *C. tinctoria*; *C. bicolor*. On stems as tall as 3 feet (1 m), 2-inch (5 cm) flowers may be yellow, brown, purplish red or bicolored mahogany and yellow. 'Mahogany Midget,' an excellent container plant, has brownish red, golden-eyed flowers on 10-inch (25 cm) stems.

C. basalis; *C. drummondii* is a Texas wildflower about 16 inches (40 cm) tall whose 2-inch yellow flowers have a central reddish brown blotch.

C. stillmannii is a California native that blooms within about a month of sowing. It has 2-inch (5 cm) golden flowers.

Cosmos species

Cosmos

Delicate, fernlike foliage and almost translucent daisy flowers make cosmos a dramatic addition to any garden, especially when grown in masses or drifts. *C. bipinnatus* is the taller species, with 3-foot (90 cm) stems and 5-inch (13 cm) yellow-eyed flowers in the color range of white through pink to rose. *C. sulphureus* is generally shorter and more drought-tolerant with smaller red, yellow or orange flowers. Both species love warmth and sun and do well with occasional watering. They prefer poor, sandy soil and may become too tall and leggy in rich soil. All are easy from seeds sown directly in the garden in spring, the best plan in any case since cosmos resents transplanting. Simply thin out unwanted seedlings.

FAVORITES

Most cultivars of *C. bipinnatus*, which grows around 3 feet (1 m) tall, will self-sow, while *C. sulphureus* is less likely to do so. *C. bipinnatus* 'Sea Shells' has distinctive tubular petals. 'Picotee' has white petals outlined in dark pink. *C. sulphureus* 'Sunset' grows about 3 feet (90 cm) tall, with dark orange flowers. 'Bright Lights' is equally tall, with semidouble flowers in a blend of orange tints. For shorter plants along border fronts and pathways, look for the Cosmic series in orange or yellow that grow about 1 foot (30 cm) tall and are especially heat-tolerant. 'Cosmic Orange' was an All-America Selection.

C. atrosanguineus has been dubbed the chocolate flower because of the distinctive fragrance of its small, deep mahogany flowers with orange centers. It is hardy to zone 7. Stems are 2 to 3 feet tall (60-90 cm).

COSMOS BIPINNATUS

Cynoglossum amabile
Chinese forget-me-not,
hound's tongue

Brilliant blue flowers much like those of forget-me-nots (*Myosotis* spp.) identify this less common version, a biennial or annual that is a reliable self-sower in conditions that suit it — sandy soil, weather that is not too hot and preferably some shade. Cynoglossum grows about 12 inches (30 cm) tall, with slender mounding stems. It looks best at the front of a border, cascading down stairs or over a rock wall. Scatter the seeds in early spring directly where they will grow. Late sowings will not bloom until next year.

FAVORITES
As well as the fabulous blues that are the usual choice — selections include 'Firmament' and the taller 'Blue Shower' — there is 'Mystic Pink,' which offers another color option on a more erect plant about 20 inches (50 cm) tall.

Echeveria species
Hens-and-chicks

This is one annual you will most likely find in a florist shop, since its usual role is houseplant. Native from Mexico to northern South America and hardy only to zone 9, it is otherwise wintered indoors in a cool, bright window and, if you like, taken outdoors for summer. Like sempervivum, which it resembles in almost every way except hardiness and color, echeveria is a succulent that produces a fleshy, ground-hugging rosette of leaves and gradually spreads outward, forming new rosettes. The foliage is distinctly bluish, blue-gray, blue-green or

white, sometimes tinted red, pink or buff, especially in sun. In summer, from the center of a mature rosette a long slender stem may grow, topped with tubular or bell-shaped yellow or red flowers. After flowering, that rosette will die. The lower leaves eventually wilt and should be trimmed off. When the plant looks untidy, re-root the main rosettes and divide off the smaller ones. Echeveria makes an excellent container plant, on its own or in a collection of succulents, cacti and other drought-tolerant species.

FAVORITES
There are many species and cultivars. Choose what you like from the florist shop or from a cactus specialist, some of whom deliver by mail order. See Sources. If you feel adventurous, buy a packet of seeds of mixed varieties from a source such as Chiltern.

Eschscholzia californica
California poppy

Considering that it is native to California, where it is perennial, this lovely poppy is surprisingly tolerant of bitter winters — or, rather, its seeds are. Not long after the snow has gone, the appearance of delicate blue-green foliage, similar to that of young dill, shows that California poppies have self-seeded and will bloom again by midsummer. The easiest way to start a patch is simply to broadcast the seeds on the ground anytime in spring; they will await the right soil temperature and moisture level for sprouting. Like all poppies, *E. californica* resents transplanting, so seeds are the best option. Although drought-tolerant once rooted, they will not sprout or

begin growing without moisture. Seeding can be done until the end of June for flowers the same season. A lax stem about 1 foot (30 cm) tall grows a mass of bluish foliage. When the plants are 2 inches (5 cm) high, thin them to 4 inches (10 cm) apart. Although California poppy is drought-tolerant, it flowers better when the weather is not hot. If the plants receive some water during the hottest weather, they may bloom again as temperatures fall.

ESCHSCHOLZIA CALIFORNICA

FAVORITES
The color of the wild species is brilliant orange, beautiful enough in its own rite. If you prefer, there are whites, yellows, pinks, purples and crimsons, in single-, semidouble- and double-flowered forms. Among the best are the 'Mission Bells,' whose semidouble blooms in shades of gold, pink, rose and scarlet look as though they have been fashioned from silk. 'Thai Silk' is similar but the petals are subtly streaked.

E. caespitosa (tufted California poppy) is smaller, just 6 inches (15 cm) tall, with scented yellow flowers.

Everlastings

There are several similar daisies whose papery-looking flowers are actually brightly colored bracts that dry on the stem in the garden and keep their shape all winter without water. Keep the arrangements out of sunlight to preserve their colors. All are best picked in bud or when they are just beginning to bloom, as they will open a little more after picking and are less attractive when fully open. They can be wired if stiff stems are needed. They are easy from seed sown directly in the garden around the last spring frost date or planted indoors several weeks earlier, then transplanted out after the last frost.

FAVORITES
Ammobium alatum (winged everlasting) has winged 2-foot (60 cm) stems bearing silvery white flowers with yellow centers.

Helichrysum bracteatum; H. monstrosum (strawflower) is the most common of the everlastings, available in a choice of heights up to 3 feet (1 m) and in shades of yellow, orange, pink, violet, red and white. 'Porcelain Rose' grows just 8 inches (20 cm) tall with pink to salmon flowers. *H. cassianum* bears sprays of small, starry white flowers. Additional species of everlasting *Helichrysum* are available from specialists.

Helichrysum petiolare (licorice plant) is a moisture lover and a hanging basket favorite grown not for its flowers but for its downy silver foliage on trailing 20-inch (50 cm) stems. There are also cultivars with chartreuse or variegated foliage.

Helipterum roseum (rose everlasting) is available in shades of pink, rose and white. Leaves are grayish, and stems are generally about

18 inches (45 cm) tall. 'Pierrot' is a Fleuroselect winner whose white flowers have yellow-and-black centers.

Xeranthemum annuum, the best of the everlastings for poor, dry soil, has single or double white, pink, rose or purple flowers and woolly white foliage on 20-inch (50 cm) stems.

Additional annual everlastings for the dry garden include *Gomphrena* (see next page), *Limonium* (page 146) and seed heads of poppies and of the grasses listed in Chapter 4.

Gazania rigens; G. splendens
Gazania; treasure flower

Gazania is one of the South African wildflowers that closes at night and on cloudy days. Petals in shades of yellow, orange, russet, gold, pink, scarlet, white and bicolors have a contrasting darker ring around a yellow center, making these daisies some of the showiest in the garden. Stems are generally about 8 inches (20 cm) tall, with 6-inch (15 cm) leaves with hairy undersides. It does best in full sun and in well-drained soil, even sandy, light and dry. It will rot in soil that is too wet. It will put up with windy places, including salty winds. It is an excellent choice for a container in sun. Buy plants or grow your own from seeds sown indoors about 10 weeks before the last frost.

FAVORITES
Among the best are the Sunshine series, 10 inches (25 cm) tall with especially vivid colors and contrasts, and the Talent series, 8 inches (20 cm) tall with unusual silvery white foliage. The Harlequin hybrids grow as tall as 15 inches (38 cm) with a dark central zone. The Daybreak series, with 4-inch (20 cm) flowers on 8-inch (20 cm)

GAZANIA 'KISS MAHOGANY'

stems, includes the Fleuroselect winner 'Daybreak Red Stripe,' bright yellow with a red stripe. The Mini-Stars are a little shorter, with silvery green foliage. 'Mini-Star Yellow' and 'Mini-Star Tangerine' are both Fleuroselect winners. The Kiss series, such as 'Kiss Mahogany,' has large flowers on short, sturdy stems.

Gomphrena species
Globe amaranth

Globe amaranth, with its papery, 1-inch (2.5 cm) balls atop stiff, 2-foot (60 cm) stems, was a favorite of the pioneers because it was easy to grow, was pretty in the garden and lasted all winter in a vase without water, but they knew it only in shades of purple, pink and white. The palette now includes orange, red and bicolors. For dried arrangements, cut the stems when the flowers are newly opened; the bracts keep their color well, and the stiff stems need no wiring. Seeds can be sown directly in the spring garden, in well-drained soil in sun or part shade.

FAVORITES
All are good, so the choice is color and flower size. The bright red 'Strawberry Fields' makes a flower bed resemble a berry patch. The QIS series has flowers about twice the usual size. Both the Gnome series and Buddy series are 6-inch (15 cm) dwarfs.

Gypsophila elegans
Baby's-breath

Like its perennial cousin *G. paniculata* (page 111), annual baby's-breath prefers dry, alkaline soil, where its wiry stems yield a crop of tiny, white or pink flowers that are perfect fillers for garden, container, window box or vase. If you want continuous cutting, sow the seeds every couple of weeks through spring and early summer. Plants take three months to flower from seed. Stems grow 8 to 30 inches (20-75 cm) tall, depending on the cultivar and growing conditions.

GYPSOPHILA ELEGANS 'SNOW MOUNTAIN'

FAVORITES
G. 'Gypsy Deep Rose' grows 8 to 10 inches tall (20-25 cm) and a little wider, with finely textured foliage and deep rose, semidouble to double flowers. The pastel pink version, also an All-America Selection, is 'Gypsy.' 'Snow Fountain' produces a prolific crop of white flowers on stronger stems.

Helianthus annuus
Sunflower

Sunflowers are the crowning glories of hot, sunny gardens, although not necessarily the driest ones. Like many other daisies, they do best in rich soil and with some moisture, especially in early summer, when they are growing rapidly. There are many varieties: short-stemmed types with huge flowers, taller-stemmed branching types with small flowers — excellent for cutting — and the tallest-stemmed types with large flowers, including those, such as the 10-foot (3 m) 'Russian Giant,' grown for their large, edible, protein-rich seeds. Flower colors range from white and the palest yellow through golden to dark orange, bronze and red, sometimes bicolored. All are easy from seeds sown directly in the garden anytime in spring, watered until they sprout, then thinned to stand about 1 foot (30 cm) apart, farther for the tallest types. In a windy spot, the tallest may need staking. Deadhead the finished flowers, and save their seeds for planting or for the birds in winter. Sunflowers often self-sow, and seedlings transplant well. All make excellent cut flowers.

Many parts of sunflowers are toxic to neighboring plants, especially the hulls on any seeds that fall. Grow them where they will neither shade nor compete with other flowers. They are excellent for mass plantings.

FAVORITES
Sunflowers are the darlings of flower arrangers. If you intend to bring the blooms indoors, look for multi-branching types with medium-sized flowers in a variety of colors. Although some have very short

HELIANTHUS ANNUUS 'RING OF FIRE'

stems, such as the 2-foot (60 cm) tall 'Sundance Kid,' stubby sunflowers are not the most graceful flowers in the garden. Better are taller-stemmed beauties for the back of the bed such as 'Razzmatazz,' 6 feet (180 cm) tall with flowers in shades of pink, purple, yellow and white; 'Ring of Fire,' 4 1/2 feet (135 cm) tall with flowers ringed burgundy and yellow; or another award winner, bright orange, 5- or 6-foot-tall (150-180 cm) 'Soraya,' with about twenty 4-to-6-inch (10-15 cm) flowers per plant. There are also pollen-free cultivars especially selected for indoor arrangements. Check the seed catalogs if this is a priority.

Lantana camara (L. hybrida)
Lantana; yellow sage

A tender shrub (zone 8 or 9) that has become weedy in places that suit it, such as the southern states and Hawaii, lantana is coaxed along in cooler places as a houseplant or a tender annual especially prized for containers in sun or part shade, where it will bloom nonstop until the weather turns cold. Although lantana can exceed 6 feet (1.8 m) where it is perennial and can be trained as a show-stopping standard, newer forms grown as annuals are smaller, usually about 2 feet (60 cm) tall and somewhat wider. On the species, rounded 1 1/2-inch (3 cm) heads of tiny verbena-like flowers open bright yellow and then mature to red or white, so several colors appear on the same stem. The flowers are loved by butterflies. The bluish fruits are eaten by birds, who distribute the seeds far and wide. Lantana needs regular watering until it becomes established but, by midsummer, is very drought-resistant. It is usually grown from

purchased plants. Seeds are not difficult but must be sown indoors about eight weeks before the last spring frost date. Some cultivars cannot be grown from seed.

FAVORITES
Where lantana is perennial, gardeners are urged to grow sterile cultivars such as 'New Gold,' an all-yellow cultivar that sets no seeds and blooms nonstop. It may require severe pruning in midwinter. 'Samantha' is similar but has the bonus of variegated foliage. Although other varieties feature flower colors including white, yellow, orange, deep red, hot pink and purple, the selection is limited in cooler zones.

LANTANA CAMARA

LIMONIUM SUWOROWII

Limonium species
Statice

Best known for papery light or dark blue flowers on spikes as tall as 2 to 3 feet (60-90 cm), this everlasting annual also blooms in shades of purple, white, rose, orange, tan and yellow. The flowers dry naturally right in the garden and should be cut for everlasting arrangements as soon as they begin to open. Kept out of direct sunlight, they keep their color indefinitely. Give statice sandy soil mixed with plenty of compost, and grow it in sun or a little shade. Seeds are best sown indoors about eight weeks before the last spring frost date.

FAVORITES
There are several types of statice. Most common is *L. sinuatum*, available in a good selection of cultivars offering different colors and heights. The Forever, Pacific and Soiree series grow about 2 feet (60 cm) tall with dense flower spikes. 'Sunset Blend' is a little taller, in shades of orange, apricot, peach and rose. 'Forever

Gold,' a Fleuroselect winner, is golden yellow. Dwarf strains include the 12-inch-tall (30 cm) Petite Bouquet series.

L. suworowii has slender, 8-inch (20 cm) spikes of rose-colored flowers that resemble chenille. This species is best used in fresh arrangements.

Melampodium paludosum; Leucanthemum paludosum
Melampodium, African zinnia

This recent garden arrival, which forms a neat, 8-to-10-inch-tall (20-25 cm) shrubby mound of bright green leaves and small white, yellow or orange daisies, has been winning good reviews wherever it is grown, but especially in hot, dry places. It is an excellent cut flower that is perfect for containers or window boxes in sun. It also does well on a border front or along a pathway. It survives drought, but even in poor soil and humid heat, it blooms all summer, requires no deadheading and sometimes self-sows. Buy plants or sow seeds two weeks before the last spring frost date, and transplant into the garden four weeks later.

MELAMPODIUM PALUDOSUM

FAVORITES
'Showstar' grows 10 inches (25 cm) tall with yellow flowers. 'Million Gold' has orange flowers on a dwarf, 8-inch (20 cm) plant. 'Lemon Delight' is similar with light lemon yellow flowers. 'Derby' is gold.

Mesembryanthemum criniflorum (Dorotheanthus species)

Ice plant, Livingstone daisy

Succulent foliage that looks as though it's been frosted with ice crystals is well adapted to deflecting summer's heat. Daisies a little wider than 1 inch (2.5 cm), in bright, cheery shades of pink, peach, orange and rose, bloom just above the ground on reclining stems. The flowers close at night and in cloudy weather and do not open until afternoon. *Mesembryanthemum* is a favorite plant for dry southern roadsides and is just as adaptable to the front of a sunny bed or to northern containers that are never watered. It needs full sun. Buy plants or sow seeds in spring where they will grow.

FAVORITES
The Harlequin mix bears 1½-inch-wide (5 cm) flowers all summer in brighter-than-usual shades of orange, yellow, salmon, red, pink and magenta, sometimes bicolored.

MESEMBRYANTHEMUM CRINIFLORUM

OSTEOSPERMUM HYBRID

Osteospermum species (Dimorphotheca species)

Cape marigold; African daisy; Star of the Veldt

Many of the choice daisies for dry places hail from southern Africa. Unlike native American daisies, they are less likely to be yellow or orange, more likely to be pink, violet or white, with petals that look more waxy. Flowers close at night and in cloudy weather. Blooming is best in coolish weather, so expect these daisies to attract attention in spring and fall. On stems generally about 2 feet (60 cm) tall, the *Osteospermum/ Dimorphotheca* group blooms in shades of white, cream, pink, buff and purple with dark brown centers. There are a few yellows and oranges. The undersides of the curving petals are often purplish or brown. Buy transplants, or start seeds indoors several weeks before the last spring frost date, as they need a long season for the best show. Choose very well-drained, even sandy soil, and stake them in groups, grow at the edge of a container or crowd between other plants, since they tend to flop. Deadheading prolongs flowering.

FAVORITES
'Malindi' is deep purple. 'Highside' is pink. 'Symphony' is orange. 'Glistening White' has pure white petals and black centers on dwarf 8-inch (20 cm) stems. The Passion series, with 2-inch (5 cm) pink, rose, purple or white 2½-inch (6 cm) flowers on 12-to-18-inch (30-45 cm) stems, is an All-America Selection, chosen for compactness and profuse flowering. New cultivars appear on the market every year, some with odd spoon-shaped or pinched petals, such as the Whirligig series.

Papaver species
Poppy

The annual poppies are some of the flowers apt to self-sow and put their roots into the soil while there is still spring moisture. The first season, you'll have to scatter their seeds to start the cycle. Since they have tap-roots and resent transplanting, this is the safest way to grow them. About 2 feet (60 cm) tall and a month or so in bloom in midsum-mer, they look best growing in and among other annuals and perenni-als in a bed or a wildflower meadow. Stiff stems may hold the flowers upright if they grow in a sheltered place or between stronger plants, but entire plants may flop in wind or heavy rain — be prepared to stake them. After flowering, leave a few of the pods on the stems for seed or flower arrangements, but otherwise, remove all the stems when bloom-ing is done.

FAVORITES
Papaver rhoes (field poppy; Shirley poppy) is breathtaking when allowed to grow through the garden in scarlet drifts, although there are also whites, oranges, yellows and pinks, both single and double. With large, 4-inch (10 cm) flowers and slender stems, it is the most graceful of the annual poppies. The true Shirleys, which orig-inated in a garden in Shirley, England, more than a century ago, are single, with a white base and yellow or white stamens. All others might best be called field poppies, although the dis-tinction has been blurred with time. All self-sow dependably. The 'Mother of Pearl' mixture is unusual, with a grayish or dusty cast to all the colors. 'Angel's Choir' is a double mixture.
  Papaver somniferum (peony poppy) grows about 3 feet (90 cm) tall. Petals may be fringed or plain, single or double in pink, red, maroon or white. Many have a contrasting blotch at the base of each petal. Stems are thicker than other poppies, and foliage is blue-green. The globe-shaped seed heads are large and woody when dry, cherished by flower arrangers and by cooks, who use the seeds in baking.

PHACELIA CAMPANULARIA

Phacelia campanularia
Desert bluebell; California bluebell

You may have to search the specialist seed houses to find this native of the California deserts, but it is worth the trouble. The plant is tough enough to survive in the cracks in a side-walk, a perfect partner, in color and form, to its wildflower companion the California poppy. Relaxed stems grow 6 to 24 inches (15-60 cm) long, and the 1-inch (2.5 cm) flowers are an intense deep blue. It is excellent massed along a border's edge, between taller plants or in a con-tainer filled with sandy soil. It flowers in about two months from seeds sown directly in the garden a couple of weeks before the last spring frost date.

PORTULACA GRANDIFLORA 'SUNDIAL PEACH'

Portulaca grandiflora

Rose moss

In hot dry sun, portulaca forms a carpet of tiny leaves and brightly colored flowers with the texture of tissue paper. Of all the annuals suited to dry places, portulaca is the easiest to find as a bedding plant in spring, which is not a bad way to go unless you want to start the tiny seeds several weeks early indoors or sow them directly in the garden anytime in spring. One advantage of growing from seed is that you can buy a single color instead of the mixtures generally available as transplants. Mass planted, a single color makes an especially effective temporary ground cover, whether on the ground or in a container. Colors available from good seed houses include cream, pink, magenta, yellow, orange and mango. The seeds are simply scattered on the soil surface, which should be kept moist until germination. An individual plant will form a mound 4 to 6 inches (10-15 cm) high and about 1 foot (30 cm) wide. Portulaca

sometimes self-sows. In my zone 4 garden, seedlings are 1/2 inch (1 cm) high by the first week of June and are easy to transplant elsewhere.

FAVORITES
Portulaca flowers normally close at night and on cloudy days and are late to open in the morning — one old name is eleven o'clock. The Sundial series is one group that stays open longer, and its flowers, available in 11 colors, are larger than most at about 2 inches (5 cm) wide. 'Sundial Peach' is an All-America Selection.

SALVIA SPLENDENS

Salvia species

Salvia, sage

Salvia splendens, the common annual bedding salvia with its bright plume flowers, mostly red, needs a fairly steady water supply, although it does well in heat and sun. An exception may be the Hotline series developed by Park Seeds, promoted as tolerant of both heat and drought. Available in burgundy, white, red, violet and the blue-white bicolor 'Blue Streak,' this series grows about 1 foot (30 cm) tall. There are other annuals that live up to the salvia reputation as plants for dry places.

FAVORITES
S. coccinea (Texas sage) tolerates heat and drought, as one might expect of a Texas wildflower. 'Lady in Red,' a favorite of hummingbirds, has brilliant scarlet flowers on spikes 12 to 16 inches (30-40 cm) tall. The Nymph series is taller, about 2 feet (60 cm). 'Coral Nymph' has bicolored flowers, coral pink and white.

S. viridis; S. horminum (clary sage) is one of the best flowering annuals for dry soil. It will grow in sand, with very little watering after germination. It has grayish leaves and 2-foot (60 cm) stems and looks modest until its flowers appear; pastel-colored petal-like bracts, often veined with green. Colors include white, pink, rose, lilac, purple and blue. All are great in wildflower meadows, mass planted or combined with other drought-tolerant annuals in a sunny container. It often self-sows.

SANVITALIA PROCUMBENS

Sanvitalia procumbens
Creeping zinnia

Trailing 6-inch (15 cm) stems tipped with 1-inch (2.5 cm) yellow or orange daisies make sanvitalia a good choice for the front of a border, a hanging basket or a container. Once blooming starts in mid-summer, it continues until fall frosts. In warm zones, seeds can be sown in fall. Sanvitalia prefers light, sandy soil in sun or part shade and needs careful transplanting.

FAVORITES
'Mandarin Orange' is an All-America Selection whose brilliant orange flowers have contrasting black centers. 'Aztec Gold' is golden yellow with gold-and-green centers. 'Yellow Carpet' has lemon yellow flowers with black centers. 'Irish Eyes' is buff orange with green centers. 'Orange Sprite' is a double orange on 12-to-14-inch (30-35 cm) stems. There are also whites.

Tagetes species
Marigold

There are several marigold species, all with flowers mostly in the bright color range of yellow through orange. The largest, showiest and best-known are the African marigolds (*T. erecta*), 2 to 4 feet tall (60-122 cm), and the French marigolds (*T. patula*), 9 inches to 2 feet (23-60 cm) tall, and their hybrids. Despite the labels, both species are natives of Central and South America. Less well-known are the small signet marigolds (*T. tenuifolia; T. signata*), which form bushy plants about 1 foot (30 cm) tall, and the taller Mexican tarragon (*T. lucida*). Although all marigolds are lovers of sun, hot days and coolish nights, not all fare well in dry places. As with most other flowers, the large-flowered varieties, the hybrids and the triploids tend to need more coddling in the form of richer soil and more water. All are easy from seeds sown indoors a few weeks before the last frost date, but since there is a good selection available from garden nurseries in spring, most gardeners opt for buying plants.

FAVORITES
Among the French marigolds and the hybrids, the most self-sufficient are the smaller — 1 foot (30 cm) or shorter — and single-flowered varieties, which can be found in abundance in seed catalogs and nurseries. Examples include the 12-inch (30 cm) 'Red Cherry,' the All-America 'Golden Gate' and the heat-tolerant Bounty and Little Hero series.

 T. tenuifolia; T. signata (signet marigolds) are some of the best for dry places. The Gem series including 'Lemon Gem,' 'Golden Gem' and 'Tangerine Gem,' all colored as the names suggest, have finely divided foliage and 1-inch (2.5 cm) single flowers on 4-inch (10 cm) stems. All are excellent at the front of a border, as accents in vegetable gardens, along pathways and in containers. These produce large quantities of seed that the gardener can gather in late summer; they sometimes self-sow. If the season is extended, a second crop of summer seedlings may reach blooming size before fall frosts.

 T. lucida (Mexican tarragon), hardy in zone 7, has 3-foot (90 cm) stems with small yellow flowers and aromatic foliage that smells like anise. It is a favorite of xeriscape demonstration gardens.

**TAGETES PATULA
'RED CHERRY'**

TITHONIA ROTUNDIFOLIA 'TORCH'

Tithonia rotundifolia (T. speciosa)
Mexican sunflower

In hot sun and fertile soil that is well drained but occasionally moist, this impressive annual can form a bush of stiff stems as tall as 6 feet (1.8 m), with large, velvety leaves and sunflowers about 3 inches (7.5 cm) wide. In dry, poor ground and where nights are cool, it may grow only half as tall, although height varies with each cultivar. The flowers, which attract butterflies, bloom freely from summer until fall frost. Sow the seeds indoors six to eight weeks before the last spring frost date, and set the plants out 2 feet (60 cm) apart in sun. *Tithonia* is good at the back of a sunny border or as a specimen.

FAVORITES
The profusely flowering dwarf 'Fiesta del Sol,' an All-America Selection, forms a compact, wind-tolerant bush about 24 inches (60 cm) tall with bright orange flowers. 'Aztec Sun' is 4 feet (120 cm) tall. Its butterscotch-colored flowers have yellow centers. 'Sundance' blooms scarlet-orange on 3-foot (90 cm) stems. 'Goldfinger' is the same height but bright gold. 'Torch,' the tallest, grows about 6 feet (180 cm) with scarlet-orange flowers.

Verbena species
Verbena

The usual garden verbenas are somewhat drought-resistant, almost constant bloomers popular for hanging baskets and window boxes in fertile soil in sun. Most have relaxed stems about 10 inches (25 cm) long, and flattish heads of small flowers in bright colors of red, blue, purple, mauve, pink, white and bicolors, sometimes with a white eye. All verbenas attract butterflies.

FAVORITES
Verbenas can now be divided into two large groups; those grown from seeds and those that can be grown only from cuttings. Among seed-grown types for hanging baskets and containers that occasionally dry out, 'Peaches and Cream' is an All-America winner whose flowers combine peach-pink and cream. 'Imagination,' with intense violet-blue flowers all summer, was both an All-America Selection and a Fleuroselect winner.

More prevalent today, especially for containers, are hybrid verbenas that must be grown from cuttings, not seeds. New ones appear every year. Their advantage is greater flowering and generally larger flower clusters on bigger plants. None are especially drought-tolerant, but all do best in sun and should be allowed to dry out between waterings. There are two types; those with broad leaves that grow upright, such as the Tamari, Lanai, Tortuga and Tukana series, and those with fine leaves that creep or hang, such as the Tapien and Rapunzel series.

V. bonariensis is an upright species that grows 3 to 4 feet (90-120 cm) tall and has dark purple ball flowers. It often self-sows.

**ZINNIA HAAGEANA
'SOMBRERO'**

Zinnia species
Mexican zinnia

Like marigolds, zinnias have been selected and hybridized into hundreds of forms, some so mop-headed that they have to be tended like lapdogs. These dahlia look-alikes are not good candidates for dry or windy places. On the other hand, the less-celebrated singles and wilder doubles, many of which are lovely and graceful, have retained their inborn ability to withstand stressful weather. These zinnias are easiest to grow by sowing the large seeds directly in the garden after the last spring frost date. They do best in fertile soil in full sun with some moisture, especially until they germinate and for a couple of weeks afterward.

FAVORITES
Z. angustifolia (*Z. linearis*) is not only drought-tolerant but is also so capable of blooming in heat and humidity that it is a favorite where summers are muggy. The Star series, which includes orange, yellow and white selections, were 2003 winners of the Georgia Gold Medal. 'Crystal White,' an All-America Selection, has white daisies with yellow centers on a compact plant. Leaves are small and narrow and the single flowers, about the size of a quarter, are produced in great quantity on mounding 10-to-12-inch (25-30 cm) plants. Grown in masses planted 6 inches (15 cm) apart, *Z. angustifolia* makes a good temporary ground cover in sun. It is also an excellent plant for hanging baskets as well as other containers.

Z. angustifolia x *elegans* hybrids are represented mainly by the All-America award-winning Profusion series, including white, orange, cherry and apricot flowers. All form shrubby mounds about 16 inches (40 cm) tall and 24 inches (60 cm) wide with single flowers 2 or 3 inches (2.5-4 cm) wide. The last two colors are apt to fade in bright sun, but 'Profusion White' and 'Profusion Orange' look good all season. They require no deadheading.

Z. haageana (Mexican zinnia) is disease-resistant, tolerates heat and drought and grows about 15 inches (38 cm) tall with small, narrow leaves. Single or double, bicolored flowers bloom in shades of orange, maroon, red, brown, cream, pink and purple, all with a contrasting color on each petal tip. 'Persian Carpet' and 'Old Mexico' are dwarf versions that have both won All-America awards. 'Chippendale' is bright red with yellow tips. 'Sombrero' is similar but about half as tall, at 15 inches (38 cm).

CHAPTER EIGHT

SHRUBS

Many shrubs and trees are suited to dry gardens. Some may seem surprising. Willows, for instance, are appreciated for their tolerance of very wet ground but will survive in dry conditions after they have rooted for a couple of years. Because most trees once established can survive short droughts, this chapter concentrates, instead, on shrubs. Shrubs living at the edge of their limit of hardiness may act like herbaceous perennials, dying back to the ground in winter and resprouting in spring. Many roses do this.

This plant list is confined to the types that are hardy to at least zone 7 and mature under about 20 feet. If left unpruned, they will likely have several stems. Note that although some shrubs are listed as suitable for zones 9 and 10, they may not do well in southern Florida and the Gulf Coast because of the combination of high humidity and warm winters.

Rosa rugosa is known for fragrant flowers, unusual pleated foliage and ruggedness that is manifested by cultivars both single and double.

AESCULUS PARVIFLORA

Aesculus parviflora
Bottlebrush buckeye
Zones 4 to 10

With foliage and flower clusters reminiscent of its tree cousin the chestnut, bottlebrush buckeye is attractive all season. The long, narrow leaves grow in groups of five to seven radiating from a common center. Stems grow quickly and can be cut back severely, even back to the ground if the shrub becomes too tall or too leggy. It normally reaches 8 to 12 feet (2.4 to 3.6 m) and just as wide, so give it plenty of space or prepare to move other plants away as it grows. The upward pointing spires of white summer flowers can be a foot (30 cm) tall. It tolerates shade and average soil.

Aronia species
Chokeberry
Zones 4 to 10

Chokeberries are native North American shrubs with showy white or rose-colored spring blossoms, followed by decorative, edible but bitter-tasting fruits that last well into winter. The toothed green foliage is brightly colored in fall. All are excellent for massing or for including in shrub or perennial borders in either wet or dry soil.

FAVORITES
A. arbutifolia (red chokeberry) is named for a big crop of glossy red fruits (technically pomes) that resemble tiny pears. The cultivar 'Brilliantissima' has white blossoms, and bright scarlet fall foliage. Red chokeberry grows 8 feet (2.4 m) at most.

A. melanocarpa; A. nigra (black chokeberry) is somewhat hardier, to about zone 3. It grows roughly half as tall. The cultivar 'Autumn Magic' has wine-red foliage in fall and shiny purple-black fruits that do not persist like those of red chokeberry.

Buddleia davidii
Butterfly bush
Zones vary

Butterfly bush is well named for the magnetic effect its flowers have on butterflies, bees and other flying insects. The dense spikes or clusters of small blooms, showy for weeks, are typically bluish, lilac or purple, although there are also whites. The shrub does best in sun and any soil that is well drained. Prune it hard every year to keep it floriferous and shapely. After flowering, deadhead to avoid an abundance of seedlings.

FAVORITES
B. davidii is most widely available and the hardiest species, zones 5 to 9. The outward-pointing spikes of flowers are typically blue, but there are also pink, lilac, purple, reddish purple and white versions, all fragrant. It blooms in late summer on new wood, so it can be pruned back hard in spring or after flowering. This sun-loving shrub grows quickly and unevenly to about 10 feet (3 m), can be invasive and has become a weedy pest in some places. In zone 5, it is often grown as an annual or as a perennial that dies back to the ground most winters and reappears in spring. There are many cultivars and hybrids offering a variety of flower colors, including the yellow-flowered hybrid 'Sun Gold,' zones 7 to 10, and about 15 feet (4.5 m) tall. 'Santana' has green-and-yellow variegated foliage and dark purple flowers; Strawberry Lemonade™ ('Monrel') has pink flowers and variegated foliage. Both grow 6 to 8 feet (180-240 cm) tall.

B. alternifolia, which has alternate, grayish leaves, is more winter hardy, zones 4 to 8, and blooms in late spring. It grows about 6 feet (2 m) tall. Its lavender pink flowers are borne in clusters on year-old wood, so prune after flowering to encourage more blooms for next year. The leaves of 'Argentea' have a silvery cast.

CARAGANA ARBORESCENS

Caragana species
Siberian pea shrub, pea tree
Zones 2 to 7

Many drought-tolerant shrubs are members of the pea family (Leguminosae) with characteristic roundish, opposite leaves, intricate flowers and, later, seed pods. These plants are capable of synthesizing their own soil-nitrogen supply, enriching the soil for neighboring plants, and can be relatively self-sufficient otherwise. Many will put up with dry, alkaline, even salty soil. Too much fertilizing can make them leggy and weak. Caragana, whose chief attribute is its ability to thrive despite cold winters and dry weather, produces a brief but bright show of spring flowers that are usually yellow. Prune immediately after flowering. Following 11 years of trials to determine the most self-reliant plants for the Midwest, the University of Minnesota recommended caragana for hedges and screens in difficult places. This shrub is easy from seed, which is the best way to obtain unusual species. Some plants have spines.

FAVORITES
C. arborescens (common caragana) is a plant for dry, windy situations, where it can grow as tall as a leggy 18 feet (5.5 m) but should be pruned to stay shorter and denser. In rich soil, it is invasive. The variety 'Sutherland' has a vertical shape as tall as 20 feet (6 m), ideal for windbreaks. 'Fernleaf,' named for its distinctive foliage, is about the same height. More suitable for the garden is the justifiably popular weeping form, 'Pendula,' usually sold grafted to a standard. It looks unpleasantly like an umbrella for the first couple of years but becomes increasingly graceful as its branches multiply and lengthen. It is so top-heavy that it should be staked for at least the first year, longer in a windy spot. Pull out suckers that grow from base. 'Walker' is another weeping form, to about 5 feet (1.5 m) tall and wide.

C. pygmaea; C. aurantiaca (pygmy caragana) forms a compact fine-textured mound of arched, spreading branches only 2 to 4 feet (60-120 cm) tall, suitable for the perennial border. The Devonian Botanic Garden near Edmonton, Alberta, uses this species as a low hedge around its herb garden. More difficult to find, although more ornamental, are the equally hardy *C. jubata, C. frutex* and *C. sinica.*

Caryopteris x clandonensis
Blue mist shrub, bluebeard, blue spirea
Zones 5/6 to 9

As its common names indicate, *C.* x *clandonensis* is known for a beautiful show of blue flowers. The fuzzy-looking flowers, which may also be white, attract butterflies for several weeks in late summer and early fall. The shrub can become ragged-looking, but it blooms on new wood, so if you prune off about half of the old wood every year in early spring, the shrub can be maintained as a neat mound of floriferous grayish foliage around 2 to 3 feet (60-90 cm) tall and wide. Give caryopteris sun or light shade and preferably a light-textured limy soil.

Although caryopteris was one of the star performers during the 1995 drought at the Xeriscape Demonstration Garden in Plainview, New York, it was not sufficiently winter-hardy to survive at the trial garden at the University of Maine at Orono (zone 4). It is hardy in protected places in zone 5 but may suffer tip dieback in winter; it is safer in zone 6. Farther north, it can be grown in a cool greenhouse.

FAVORITES
The flowers of 'Dark Knight' are violet-blue, and those of 'Heavenly Blue' are medium blue. 'Sunshine Blue' is the most eye-catching of all, with purplish blue flowers and bright yellow foliage.

Cistus species

Rock rose, sun rose
Zones 7 to 10

Lovers of sun, heat and well-drained, alkaline, even sandy soil and easily damaged by cold and wet, rock roses are shrubby plants that produce delicate looking poppy- or roselike flowers in shades of pink, rose and white. Each flower lasts just a day but flowering lasts for weeks. Plant where you want them, since they do not transplant well. Where they are hardy, plants eventually become open and leggy and should be replaced.

FAVORITES
The hardiest, to zone 7, is *C. ladanifer*, which has sticky branches and reaches about 4 feet (120 cm) tall. The white flowers, almost 3½ inches (9 cm) wide, have a yellow center and purple blotch on each petal. They bloom in summer. The other species are reliably hardy only to zone 8.

COTINUS COGGYGRIA

Cotinus coggygria

Smoke bush, smoke tree
Zones 4 to 9

This heirloom is named for the unusual foggy appearance of the shrub in bloom. The misty look comes from thousands of hairs that extend from clusters of tiny flowers. After the flowers fade, the hairs continue to grow, so the effect can last for weeks. Cotinus grows as tall as 10 to 15 feet (3-4.5 m) and almost as wide, with oval leaves. It needs watering until it is established, then does best in rather poor, dry soil. The lower branches can be removed to create a small multi-stemmed tree, or the entire plant can be cut back to 2 feet (60 cm) or so every winter or early spring to keep it growing as a small, dense, profusely flowering shrub, since cotinus blooms on new wood. Leaf color is remarkably intense on new growth, another incentive to prune heavily. In zones 3 and 4, this annual die-back happens naturally, and the shrub may act much like a herbaceous perennial. Such was the case when the cultivars 'Nordine,' 'Royal Purple' and 'Velvet Cloak' were grown in the trial garden of the University of Maine at Orono (zone 4). The hardier 'Pink Champagne' suffered little or no winter damage. There are many additional cultivars, most with green leaves. Give smoke bush sun for most of the day. It can put up with almost any soil and has no major pest or disease problems. A relative of sumac (*Rhus* species), smoke bush is sometimes labeled *Rhus cotinus*.

FAVORITES
While there are many green cultivars, those with differently colored leaves have greater appeal throughout the season. 'Royal Purple' has dark purple foliage. 'Velvet Cloak' is red. 'Golden Spirit' is a golden-leaved form that grows to only about 7 feet (2.1m) in 10 years. Its fall color is bright orange. It will pair beautifully with 'Royal Purple.' 'Daydream,' a green-leaved release from the Arnold Arboretum in Boston, is also valued for its smaller size, about 10 feet (3 m).

Cotoneaster species

Cotoneaster
Zones vary

Cotoneasters are members of the rose family, mostly from China, known for small, dark green leaves that are shiny and waxy-looking. In spring, they bear small white or pink flowers, followed by tiny red or black applelike fruits correctly called pomes. These fruits persist into winter and attract birds, contributing to the year-round appeal of the shrubs. Fall leaf color is often excellent. If you look far enough, you can find at least 13 species of cotoneaster on the market. All prefer sun and well-drained soil, preferably alkaline. They resent transplanting, so choose their position carefully at the outset. Several grow laterally and so create a good ground cover (page 64). Others, listed here, form neat shrubs. For maximum fruit production, prune cotoneaster only as needed.

FAVORITES
The hardiest cotoneasters proved self-reliant after 11 years of field trials at the University of Minnesota, maintaining a good appearance whether

**COTONEASTER
RACEMIFLORUS AUREUS**

they were irrigated or not. In trials at the garden of the University of Maine at Orono (zone 4), two species thrived: *C. lucidus* (hedge cotoneaster), which is deciduous, often used for hedges and grows about 10 feet (3 m) tall, with black fruit; and *C. racemiflorus aureus*, deciduous, to 8 feet (2.4 m) tall, with bright red fruit. Not included in the Maine trial but hardy to zone 2 are *C. acutifolius* (Peking cotoneaster), which is deciduous, to 10 feet (3 m) tall, with black fruit; and *C. integerrimus* (European cotoneaster), also deciduous, 4 to 7 feet (1.2-2 m) tall, with red fruit.

In warmer zones, cotoneaster is at least somewhat evergreen. The following examples are recommended as drought-tolerant shrubs for North Carolina:

C. apiculatus (cranberry cotoneaster), zones 4 to 7, grows 3 feet (1m) tall and twice as wide, with erect branches in a herringbone pattern, pink flowers and red fruit. The fall foliage is red to purple. 'Blackburn' is more compact.

C. lacteus (Parney cotoneaster), zones 6 to 8, grows 6 to 10 feet (2-3 m) tall with dark green leaves, white flowers and red fruit.

C. microphyllus (little-leaf cotoneaster), zones 5 to 7, forms a low shrub just 21 inches to 3 feet (60-90 cm) tall with white flowers and red fruit. The dark green leaves are woolly underneath.

C. salicifolia (willowleaf cotoneaster), zones 5 to 7, is taller than most at 7 to 15 feet (2.1-3.5 m) with white flowers and red fruit that does not persist. 'Autumn Fire' ('Herbstfever') is a dwarf 2 to 3 feet (60-90 cm) tall. 'Repens' is a spreading, prostrate form for use as a ground cover. 'Scarlet Leader' has scarlet new growth.

Eleagnus species

Silverberry
Zones vary

Two members of this genus, *E. angustifolia* (Russian olive) and *E. umbellata* (autumn olive), are Asian imports that have become invasive in parts of midwestern and eastern North America and so are generally not recommended.

FAVORITES
A North American cousin, *Eleagnus commutata* (silverberry, wolf willow) also suckers profusely and can be invasive, so it should be used with caution. It is extremely hardy, to zone 2, and is a good choice for poor ground on dry, windy hillsides or for places where it can be controlled with mowing or by pavement. A shrubby version of the Russian olive tree as tall as 12 feet (3.7 m), it has beautiful silvery leaves and fragrant flowers followed by silvery fruit.

For zones 7 to 10, the evergreen, slightly spiny *E. pungens* 'Fruitlandii' (Fruitland eleagnus) is recommended. It forms a large mound 8-10 feet (2.4-3 m) high and 6-9 feet (1.8-2.7 m) wide. Clusters of silvery flowers are followed by red fruit.

Euonymus species

Spindle tree
Zones vary

Euonymus is known for its showy, shiny, often brightly variegated foliage. Some plants will climb if they are grown by a rough-textured wall. Small white, greenish or yellow spring flowers are followed by poisonous fruit capsules that persist from summer till fall. All tolerate sun or shade.

FAVORITES
E. alatus (winged euonymus, burning bush), noted for its brilliant red fall color on mature specimens, is recommended for zones 4 and 5 but should be avoided where it is considered invasive in midwestern and eastern states. It has corky protrusions on the bark — the wings described by its common name — which add to its interest. The cultivar 'Compacta' reaches only about 4 feet (1.2 m), while most others grow twice as tall.

E. fortunei (wintercreeper) looks very different from *E. alatus*. A low, spreading plant with waxy leaves in variegated shades of gold, cream and green, it attracts a lot of attention at plant nurseries in spring. Despite its showy looks and evergreen foliage, it is an easy shrub where it is hardy, prized for foundation or specimen plantings and for sunny or lightly shaded perennial borders — anywhere the soil is not wet. Some plants grow no taller than a foot (30 cm), and others can be maintained at 3 to 4 feet (90-120 cm). *E. fortunei* is most safely grown in zone 6 or warmer gardens, but among the hardiest cultivars, suitable for protected places in zone 5 are 'Emerald Cushion,' 'Emerald Gaiety,' 'Green Beauty,' 'Silver Edge,' 'Sunspot,' 'Vegetus' and 'Waterdown.'

EUONYMUS FORTUNEI 'GREEN BEAUTY'

E. japonica is less hardy, zones 7 to 10, and taller, to about 15 feet (4.5 m). It is most often used for hedges. The dense evergreen foliage may be green, gray, gold or variegated. The fruit is bright red and showy. There is also a hardier, smaller form, microphyllus.

Exochorda species

Pearlbush
Zones 4 and 5

Pearlbush is an old-fashioned favorite that is showiest at lilac time in midspring, when it is covered with racemes of white flowers. The leaves are small and oval. Pearlbush will grow in any well-drained soil, preferably acidic, in sun or shade. Flowers bloom on old wood, so prune soon after blooming.

E. racemosa (common pearlbush) grows about 10 feet (3 m) and equally wide. The flower racemes are about 2½ inches (6 cm) long.

FAVORITES
E. x *macrantha* 'The Bride' is a weeping form that grows to only about 4 feet (120 cm), but the flower clusters are twice as long, and flowers wider. The foliage is gray-green.

Forsythia species
Forsythia
Zones 4 to 8

Forsythia is nothing more than a modest green shrub after the flowers are gone, but that matters little to northern gardeners who eagerly await its early show of bright yellow, four-petaled flowers which appear before the leaves. It is the first garden shrub to bloom — if it blooms at all. Older cultivars may bloom only at the base where buds were protected by snow. Newer cultivars have buds that are later developing or more cold-resistant. Give forsythia sun or part shade, and allow it plenty of room to grow, roughly 3 feet (1 m) all around, so that it can be allowed to reach its full height of 7 to 9 feet (2-2.7 m). Soon after blooming, prune to shape, trimming the oldest stems close to the ground to create replacements. An overgrown plant can be cut back almost to the ground immediately after blooming. Branches cut several weeks before flowering time can be forced indoors.

FAVORITES
Reliable bloomers are mostly hybrids of *F. ovata* and *F. europaea*. At the Minnesota Landscape Arboretum, 'New Hampshire Gold,' 'Northern Gold' and 'Northern Sun' were found best able to withstand average Minnesota winters, including temperatures as low as minus 33 degrees F (−36°C), although all suffered flower-bud death when temperatures fluctuated. ('Happy Centennial,' a good Canadian introduction, was not included in the Minnesota trial.) 'Vermont Sun,' a selection of *F. mandschurica*, came out of dormancy earliest of the plants in the Minnesota trials and ended up less hardy than the others

by mid-March. For zone 5, there are more profusely flowering species and cultivars, such as the hybrid *F.* x *intermedia* cultivars including 'Lynwood Gold' and 'Beatrix Farrand,' an Arnold Arboretum release with 2-inch (5 cm) flowers.

Genista species
Dyer's greenwood, Spanish gorse
Zones 5 to 9

Very similar to their relatives in the aggressively weedy genus *Cytisus* (Scotch broom) and often grouped with them, these shrubs also thrive in poor, dry soil in sun, and most are resplendent with golden pea flowers in spring, although some bloom white. Long flat pods follow. Stems are striped green and may be spiny. Genistas grow 1 to 3 feet (30-90 cm) tall, depending on the species and cultivar. Prune soon after blooming. Like most legumes, genista resents transplanting. It should be obtained as a container-grown plant and moved only when small.

GENISTA TINCTORIA

FAVORITES
Utah's Water-Wise Plants list recommends three species: *Genista hispanica*, *G. pilosa* and *G. tinctoria*. *G. pilosa* is a ground cover, page 66. *G. hispanica* (Spanish gorse, broom) has become a prickly pest in the mildest parts of the Pacific Coast, zones 6 to 9, but is more polite where winters are colder and conditions are more harsh. It forms a low mound about 2½ feet (76 cm) tall, covered with bright gold flowers in spring. The best-known species for places with colder winters is *G. tinctoria* (dyer's greenwood, used as a source of green dye), about 3 feet (1 m) tall, and its dwarf forms 'Golden Dwarf' and the double-flowered 'Plena,' all hardy to zone 4 or 5. One of the prettiest is the smaller *G. lydia* (Lydia woadwaxen) about 2 feet (60 cm) tall and somewhat wider, with weeping branches, and suited to zones 5 to 7.

Hamamelis species
Witch hazel
Zones vary

Witch hazel is famed for fragrant golden to reddish flowers that bloom in late winter or very early spring before the leaves develop. The two species below do best in well-drained, acidic soil in part shade. The foliage turns yellow in fall.

FAVORITES
These two species are recommended for drought-tolerance:

H. mollis (Chinese witch hazel), zones 5 to 8, is a shrub or small tree about 20 feet (6 m) tall and wide with hairy leaves and very fragrant flowers about 3/4-inch (2 cm) long. 'Westerstede' has pale yellow flowers and bright orange fall foliage.

H. x *intermedia* hybrids of *H. mollis* with Japanese witch hazel include 'Arnold Promise,' with larger, longer-lasting flowers; 'Diane,' with red flowers that fade to orange; 'Jelena,' whose flowers appear orange and whose fall color is excellent; and 'Ruby Glow,' with red flowers.

H. vernalis (vernal witch hazel) is a North American native shrub that is hardier, zones 4 to 8, and smaller, about 10 feet (3 m) tall and wide. It blooms earlier than *H. mollis* and has smaller flowers that are yellow and fragrant. 'Sandra' has larger petals, purplish or bronze new growth and reddish orange fall foliage.

Heptacodium miconioides
Seven son flower
Zones 5 to 8

This native of China is still little known in North America but is already acclaimed, especially for flowers in fall when few other shrubs bloom, and dark green foliage that lasts well into late fall, then turns yellow. It was introduced to the United States in 1980 by the Arnold Arboretum in Boston and was awarded a Gold Medal in 1994 by the Pennsylvania Horticultural Society for its beauty, uniqueness and resistance to pests and diseases. It can be kept smallish as a shrub or allowed to grow into a tree about 20 feet (6 m) tall and almost as wide. Clusters of small, creamy white flowers are followed by fruit that is purple when ripe. The tan-colored, shredding bark is attractive in winter. Seven son flower does best in sun but will tolerate shade and almost any soil from sandy to heavy clay.

Hippophae rhamnoides
Sea buckthorn
Zones 3 to 7

There are several dry-garden plants whose common name includes the word "sea" — such as sea lavender, sea holly and this shrub — indicating a plant that can grow in salty, sandy seaside gardens. Sea buckthorn can even be used to create a windbreak on a beach. These large, spiny shrubs or small trees have an airy look thanks to narrow silver leaves resembling willow. There are separate male and female plants. Provided you grow at least one male for as many as six females — one reason sea buckthorn is often used as a hedge — the females bear inconspicuous yellow flowers followed by their showiest feature, clusters of bright orange fruit. The berries will last all winter, since although they are edible, they are too acidic to be eaten by birds. The species generally grows about 12 feet (3.7 m) tall and equally wide, although there are taller cultivars. As is the case with many tough plants, sea buckthorn can be aggressive and hard to get rid of. It suckers freely, so keep it out of perennial borders. It is easiest to control and looks best when given its own corner. Prune it back in summer. Sea buckthorn is quite easy from ripe seeds sown outdoors in fall.

FAVORITES
The cultivar 'Leikora' is a heavy fruiting female. 'Pollmix' is a male pollinator for 'Leikora.' 'Sprite,' a male that stays under 5 feet (1.5 m) tall and wide, is grown not for fruit but for its dense silver foliage.

Hypericum species

St. John's wort
Zones vary

There are herbaceous and woody forms of this genus, known for flat, sunny yellow summer flowers with a central pincushion of yellow stamens. The common name attests to its use in medicine — some species have proven antibiotic qualities. "Wort" is simply an old name for any healing plant. Some herbaceous types of hypericum are weedy and all are easy to grow, provided you choose a species hardy and drought-resistant enough for your garden. Most thrive in full sun to full shade and dry, sandy soil but do less well where summers are hot and humid. Because they have a mounding habit, they can be used as ground covers. They are evergreen in warmer zones and deciduous where winters are severe.

FAVORITES

Among the hardiest, zones 4 to 7, are *H. patulum* (goldencup St. John's wort) 'Sungold,' about 18 inches (45 cm) tall and equally wide, and *H. kalmanium* (Kalm St. John's wort). The latter is a North American species about 3 feet (1 m) tall with flowers an inch (2.5 cm) wide. These two were the only hypericums to survive winter in the trial garden at the University of Maine at Orono (zone 4).

Also hardy to zone 4 is *H. prolificum* (bush broom, shrubby St. John's wort), an evergreen North American native that grows 3 to 5 feet (1-1.5 m) tall or more, with clusters of 3/4-inch (2 cm) flowers throughout much of the summer.

H. patulum (goldencup St. John's wort), zones 6 to 8, grows about 3 feet (90 cm) tall and wide.

H. calycinum (Aaronsbeard St. John's

wort), only about a foot (30 cm) tall. It does best in sandy, alkaline soil.

H. frondosum (shrubby St. John's wort) about 4 feet (120 cm) tall, with bluish green, 2-inch (5 cm) leaves and reddish, peeling bark. 'Sunburst,' developed at Cornell University and Longwood Gardens in Pennsylvania, is suited to zones 5 to 8, although it should be mulched in colder gardens. It is recommended for dry gardens in New York and Colorado. It is more compact than the species, and the flowers are larger.

For zones 7 to 9, *H. xinodorum* 'Summergold' offers foliage that is gold when young, becoming splotched with green as it matures. It grows to 4 feet (120 cm).

Ilex glabra and I. vomitoria

Inkberry and Yaupon holly
Zones vary

Hollies are associated with benign climates and wet, organic soils, but these two species, one for cold winters and one for warm, are exceptions. Inkberry, named for its black berries, is hardy to zone 4, or protected spots in zone 3. Yaupon holly, also drought-tolerant, is suited to zones 7 to 10. *I. glabra* is a native of eastern North America. A list of common names, which include winterberry and Appalachian tea, attests to its versatility. In common with all broad-leaved evergreens, it isn't suitable for exposed places, windbreaks or south- or west-facing positions but can be included in a perennial border or a sheltered corner in sun or part shade. The small flowers attract bees.

On both species, fruit appears only on females, but since the fruit is pea-sized and mostly hidden, plants sold are generally males,

grown for their lovely, dark green, leathery foliage, which remains green in warmer zones but turns rust-colored where winters are more severe. Winter burning of the foliage occurs at minus 15 degrees F (−26°C).

FAVORITES

I. glabra grows around 5 to 6 feet (1.5-1.8 m) tall and equally wide. It puts out suckers, so it is easy to transplant or divide, but it is not badly invasive. Shear it lightly every year to encourage dense growth. The cultivar 'Compacta' is smaller and more dense than the species. 'Shamrock' grows only about 2 feet (60 cm) tall with dense foliage. 'Nordic' is a male that grows 4 feet (120 cm) tall, hardy to zone 3.

I. vomitoria is an evergreen that grows in dry or wet soil and tolerates salt spray. Cultivars include 'Stokes Dwarf,' a compact male 3 to 4 feet (1 -1.2 m) tall and wide, the slightly taller 'Nana,' a female with scarlet fruit; 'Condeaux' or 'Bordeaux,' which has red new growth, maroon winter foliage and grows 4 to 5 feet (1.2-1.5 m) tall and a bit wider, and 'Will Fleming,' a male that is narrow and 10 to 12 feet (3-3.6 m) tall.

Itea virginica
Virginia sweetspire; Virginia willow
Zones 5 to 9

Virginia sweetspire is grown for its 2-to-4-inch (5-10 cm) drooping spires of small, fragrant white flowers in early summer and its red foliage in fall. Suited to either wet or dry places in sun or shade, this native of eastern North American swamps and woods grows 4 to 10 feet (1.2-3 m) tall and half as wide. In the warmer zones, it is semi-evergreen.

FAVORITES
I. virginica 'Henry's Garnet' is an award-winning cultivar a little shorter than the species, about 6 feet (1.8 m) tall and wide, with deeper red-purple fall foliage color and longer, 6-inch (15 cm) flower spikes. 'Long Spire' has even longer racemes, about 8 inches (20 cm), but the fall color is not as good.

Juniperus species
Juniper
Zones vary

One of the evergreen shrubs most likely to succeed in dry, sunny gardens — and least happy in shade and damp — juniper is available in so many shapes, sizes and foliage colors that an attractive minimal-care garden could be created using little else. The ground-covering types are described on page 67, the upright types here. Because some junipers grow very large and do so quite quickly, make sure that the diminutive plant you buy will not overwhelm your garden, or be prepared to move neighboring plants outward every couple of years.

Upright junipers should be spi-

JUNIPERUS COMMUNIS

raled round with twine in late fall to prevent snow and ice damage. If grown in a windy place, they may need staking for the first year or two. In spring, wearing gloves, shear junipers if you want to retain a tight, formal shape. Trim away any dead needles and cut broken branches back to the closest joint.

FAVORITES
J. chinensis (Chinese juniper) is available in an array of cultivars, some hardier than others. The best-known Chinese junipers are called pfitzers, selections with ascending branches. The first of these, 'Pfitzeriana,' bred in Germany in 1899 and still recommended as an easy hedge for full sun in zones 5 to 9, has been hybridized into green-, blue- and gold-tipped cultivars, usually 3 to 4 feet (90-120 cm) tall but sometimes dwarf and sometimes much taller; 'Hetzii' may reach 15 feet (4.5 m). 'Gold Star,' hardy to zone 2, forms a dense, low-growing mound up to 2 feet (60 cm) tall. Its juvenile foliage, produced at the branch tips, is bright gold throughout the life of the plant. The greens are reliable in zones 4 to 9. 'Mint Julep,' also known as 'Seagreen,' is one of the best of the greens.

J. communis (common juniper) is hardy to zone 3. It tolerates salty soil.

J. scopulorum (Western red cedar, Colorado red cedar, Rocky Mountain juniper) is hardy to zone 2 or 3. It forms a pyramidal shape. 'Blue Heaven' and 'Wichita Blue' both grow quickly to a height of 10 to 20 feet (3-6 m), too tall for foundation plantings and small gardens but good as specimens in a lawn or along a driveway. 'Skyrocket' is about 3 feet (90 cm) wide and 15 feet (4.5 m) tall.

J. virginiana (Eastern red cedar) is also very hardy, zones 2 to 9, and can reach 30 feet (9.1 m) tall. It should be kept out of apple-growing areas and should not be planted near hawthorn (*Craetagus*), an alternate host for cedar apple rust, a fungus that produces ugly growths on junipers and damages apples. Most cultivars, such as the dark green 'Emerald Sentinel,' are pyramidal, although some, such as the silver-blue 'Gray Owl,' are wide-spreading.

KERRIA JAPONICA 'PLENIFLORA'

Kerria japonica
Japanese kerria
Zones 4 to 9

This Chinese (not Japanese) member of the rose family is an old-fashioned favorite with bright yellow, inch-wide (5 cm) spring flowers that may be hidden somewhat by the coarse-looking foliage. The shrub grows about 4 to 6 feet (1.2-1.8 m) tall and somewhat wider. It is deciduous, but the stems remain green and decorative all winter. Kerria needs well-drained soil and should be grown out of the wind in sun or part shade. In the coldest part of its range, in sheltered spots in zone 4, branch tips may be lost to winterkill and should be pruned off, but the shrub generally recovers quickly in spring. Prune off flowering shoots soon after blooming. It spreads quickly, but suckers can be easily removed.

FAVORITES
More often grown than the species, whose single flowers resemble butter-cups, is 'Pleniflora' (Japanese rose; gypsy rose), which is taller and has double, ball-shaped, long-lasting flowers. 'Picta' ('Variegata'), a smaller shrub that offers white-edged green foliage and single flowers, thrived during the 1995 drought at the Xeriscape Demonstration Garden in Plainview, New York. 'Golden Guinea' has 2-inch (5 cm) flowers. 'Kin Kan' ('Aureovittata') has yellow stems striped with green. The cultivars are somewhat less winter-hardy than the species, to zone 5.

Kolkwitzia amabilis
Beauty bush
Zones 4 to 8

An old-fashioned favorite resembling weigela, this honeysuckle cousin is valued for its spectacular crop of fragrant, 1/2-inch (1 cm) yellow-throated, pink, starry flowers in late spring. Branches can be pruned off several weeks early and forced indoors. Beauty bush can be overly eager. It is too large for most small gardens and not especially interesting when blooming is over, so it needs pruning as soon as the flowers fade to keep it from becoming too large and too leggy. Allowed to grow, it forms an arching shape 6 to 10 feet (1.8-3 m) tall and about the same width, with heavily textured leaves. It will put up with virtually any soil if given full sun.

KOLKWITZIA AMABILIS

FAVORITES
'Pink Cloud,' developed in England, is the cultivar usually offered. The flowers are bigger and brighter than the species, but it may be less winter-hardy.

Lespedeza species
Bush clover
Zones vary

Lespedeza can be useful in a garden where winters are harsh, but in its most southerly reaches, such as Virginia, it is a weedy pest and should be avoided. Its clusters of white or rosy purple pea flowers bloom in late summer or early fall, when few other shrubs bloom. The foliage is blue-green and opposite. Lespedeza does best in well-drained, even sandy soil in sun or part shade. It can be considered a shrub or a perennial, because after a cold winter, it may die back to the ground but then grows rapidly in spring. In any case, it should be cut back hard early in spring to keep the growth dense and to ensure a good crop of flowers, which bloom on new growth. Lespedeza is very easy from seeds, which are large and can be sown outdoors in spring just like sweet peas. Since it resents transplanting, this may be the easiest way to grow it.

FAVORITES
L. bicolor, the hardiest species, zones 4 to 7, has a vertical habit that can exceed 6 feet (2 m.) tall and half as wide, with arching branches and purple flowers in summer and fall.

L. japonica, hardy to zone 6, has white flowers.

Lonicera species
Honeysuckle
Zones vary

There are more than 100 species of honeysuckle, both tender and hardy, moisture-loving and drought-tolerant, and there are a few that combine the attributes of attractiveness, hardiness and drought-tolerance. Their uniquely shaped fragrant spring flowers in white or in shades of pink from pale to intense are favorites of bees, birds and butterflies. The flowers are followed by berries that may be decorative. Honeysuckle can become leggy and unkempt, so it looks and fares best if severely pruned every year immediately after flowering. Faithfully pruned, it is an excellent candidate for a flowering hedge. Reduce branch height as desired, remove the oldest branches to the base and prune hedges to the desired shape.

Certain honeysuckles are susceptible to damage by the honeysuckle aphid, which entered North America on imported plants during the 1970s. Infected plants develop the clumps and deformities known as witches'-broom. Twigs and sometimes entire plants may die.

LONICERA TATARICA 'ARNOLD RED'

FAVORITES

Horticulturists at North Dakota State University evaluated honeysuckles' aphid-resistance. Among the plants that fared best were a few that also have considerable drought-resistance:

L. maackii (Amur honeysuckle) and its cultivars 'Cling Red' and 'Rem Red'; and *L. tatarica* (Tatarian honeysuckle) 'Arnold Red.' *L. maackii* can reach 10 to 15 feet (3-4.5 m) tall and wide, with a fabulous show of fragrant flowers followed by bright red berries. It can be invasive, so is best confined to places where conditions are difficult. It is hardy to zone 2.

L. tatarica grows 8 to 10 feet (2.4-3 m) tall and almost as wide and bears white, pink or red flowers in spring, followed by red berries that are decorative in summer. The species is hardy to zone 2 but invasive because of suckering and seeding. 'Arnold Red,' which has dark pink flowers, is a bit less hardy (zone 3) and not invasive.

L. xylosteum (zones 4 to 6), with yellow flowers and red fruit, is invasive in some areas. For yellow flowers on less invasive plants, choose *L.* x *xylosteoides* hybrids, which include 'Clavey's Dwarf,' about 7 feet (2.1 m) tall and almost as wide, 'Emerald Mound,' which forms a dense mound about 3 feet (1 m) tall and twice as wide, and is resistant to the honeysuckle aphid, and 'Hedge King,' an upright form especially selected for hedges.

Myrica species
Bayberry, wax myrtle
Zones vary

Two aromatic plants that originated in eastern North America are uncommon in gardens, but nevertheless good choices for dry places, especially if you prefer native plants. Both need very well-drained, even sandy or rocky soil, preferably acidic. They spread by suckers to form thickets so should be kept out of perennial borders but can be used to stabilize dry hillsides in full sun to light shade.

FAVORITES

M. pensylvanica (bayberry), zones 4 to 9, is a shrub of the seashore. It grows about 8 feet (2.4 m) tall and wide, with elliptical dull green foliage. Nurseries generally sell plants with both male and female flowers so there will be at least some fruit. Gardeners who want heavier fruit production should choose a female such as 'Myda' and grow at least one male such as 'Myriman' for every five females. The pea-sized berries, which are waxy and grayish and have a distinctive fragrance, are used to make bayberry candles. The fruit persists into winter unless eaten by birds.

For warmer gardens, zones 7 to 9, a better choice, although less available commercially, is *M. cerifera* (southern wax myrtle), the plant that gave Myrtle Beach its name. It also produces fragrant grayish fruit used for candles. It can be grown as a tall evergreen shrub or small tree as tall as 20 feet (6 m) in the same conditions as bayberry.

PHILADELPHUS CORONARIUS

Philadelphus species

Mock orange
Zones vary

Mock orange is one of many flowering shrubs that is interesting only when in bloom, unless you choose a variety with foliage other than plain green. The flowers, however, are lovely: white, spring-blooming and, best of all, strongly and sweetly perfumed. Double flowers last longer than singles. Mock orange will grow well in any decent soil, provided it is well drained, and can reach 12 feet (3.6 m) high and wide if allowed. Prune the branches back immediately after blooming every spring, in the manner of forsythia, to prevent legginess and so that new wood can produce flowers next spring. Overgrown plants can be cut back entirely to just above the ground and will regrow, although blooming may be delayed a year.

FAVORITES

Species and cultivars range from hardy to tender, so if you live where winters are harsh, choose carefully. Gardeners in zone 2 can grow *P. schrenkii* (Manchurian mock orange). *P. coronarius* is the usual species for zones 3 or 4 to 8. The cultivar 'Aureus' is a choice selection with golden leaves that turn greener in summer heat. 'Variegatus' grows slowly and has leaves bordered with white. Double-flowered cultivars include 'Glacier,' 'Polar Star' and the hybrids 'Minnesota Snowflake,' 'Snow Goose' and 'Miniature Snowflake,' which grows only 3 feet (1 m) tall and wide.

Phlomis fruticosa

Jerusalem sage
Zones 6 to 10

This bold, silvery, evergreen shrub grows about 3 feet (90 cm) tall and wide, with bright mustard yellow, 1-inch-wide (2.5 cm) flowers in whorls around the stem tips in early summer. Both the new shoots and evergreen foliage are furry and are good for flower arrangements. The foliage is aromatic when crushed. Deadheading will prolong flowering. Like other members of the mint family, Jerusalem sage has square stems. It needs full sun and well-drained, mostly dry soil and can survive in sandy, salty seaside gardens. Too much moisture in winter or spring will kill it. Cold winds are also harmful, so it should be given a warm, sheltered position. In marginal areas (zone 6), it may die back in winter and emerge again in spring, acting like a hardy perennial. Hard frosts in spring will damage shoot tips. Jerusalem sage has an uneven appearance that suits it best to informal gardens. In fall, prune the stems back to keep its shape. Prune out frost-damaged branches in spring.

FAVORITES

The species received the Royal Horticultural Society Award of Merit and is the usual plant grown. The hybrid 'Edward Bowles' has large green leaves. It is probably the same plant as 'Grande Verde.'

PHYSOCARPUS OPULIFOLIUS 'LUTEUS'

Physocarpus opulifolius
Ninebark
Zones 2 to 7

Ninebark is fast-growing to a height of 5 to 8 feet (1.5-2.4 m) and equally wide, flowers profusely in early summer and, if pruned every year, can make an easy and informal hedge. The small white flowers are produced in 2-inch (5 cm) clusters in late spring. Peeling bark that reveals beautiful brown inner bark is a winter feature. The species, a North American native, is seldom grown, because cultivars with yellow-green spring foliage or purplish foliage are more decorative and just as hardy. Plant them near shrubs with dark green foliage for a good contrast. Ninebark does fine in ordinary soil and full sun or part shade. It is easy to propagate from rooted side shoots or from stem tip cuttings taken in late summer.

FAVORITES
For dark green foliage, choose 'Snowfall,' which has improved flowering. It grows about 7 feet (2.1 m) tall and somewhat wider. The variety intermedius has dense growth to 4 feet (1.2 m). 'Nanus' or 'Nana' is half as tall. Among yellow-green cultivars, all of which fade to green in summer, one of the best is the 6-foot (1.8 m) 'Nugget, which stays gold longer than 'Luteus.' 'Dart's Gold' is shorter, about 3-4 feet (90-120 cm) tall. 'Pygmy Gold' is similar but has pinkish flowers. Diabolo™ ('Monlo') has unusual bronzy purple foliage that fades to purplish green in hot climates and is best with some shade. I have seen multi-stemmed specimens 10 feet (3 m) tall and twice as wide looking splendid when given enough space to reach their full size. It can be kept smaller with hard pruning in spring.

PINUS STROBUS 'CONTORTA'

Pinus species
Pine
Zones vary

Pines are most impressive when tree-sized, but there are many small species and cultivars that are among the best evergreens for rock gardens and other dry, sandy places in sun. Shrubby pines can also be pretty along paths, in foundation plantings and in perennial borders, providing long-lasting color after their deciduous or herbacious bedmates fade in winter. To keep pines small and dense, pinch off all or a portion of the new candles of growth each spring. They suffer in polluted air.

FAVORITES
P. mugo (mugho, or mountain pine), hardy to zone 2, is the most popular small pine for landscaping, although it is extremely variable in eventual size. Left unpruned, some may grow 30 feet (9 m) tall and wide, overwhelming demure foundation plantings and shrub borders. Unfortunately, potted mugho pines are often unpredictable and unnamed. If you want a small mugho without pruning, search for named cultivars such as 'Mops,' about 5 feet (1.5 m) tall; or the smaller 'Allen's Dwarf,' 'Gnome,' 'Valley Cushion,' 'Oregon Jade' or 'Green Candle.'

Other dwarf or slow-growing pines include *P. densiflora* 'Umbraculifera,' hardy to zone 5; the silvery blue-green *P. strobus* 'Nana,' zone 3; and dwarf forms of *P. sylvestris* (Scots pine), such as 'Beuvronensis,' which grows about 2 feet (60 cm) tall and twice as wide, zone 3.

There are many other lovely small pines, such as the unusual *P. strobus* 'Contorta' (also known as *P.s.* 'Tortulosa'). Check the labels at good nurseries, or read the listings in mail-order catalogs or on the Internet.

Potentilla fruticosa
Cinquefoil
Zones 2 to 6

A shrub or ground cover that prefers cold winters, potentilla is easy in poor, dry soil in sun, where its flat, five-petaled flowers may bloom through most of the summer. Its small, narrow leaflets grow in groups of five — thus the common name cinquefoil, meaning five leaves. The usual flower color is sunny yellow, but there are also whites, light and dark oranges, reds and pinks, all with yellow undertones. Shrubs grow 1 to 4 feet (30-120 cm) tall and slightly wider, but the shorter types are often spreading, with stems that root where joints touch the ground. Examples are 'Longacre' and 'Yellow Gem.'

Clip back potentilla branches, and cut out one-third of the canes every year after flowering to keep the shrub dense and floriferous. It can be cut back to the ground every three to five years. Potentilla is susceptible to infestation by spider mites, which can be killed with insecticidal soap spray.

FAVORITES

There are many good cultivars, differing mostly in size and color of the flowers and in size of the shrub. The newest flower color is pink, which looks brightest in cool weather and fades in hot. Cultivars include 'Pink Pearl' and 'Pink Whisper' and the double 'Pink Beauty.' The whites, which always look crisp and fresh, include 'Abbotswood,' 'McKay's White' and the double 'Snowbird.' From North Dakota come two excellent potentillas that grow 3 feet (1 m) tall with large yellow flowers, 'Absaraka' (Dakota Goldrush™) and 'Fargo' (Dakota Sunspot™). Another excellent full-sized yellow is 'Gold Star.' 'Goldfinger' has foliage that stays dark green until fall. 'Sutter's Gold' is one of the smallest, about 1 foot (30 cm) tall. 'Primrose Beauty' has silvery foliage and pale yellow flowers. Newest developments in color are the orange-yellow flowers on 'Sunset,' a spreading shrub just 16 inches (40 cm) tall; and copper-colored flowers on the 2-foot (60 cm) 'Tangerine.'

Prunus species
Cherry, plum
Zones vary

The flag bearers of the genus *Prunus* are the sweet cherries, apricots, almonds, peaches and plums that need plenty of water in hot weather to produce their large, luscious fruit, but there are smaller-fruited types that are remarkably less demanding. All produce spring flowers and edible fruit that, if not sweet enough for humans to eat straight off the branch, is cherished by birds and other wildlife and makes delicious preserves. Give these shrubs or small trees full sun or only a little shade. An exception is *P. laurocerasus*, which tolerates full shade. Prune them back in early spring to keep the growth dense. Many make good hedges. Once established, the plants survive dry summers, but the soil must be well drained. All prunus are among the favorite choices of tent caterpillars, but colonies can be destroyed with the careful use of a flame. Prunus are also vulnerable to the pests, fungal diseases and blights that infest their cousins, the roses.

FAVORITES

P. besseyi (Western sand cherry, bush cherry), hardy to zone 3, is a North American prairie native with sweet black fruit. It grows 4 to 6 feet (1.2-1.8 m) tall. Hybrids of sand cherry and plum have produced so-called cherry plums, small trees hardy to zone 4 that bear sweet, edible fruits that look like cherry-sized plums. Cultivars include 'Opata' and 'Sapa.'

P. x *cistena* (purple sand cherry), hardy to zone 3, is valued as one of the few hardy shrubs with reddish magenta foliage that keeps its color all season. Small fragrant pink flowers

POTENTILLA FRUTICOSA 'ABBOTSWOOD'

PRUNUS X CISTENA

are followed by dark purple fruit. It can reach 10 feet (3 m) in protected places but is best kept shorter and dense with an annual hard pruning in spring. Use prunings in flower arrangements.

P. glandulosa (dwarf flowering almond), zones 4 to 8, is grown for a profuse crop of clusters of white or pinkish flowers before the leaves open. Some cultivars produce tiny red fruit. 'Alba' has single white flowers. 'Rosea Plena' is double pink. It reaches 5 feet (1.5 m) and is almost as wide.

P. laurocerasus (cherry laurel, English laurel) is valued for its shiny, ever-green foliage more than its flowers or fruit, one reason it does fine in shade. In fact, it can sunburn, especially in winter. It grows as tall as 20 feet (6 m). Candles of small fragrant white flowers bloom in spring, followed by dark purple 1/2-inch (13 mm) fruit. 'Otto Luyken,' which tolerates deep shade, is about 4 feet (120 cm) tall and some-what wider. It is hardy to zone 6 or even farther north with mulching. 'Schipkaensis,' the hardiest (zone 5), has dark green, narrow foliage and grows about 5 feet (1.5 m) tall and somewhat wider. 'Zabeliana,' also hardy, has narrow, willowlike leaves. *P. laurocerasus* will survive in dry or moist ground but needs good drainage.

P. maritima (beach plum) is native to the east coast of North America and hardy to zone 4. As its common name suggests, it grows well in sandy soil. Masses of white spring flowers that bloom before the leaves appear are followed by sweet purple or yellow fruit. It grows 3 to 6 feet (1-1.8 m) tall and can grow twice as wide.

P. tenella (dwarf Russian almond) zones 2 to 6, like *P. glandulosa*, is grown chiefly for its profuse crop of spring flowers. They may be white, pink or red. It grows about 4 feet (1.2 m) tall and wide with small narrow leaves. Since it flowers on old wood, it should be pruned directly after flowering.

P. virginiana (chokecherry), zones 2 to 9, is named for its bitter-tasting fruit, which is red to dark purple. Tassels of white flowers bloom in early spring. This is a North American native that grows wild from the Northwest Territories to Texas.

Pyracantha species
Firethorn
Zones 5/6 to 10

These spiny evergreen shrubs, closely related to cotoneaster, are grown mostly for their bright red or orange fruit that persists into winter, although they also feature decorative glossy foliage and clus-ters of white spring flowers. The foliage is evergreen in warmer areas, but in colder zones, it turns bronze in fall and may drop. Pyracantha does best in full sun in dry, well-drained soil. Late-spring frosts or cold winds interfere with pollina-tion, so in colder zones, it needs a sheltered position if you want fruit. It is often trained against a wall. Because of its long thorns and because it is difficult to transplant, choose a position for pyracantha

where it can remain and can spread, to minimize the need for pruning and handling. Some species are susceptible to scab and fireblight.

FAVORITES
P. coccinea (scarlet firethorn) grows 10 to 15 feet (3-4.5 m) tall. Hairy flower clusters are followed by bright red, pea-sized fruit. It is hardy to zone 6, but the cultivar 'Lalandei,' with orange-red fruit, is somewhat hardier. It looks best trained against a wall.

P. hybrids include 'Mohave,' zone 6, disease-resistant with bright orange-red berries; 'Navaho,' zone 7, a dense, rounded shrub 6 feet (1.8 m) tall with orange-red fruit; 'Teton,' 15 feet (4.5 m) tall and wide, with yellow-orange fruit.

Where it can be grown, zones 7 to 10, *P. koidzumii* (Formosa firethorn) is a better choice since it has the largest, showiest red fruit of the genus. It forms an arching shape and is an excellent candidate for espalier. 'Victory' is about 10 feet (3 m) tall and wide. 'Santa Cruz' is about half as tall, but 5 to 10 feet (1.5-3 m) wide. In the hottest places, *P. koidzumii* should not be planted near sunny south- or west-facing walls.

RIBES ALPINUM

Ribes species
Mountain currant, alpine currant
Zones vary

The best-known members of this family are currants and gooseberries, but smaller fruit means less water required and easier care. Many are native to North America. All bloom in early spring and produce decorative summer fruit, and all are good subjects for massing or for hedges. They are tolerant of urban air pollution but are susceptible to rust, blight, mildew, aphids, scale and mites. Grow them in sun or shade and any soil. They can be pruned at any time. Because some *Ribes* species, including females of *R. alpinum*, can be hosts of white pine blister rust fungus, a potentially devastating disease of white pines, some states prohibit importation of all *Ribes* species. Only males are now propagated, since they are resistant to the disease. Contact your extension department agent for more information.

FAVORITES
R. alpinum (mountain currant), zones 2 to 7, is a native of northern Europe considered one of the best drought-tolerant shrubs by North Dakota State University in Fargo. The foliage is dense and dark green, and the plant is strongly upright, to about 7 feet (2 m) tall, but can be sheared regularly to stay smaller. 'Aureum' is a golden form. 'Green Mound' grows 3 feet (90 cm) tall and wide, with increased disease-resistance. 'Pumila' is a little shorter. 'Spreg' has glossy, green foliage that lasts longer in fall.

R. odoratum (clove currant), zones 4 to 6, is a native of the central United States that bears showy clusters of fragrant yellow flowers followed by edible black fruit on females. It grows 4 to 6 feet (1.2-1.8 m) tall and almost as wide.

R. sanguineum (flowering currant), zones 6 to 9, is a native of the western states and British Columbia. It grows 5 to 12 feet (1.5-3.5 m). It bears racemes as long as 4 inches (10 cm) of showy red flowers, followed by bluish black fruit on females. There are many cultivars, including 'White Icicle,' with white flowers, and 'King Edward VII,' with scarlet.

Rhus species
Sumac
Zones vary

Handsome foliage that turns brilliant purplish red in fall is the chief virtue of sumac, but this deciduous North American native also has large, showy flower spikes followed by clusters of fruit on the females. All members of the genus have male and female flowers on separate plants. Sumac is unusually carefree, putting up with dry ground, wind and neglect, although it has some susceptibility to wilt and rust diseases as well as aphids, scale and mites. Most species spread rapidly by sucker and so are best kept out of perennial borders and small gardens. On the positive side, this aggressiveness suits most sumacs to colonizing dry hills and occupying gravelly beds in full sun or part shade where little else will look as comely. These shrubs can also be grown where their suckers can be controlled by mowing or pavement. At the end of winter, stems can be pruned back almost to the ground to prevent their becoming leggy and bare.

FAVORITES
R. typhina is the most widely recommended species for dryland gardens throughout zones 3 to 9. It grows 10 to 30 feet (3-9 m) tall, with extremely hairy stems and beautiful slender opposite leaves. The flower heads are bigger on the males than the females. The fruit, on females only, is a crimson panicle that fades to brown. Although there are no entirely sucker-free types of *R. typhina* yet, the cultivars are less aggressive. 'Dissecta' and 'Laciniata,' which are similar and often confused, are female forms with foliage more finely divided and fernlike than the species.

R. aromatica; R. canadensis (fragrant sumac), zones 3 to 9, has rounded leaves very different from those of *R. typhina* and *R. glabra*, although it also turns bright red in fall. It grows about 3 feet (1 m) tall and 6 to 8 feet (1.8-2.4 m) wide, making it an excellent ground cover for dry, rocky slopes or in front of taller shrubs or trees. Just as wide but only 2 feet (60 cm) tall, the cultivar 'Gro-low' is recommended for sustainable landscapes by the University of Massachusetts. 'Green Globe' is a female that forms a rounded shape 6 feet (1.8 m) tall. 'Konza' is a 2-foot (60 cm) dwarf.

R. copallina (shining sumac, flame leaf sumac), zones 4 to 9, can reach 30 feet (9 m) and has eliptical, glossy, dark green leaves that turn scarlet in

RHUS TYPHINA

fall. Showy crimson fruit persists through winter. 'Creel's Quintet' is a female 8 to 10 feet (2.4-3 m) tall and widely spreading.

R. glabra (smooth sumac), zones 3 to 8, is recommended as one of the best hardy drought-tolerant shrubs by North Dakota State University in Fargo. It has slender opposite leaves and grows 6 to 10 feet (1.8-3 m) tall. 'Flavescens' has yellow fruit and yellow fall color. 'Laciniata' is a fern-leaf form that provides a shorter substitute for *R. typhina* 'Laciniata.'

R. michauxii (Michaux's sumac), zones 5 to 7, is an endangered species native to the Carolinas. It grows just 2 to 3 feet (60-90 cm) tall with 6-inch (15 cm) panicles of yellow-green flowers in summer. The fall color is yellow to purplish.

R. trilobata (oakleaf sumac; three-leaf sumac; skunkbush) is a native of western U.S. and Canada recommended for dry, windy places in zones 4 to 8. It is a medicinal species.

Rosa species
Rose
Zones vary

To disagree with Gertrude Stein ("a rose is a rose is a rose"), there are roses, roses and roses. Gardeners dealing with drought and wind have to look past the obvious. The biggest-flowered, most luxuriant roses — the ones most gardeners want to grow — are plants for deep, fertile soils, gentle rains and mild winters. Even so, they can be touchy and susceptible to diseases. On the other hand, *Rosa acicularis* is the provincial flower of Alberta; it grows wild and untended where summers are dry and winters are cold. *R. woodsii* is the most common wild rose in Utah and is included on that state's recommended list for dry gardens. These are two among many species and selections that are very hardy and self-reliant. The trade-off for added toughness is smaller flowers that sometimes, although not always, bloom for a brief season. Shrubs may be large and thorny, so these are good plants for wild or larger gardens. The species have single flowers, the type with just five petals, but many of the cultivars are fully double. Some produce a crop of apple-shaped fruits called hips, which are edible and may last into winter.

Roses need full sun or just a little shade, protection from strong winds and, in their first year, weekly watering. Give them a spot with deep, rich, weed-free and preferably slightly acidic soil without competition from other plants. Dig a large hole so that the roots will not be cramped, and plant them in spring. On grafted plants in zones 2 to 5, make sure the bud union, where the plant is grafted onto the roots, is 2 to 3 inches (5-7.5 cm) below the soil surface. Mulch around the stem in summer with about 4 inches (10 cm) of grass clippings or straw for moisture retention, and in winter, mulch all but the toughest roses with soil and fallen leaves or pile evergreen branches around the plants.

Pruning depends on the rose type, but in general, the hardy types can put up with heavy shearing if they become overly large. In early spring, always remove any dead or damaged shoots and give the plant the shape you want. Suckers that sprout up from the base can be pruned off. This is optional in wild roses but recommended for grafted roses, as the suckers will not be the preferred variety.

Roses, even the wild ones, are susceptible to a number of diseases, especially the fungal disease black spot. Choose resistant varieties, or spray the plants weekly with a solution of 1 teaspoon (5 mL) baking soda (sodium bicarbonate) dissolved in 1 quart (1 L) water. A further refinement of this recipe, developed at Cornell University, is effective against other fungi as well. It calls for 1 tablespoon (15 mL) horticultural oil, such as Sunspray, and 1 tablespoon (15 mL) baking soda in 1 gallon (4 L) water. Spray once a week, preferably during cool, overcast weather.

FAVORITES
Among roses for dry gardens are the following:

R. blanda (smooth rose, meadow rose), zones 2 to 9, grows up to 5 feet (1.5 m) tall and blooms just once but has a long-lasting display of red hips. It can bloom at its branch tips even after winter temperatures go as low as minus 45 degrees F (−43°C).

R. carolina (Carolina rose, pasture rose), zones 2 to 9, grows about 3 feet

ROSA 'DORTMUND'

Shepherdia species
Buffaloberry; Nebraska currant
Zones 2 to 10

Grown for their pale or silvery foliage and their ability to survive in sunny, windy places where winters are harsh and the soil is rocky and dry, preferably alkaline, these native North American shrubs are seldom grown and hard to find in more temperate places. Only the females produce fruit, so you must grow both a male and a female if you want it and can beat the birds to it. Buffaloberry can be grown as a backdrop for a perennial border or used for a shelterbelt or hedge, trimmed or untrimmed.

FAVORITES
S. argentea (silver buffaloberry) is thorny and stiffly upright, with attractive, coarsely textured small silvery leaves. The sour red or yellow fruit is edible and tasty in jellies or jams. The shrub grows 10 feet (3 m) or taller and about as wide. It will also grow in moist ground.

S. canadensis (russet buffaloberry, soapberry) has leaves that are green on top and silvery underneath. It is somewhat smaller, about 6 to 8 feet (1.8-2.4 m) tall and thornless, with insipid, soapy-tasting fruit.

(1 m) tall and spreads by underground stems to form dense thickets. Small pink flowers in June — white on 'Alba' — are followed by red hips.

R. chinensis, zones 5 to 9, is best represented in the garden by *R.c. semperflorens*, also known as Slater's crimson China, about 3 feet (1 m) tall.

R. glauca; R. rubrifolia (redleaf rose), zones 5 to 8, is distinguished by dark reddish foliage. The pink flowers are single. It grows 5 feet (1.5 m) or taller. The fall fruits are edible.

Rosa rugosa (rugosa rose), zones 2 to 9, is a Japanese species extensively used in breeding hardy cultivars. These roses may bloom just once in early summer, but their wrinkled (rugose) foliage is also decorative. Many yield especially large and colorful hips that remain on the plant until winter and can be made into jellies, syrups and herbal teas. Best of all the *R. rugosa* cultivars tested at several botanical gardens in Wisconsin, Minnesota, Illinois and Ohio was 'Frau Dagmar Hastrup' ('Frau Dagmar Hartopp'), about 3 feet (1 m) tall, with fragrant, light pink single flowers and large red hips. The following all have fragrant double flowers: yellow on 'Agnes,' red on 'Hansa,' pink on 'Therese Bugnet' and white on 'Blanc Double de Coubert.'

R. virginiana (Virginia rose), zones 3 to 9, has reddish canes and single, pale pink to magenta flowers followed by red hips. It spreads by underground stems to create dense thickets almost 5 feet (1.5 m) high. It can be pruned back to the ground.

Among climbers for difficult places are several *R. kordesii* hybrids, such as the fabulous German release 'Dortmund,' zones 5 to 9. Several in the Canadian rose series are named for explorers, including 9-to-10-foot (2.7-3 m) dark pink 'John Cabot,' 6-foot (1.8 m) pink 'John Davis' and 9-foot (2.7 m) 'William Baffin.' All will survive temperatures of at least minus 35 degrees F (−37ºC). Perhaps best of all is 'Henry Kelsey,' whose rose-red semidouble flowers have golden stamens.

SPIRAEA X BUMALDA 'GOLDFLAME'

Spiraea species

Spirea

Zones 3 to 9, except as noted

Spirea is one of the best-selling deciduous shrubs, mostly because of the brightly colored spring foliage, orange, magenta and variegated, on densely twiggy shrubs that may color beautifully in fall. Spireas also offer summer flowers, winter hardiness and landscape adaptability. They are useful as hedges or specimens or within a shrub or perennial border. The selections with variegated foliage — better known for the beauty of their foliage than their flowers — can be arresting within a border of other shrubs, including evergreens. New cultivars and selections appear on the market every year.

Best known for flowers are the white-flowered types of spirea, which should be pruned immediately after blooming, both to remove old canes and to maintain the desired size. The others bloom on new growth produced in spring and therefore can be either left unpruned or pruned in early spring before

growth begins. Spireas can be pruned back almost to the ground when they look leggy and need renewing. Light annual pruning will increase flowering. They fare best in sun and will put up with almost any soil, although leaves grow larger with occasional watering.

FAVORITES

The first two groups have colorful foliage and flowers that are pink or rose-colored.

S. x bumalda is fairly small, about 2 to 4 feet (60-120 cm) and equally wide. One of the most available cultivars is 'Goldflame,' whose bright orange spring foliage lightens to pink, yellow or green. There are pink flowers in summer. The flower stalks are unattractive after blooming and should be sheared off. The foliage turns red in fall. One of the parents of this hybrid is *S. japonica*, which creates confusion in classifying the cultivars.

S. japonica hybrids are generally smaller than *S. x bumalda*, with pink or rose-colored flowers. Grown for its small size is the 12-inch (30 cm)

'Alpina.' 'Goldmound,' a Canadian introduction, grows 18 inches (45 cm) tall with golden foliage. Taller still, at 3 feet (90 cm) tall, is the British introduction 'Golden Princess,' with foliage that opens bronze-orange and stays yellow for the season.

The next three species and their cultivars have white flowers.

S. nipponica, zones 3 to 7, is usually represented by 'Snowmound,' which is 4 feet (1.2 m) and somewhat wider, and 'Halward's Silver' a dwarf 3 feet (90 cm) tall and wide.

S. trilobata, hardy to zone 2, has distinctive three-lobed foliage. 'Swan Lake,' is 3 feet (90 cm) tall with arching branches and profuse white bloom in spring. 'Fairy Queen' is a compact 3 feet (90 cm). The hybrid 'Snow White' has a 5-foot (1.5 m) arching shape. Prune immediately after flowering.

S. x vanhouttei (bridalwreath) is an old-fashioned favorite that has diminished in popularity because of its large size, about 6 feet (1.8 m) tall and wide, and lack of interest after blooming. It is distinguished by gracefully weeping branches and trusses of white flowers. Branches cut in late spring can be forced indoors. For a similar but smaller effect, grow *S. nipponica* 'Snowmound' or *S. trilobata* 'Swan Lake.'

Symphoricarpos species

Snowberry, coralberry, waxberry
Zones 2/3 to 7

Deciduous cousins of honeysuckles that attract bees and butterflies, symphoricarpos are especially valued for berries that persist into winter. The species listed here are North American native shrubs that thrive in sun or shade and almost any soil. They have attractive shiny, opposite leaves. Since they spread by sucker, they should be kept out of perennial beds. They are tolerant of city air pollution, and all are easy to grow from seed or cuttings or by simply removing a sucker.

FAVORITES
Grown chiefly for its pea- to marble-sized white berries and for its ability to flower in shade, *S. albus* (snowberry, waxberry) is hardy to zone 3. It grows about 5 feet (1.5 m) tall and almost as wide; the variety laevigatus, which is more commonly available, can be twice as tall.

  S. doorenbosii (Doorenbos hybrids) include 'Magic Berry' with purplish berries, and 'Mother of Pearl' with pearl-pink, lilac or purplish berries. Both are 4 feet (1.2 m) tall and hardy to zone 3 or 4. 'White Hedge' is more compact with white berries.

  S. orbiculatus (coralberry, Indian currant), hardy to zone 2, grows about 5 to 7 feet (1.5-2 m) tall and wide. It has persistent coral-colored or purple fruit and grayish foliage that turns crimson in fall. It suckers freely and should be kept out of perennial beds, but it can be used on a dry hillside or allowed to form a clump in an out-of-the-way corner.

SYRINGA JOSIFLEXA

Syringa species

Lilac
Zones 3 to 8

The hundreds of tall, showy common lilacs (*S. vulgaris*) with huge inflorescences will put up with dry ground once established — they have naturalized in meadows of the northeastern United States and eastern Canada — but drought before blooming time may lessen flowering and diminish flower size. Also, the vast majority of lilacs — *S. vulgaris*, *S. hyacinthiflora*, *S. josiflexa* and *S. prestoniae*, as well as most of the hybrids — need a cold winter (zones 3 to 6) for best flowering and disease-resistance. Gardeners in zones 7 to 9 can choose among some of the newer *Syringa* hybrids, as well as cultivars of the hyacinth lilac (*S. hyacinthiflora*) bred in and for warmer places. These tolerate warm winters, if properly managed, but do require irrigation. *S. hyacinthiflora* and the common lilac (*S. vulgaris*) sucker excessively, so these shrubs should be kept out of perennial borders unless you are prepared to snip suckers off at the base annually. Newly planted lilacs may not bloom for several years. Provided they are in sun and well-drained soil and not

heavily pruned or fertilized, the gardener will eventually be rewarded. Lilacs should be pruned immediately after blooming. Any later, and you risk cutting away next year's buds. Prune out the oldest stems at the base. The chief detriment of lilacs, aside from the invasiveness of some varieties, is that after their period of gorgeous, fragrant bloom, they are unremarkable — a common shortcoming of spring-flowering shrubs. Plant the non-suckering types of lilac behind and among other things, rather than as specimens on their own, so that they do not command too much attention beyond their brief spell in the limelight. Many can grow as tall as 25 feet (7.5 m) but can be kept short with hard pruning after blooming. All lilacs except some of the lesser-known species are hardy to at least zone 3.

FAVORITES
The standard by which lilacs are measured is the group of French hybrids, cultivars of *S. vulgaris* developed around the turn of the century. Fragrant flowers are blue to purple, white, creamy, pink or bicolored, single or double. Several are still popular, including 'Madame Lemoine,' whose yellow buds open pure double white. Another good *S. vulgaris* cultivar is the pink double 'Edward J. Gardner,' introduced in Minnesota in 1950. 'Krasavitsa Moskvy' is a Russian introduction with pink buds opening into white-lilac double flowers. 'Sensation' has dark purple petals edged with white. 'Dappled Dawn' and 'Aucubaefolia' have variegated green-and-white foliage.

  Better for places with occasional drought are more self-reliant lilacs. According to 11 years of field trials at the University of Minnesota, the best were *S.* x *persica* (Persian lilac), 4 to 8 feet (1.2-2.4 m) tall, and *S.* x *chinensis* (Chinese or Rouen lilac), roughly twice as tall. Both types have dark green leaves and fragrant spring flowers.

S. meyeri 'Palibin' (*S. palibiniana, S. velutina*), zones 3 to 7, known as dwarf Korean lilac, is a dependable bloomer and one of the most restrained lilacs, staying less than 5 to 6 feet (1.5-1.8 m) tall. The lavender-pink spring flowers are fragrant, and the foliage is attractive in all seasons, turning pinkish as it fades in fall. This shrub does not sucker and so is a good choice for foundation planting or a perennial border. It is also a good hedge plant, with the added bonus that it resists powdery mildew.

Around the same size as *S. meyeri* 'Palibin' is *S. patula* (Korean lilac), zones 4 to 8. The best-known cultivar, 'Miss Kim,' released from New Hampshire in 1960, bears a huge crop of fragrant, lilac-colored flowers in June. It is slow-growing, easy to restrain with pruning and resistant to powdery mildew. It is one of the best choices for zones 7 and 8.

S. reticulata (Japanese tree lilac) blooms later, into July. The flowers are creamy yellow but not especially fragrant. The cultivar 'Ivory Silk' was awarded a Gold Medal in 1996 by the Pennsylvania Horticultural Society. In 20 years, it reaches about 20 feet (6 m) high and roughly half as wide. There are also variegated versions.

Tamarix species
Tamarisk
Zones vary

These unusual and distinctive shrubs or small trees have small, delicate feathery leaves and tiny flowers, usually pink, that bloom in clusters in spring or summer. The branches are very pliable, so wind damage seldom occurs. They do best in full sun in perfectly drained alkaline soil and can withstand sandy soil, salty air and wind, so they are frequently planted on seaside slopes. In fact, some have become weedy pests on stream banks and other places that suit them. Fast growers that mostly bloom on new wood (except *Tamarix parviflora*), they should be pruned hard in early spring every year to keep them from looking leggy.

FAVORITES

T. parviflora; T. tetrandra (small-flowered tamarisk), zones 5 to 8, although stem tips may winter-kill in the colder zones, grows about 15 feet (4.5 m) tall, with reddish bark. It flowers in late spring on the previous year's growth, so it should be pruned directly after flowering. It is invasive in some coastal places, including Connecticut and California.

T. ramosissima; T. pentandra (Amur tamarisk; Five-stamen tamarisk), zones 3 or 4, grows about 10 to 12 feet (3-3.5 m) tall and not quite as wide. Cultivars are a bit smaller. The species may winter-kill to the ground in exposed places in zones 3 and 4 but will generally regrow in spring. It suffers some tip dieback at the Central Experimental Farm in Ottawa, Ontario (zone 4), as did the rosy-flowered cultivar 'Summer Glow' (also called 'Summerglow' or 'Rubra') at the trial gardens at the University of Maine at Orono (also zone 4), but 'Pink Cascade,' which has brighter flowers, did not survive. In zones 4 and 5, Amur tamarisk is useful for a hardy hedge but it should be avoided in zones 8 or warmer where it can be invasive.

Taxus species
Yew
Zones vary

Yews can be plants for lush British landscapes, where they are favorites for pruning into geometric hedging, topiary bunnies and chess pieces, or they can be among the evergreens most tolerant of dry ground, even in shade. It depends largely upon species. *T. canadensis* (Canada yew) — a straggly creeper not often available for sale — is very hardy, to zone 3, and tolerant of dry ground, while *T. baccata* (English yew) is quite tender, to zone 7, enjoys cool weather and moist soil and can become a stately tree. The ground-covering types are described on page 72. What these disparate species have in common are waxy evergreen needles, soft to the touch, and an ability to regrow from buds all along the stems, not just at the tips, so they can be repeatedly pruned, even quite far down the stems, and are amenable to shaping. Male and female flowers are largely on separate plants but inconspicuous. Berries appear on females only. All yews take full sun to part shade but should be kept out of the windiest, most exposed places to prevent sunburn and winter damage. Keep them away from ocean gardens or roads treated with winter salt. The seeds are poisonous.

FAVORITES

T. cuspidata (Japanese yew), zones 4 to 7, is the hardiest garden yew. Cultivars vary greatly in size. 'Capitata' can grow 30 feet (9 m) while 'Nana' grows about 4 feet (1.2 m) tall and somewhat wider.

The baccata-cuspidata hybrids labeled *T. x media*, zones 4 to 7, are favorites of northern gardens that are extremely varied in size. 'Brownii' and 'Densiformis,' both grow up to 8 feet (2.4 m) tall. 'Tauntonii' has a low-spreading habit, good green color all year, heat-tolerance and resistance to winter windburn. 'Hillii' is a slender column to about 8 feet (2.4 m). 'Hicksii' (Hicks' yew) reaches about 15 feet (4.5 m). 'Wardii' is a fruiting female that grows about 6 feet (1.8 m) tall and twice as wide. All may suffer from occasional winter tip dieback.

Thuja occidentalis

White cedar; arborvitae
Zones 2 to 7

Not white and not a true cedar, although it is usually simply called cedar, this North American native species has cedarlike foliage and comes in such a variety of sizes and shapes that there may be at least one for every garden. Best grown on well-drained soils, they look good in foundation plantings, in shrub borders or in perennial beds, where they provide year-long color when herbaceous plants fade. In fall, water thoroughly to prevent scorching from winter winds, most likely to happen in open, sunny sites. Surround them with burlap if you want extra protection. They will turn brown if drenched in salt spray. All can be lightly sheared in spring to maintain their shape, but they

THUJA OCCIDENTALIS 'SUNKIST'

should not be clipped back far enough to expose brown inner branches.

FAVORITES

There are more than 100 cultivars of *Thuja occidentalis,* so your choices will depend on what is available locally and what suits your needs. Among frequently sold globe-shaped plants are the 2½-foot-tall (75 cm) green 'Little Champion,' 3-foot (90 cm) 'Hetz Midget' and 4-foot (120 cm) green 'Woodwardii' or yellow 'Golden Globe.' Among pyramidal forms, green 7-foot (2.1 m) 'Smaragd' ('Emerald Green') or golden 'Sunkist.' Among tall narrow forms, the 15-foot (4.5 m) dark green 'Elegantissima' and 20-foot (6 m) 'Wareana.'

Viburnum species

Viburnum
Zones vary

Known for globes or flat disks of showy, fragrant flowers in summer, usually white, viburnums are otherwise a varied group. Some are native plants of North America, but others hail from Europe and Asia. Some are considered shrubs for kind climates and moist soil, yet there are others that can survive in trying conditions. In a spot sheltered from strong winds and with a bit of shade, some of the deciduous viburnums are hardy, self-reliant and drought-resistant, especially if the soil is acidic and rich in humus. After the flowers, many leave a crop of berries that are long-lasting if not quickly eaten by the birds. The viburnum leaf beetle, whose larvae skeletonize leaves, is a pest in the northeastern states, British Columbia and from Ontario to the Atlantic provinces.

FAVORITES

All the species and hybrids listed here come from Europe or Asia, with the exception of *V. dentatum,* a native of eastern Canada and the eastern states, and *V. trilobum,* a native of northern North America.

V. awabuki; V. odoratissimum 'Chindo,' zones 7 to 9, is a drought-tolerant release from North Carolina with fleshy foliage. It grows fast to 10 to 15 feet (3-4.5 m) tall, forming a pyramidal shape.

V. dentatum (arrowwood), zones 2 to 8, is a native of eastern North America whose common name comes from an early use of the suckers, which grow straight and strong. It grows about 9 feet (270 cm) tall and wide in full sun to part shade and any soil, dry to wet. It is the last of the viburnums to bloom in late spring,

VIBURNUM TRILOBUM

with showy 3-inch (7.5 cm) clusters of white flowers followed by attractive blue to purplish fruit. It tolerates city pollution.

V. lantana (wayfaring tree), zones 4 to 7, forms a shrub or small tree about 15 feet (4.5 m) high, with wrinkled, gray-green leaves that turn red in fall. Flat, 4-inch-wide (10 cm)

clusters of spring flowers produce bunches of red berries that turn black and are a favorite of birds.

V. lentago (sheepberry, nannyberry), zones 2 to 8, was a star performer during the 1995 drought at the Xeriscape Demonstration Garden in Plainview, New York. It can reach 20 to 30 feet (6-9 m) tall. The leaves are green and lustrous. Creamy white flowers are followed by juicy blueblack berries enjoyed by birds. 'Mohican' is smaller, about 8 feet (2.4 m) tall and wide, with orangered fruit.

V. x pragense, zones 5 to 8, is a hybrid broadleaf evergreen that forms a rounded shape about 10 feet (3 m) tall and wide. Severe winter weather can damage the rugose foliage. 'Decker' has pink buds that open into white flowers.

V. x rhytidophylloides (blackhaw), zones 4 to 8, a hybrid of *V. lantana* x

V. rhytidophyllum, is hardier than the latter, with broader and smoother leaves. Flower clusters are 3 to 4 inches (7.5-10 cm) wide.

V. rhytidophyllum (leather-leaf viburnum), zones 5 or 6 to 8, is an evergreen grown mainly for its long, oval, wrinkled leaves. It can grow 10 to 15 feet (3-4.5 m) tall, best kept in shade to protect the foliage. The yellowish white flower clusters are 8 inches (20 cm) wide. The fruit turns from reddish to black.

V. trilobum (highbush cranberry), zones 2 to 7, is a North American native that grows 8 to 12 feet (2.4-3.5 m) tall. Leaves are three-lobed and toothed. The white flower clusters are nearly 4 inches (10 cm) wide. Scarlet fruit, used to make jelly, ripens in summer and persists through the winter.

CLIMATE ZONE MAP

This simplified version of the U.S. Department of Agriculture's climate zone map illustrates general temperature trends throughout most of Canada and the United States. The temperature ranges indicate average minimum winter temperatures. Colder zones have lower numbers. Nursery catalogs usually indicate the coldest zone in which a plant will thrive. Plants that are successful in your zone and in zones with numbers lower than yours should survive winters in your garden. Plants that prefer zones with higher numbers than yours may not be winter-hardy for you. But conditions vary locally, so experimentation is often worthwhile.

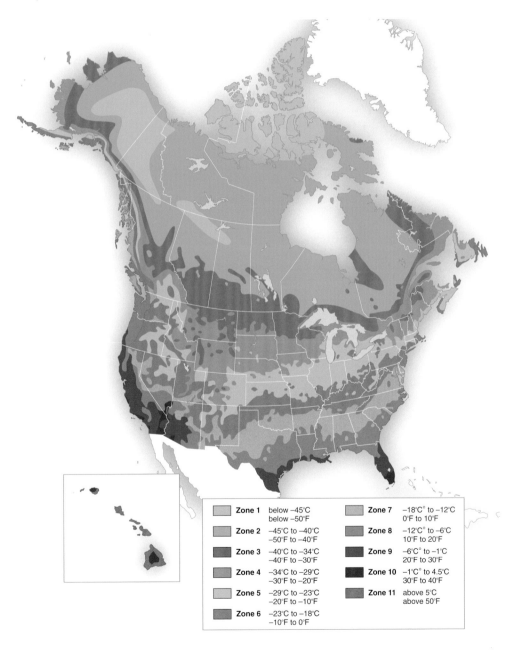

Zone 1 below –45°C / below –50°F	**Zone 7** –18°C° to –12°C / 0°F to 10°F
Zone 2 –45°C to –40°C / –50°F to –40°F	**Zone 8** –12°C° to –6°C / 10°F to 20°F
Zone 3 –40°C to –34°C / –40°F to –30°F	**Zone 9** –6°C° to –1°C / 20°F to 30°F
Zone 4 –34°C to –29°C / –30°F to –20°F	**Zone 10** –1°C° to 4.5°C / 30°F to 40°F
Zone 5 –29°C to –23°C / –20°F to –10°F	**Zone 11** above 5°C / above 50°F
Zone 6 –23°C to –18°C / –10°F to 0°F	

SOURCES

MAIL-ORDER SOURCES

All sources encourage online ordering
except where noted. Toll-free numbers
do not necessarily work in all areas.

GENERAL PLANTS AND SEEDS

United States

W. ATLEE BURPEE & CO.
300 Park Ave.
Warminster, PA 18974
(800) 888-1447
burpee@burpee.com
www.burpee.com
Seeds of vegetables and flowers.
Garden equipment, some plants. Free
catalog to U.S. only.

BLUESTONE PERENNIALS
7293 Middle Ridge Road
Madison, OH 44057-3096
(800) 852-5243
bluestone@bluestoneperennials.com
www.bluestoneperennials.com
More than 1,000 varieties. Free catalog to
U.S. only.

BUSSE GARDENS
17170 245th Avenue
Big Lake, MN 55309
(800) 544-3192
customer.service@bussegardens.com
1,000 hardy perennials. Catalog $3.

EARTHLY PURSUITS, INC.
2901 Kurtz Road
Windsor Mill, MD 21244
(410) 496-2523
mail@earthlypursuits.net
www.earthlypursuits.net
Ornamental grasses, ferns, bamboos and
perennials.

JOY CREEK NURSERY
20300 NW Watson Road
Scappoose, OR 97056
(503) 543-7474
catalogue@joycreek.com
www.joycreek.com
Catalog $3.

NICHE GARDENS
1111 Dawson Road
Chapel Hill, NC 27516
(919) 967-0078
mail@nichegardens.com
www.nichegardens.com
Native and unusual plants, shrubs
and trees. Free catalog.

PLANT DELIGHTS NURSERY, INC.
9241 Sauls Road
Raleigh, NC27603
(919) 772-4794
office@plantdelights.com
www.plantdelights.com
Send 10 U.S. stamps for a catalog.

SANTA ROSA GARDENS
P.O. Box 1187
Gulf Breeze, FL 32562
(866) 681-0856
sales@santarosagardens.com
www.santarosagardens.com
Perennials, ornamental grasses,
succulents
Ships to U.S. only. Does not ship to CA,
HI or AZ.

TWOMBLY NURSERY
163 Barn Hill Road
Monroe, CT 06468
(203) 261-2133
info@twomblynursery.com
www.twomblynursery.com
Rare and unusual plants.

WAYSIDE GARDENS
1 Garden Lane
Hodges, SC 29695
(800) 213-0379
www.waysidegardens.com
Trees, shrubs, perennials, bulbs.
E-mail newsletter. Free catalog.

WHITE FLOWER FARM
P.O. Box 50, Route 63
Litchfield, CT 06759-0050
(800) 503-9624
Garden questions:
hort@whiteflowerfarm.com
www.whiteflowerfarm.com

SPECIALIST NURSERIES

United States

ADELMAN PEONY GARDENS
P.O. Box 9193
5690 Brooklake Road NE
Salem, OR 97305
(503) 393-6185
info@peonyparadise.com
www.peonyparadise.com

ANDRE VIETTE FARM & NURSERY
P.O. Box 1109
Fishersville, VA 22939
(800) 575-5538
info@inthegardenradio.com
Daylilies and select perennials. Catalog
$7.50.

ARROWHEAD ALPINES
P.O. Box 857
Fowlerville, MI 48836
(517) 223-3581
www.arrowheadalpines.com
Alpine and rock plants, wildflowers
and dwarf conifers. Catalog $2.

B&D LILIES
P.O. Box 2007
Port Townsend, WA 98368
(360) 765-4341
help@bdlilies.com
www.bdlilies.com
Lilies and daylilies. Order online.

BOB SMOLEY'S GARDENWORLD
4038 Watters Lane
Gibsonia, PA 15044
(724) 443-6770
bsmoley@pgh.net
www.bobsmoleys.com
Cacti and succulents. Order online.

CACTI.COM
www.cacti.com
California based online source of cacti
and succulents.

SOURCES

CANYON CREEK NURSERY
3527 Dry Creek Road
Oroville, CA 95965
(530) 533-2166
johnccn@sunset.net
www.canyoncreeknursery.com
Dianthus, kniphofias, origanums, salvias and other perennials. Catalog $2.

COMPLETELY CLEMATIS
217 Argilla Road
Ipswich, MA 01938-2617
(978) 356-3197
info@clematisnursery.com
www.clematisnursery.com

COOLEY'S IRIS GARDENS
P.O. Box 126
Silverton, OH 97381
(800) 225-5391 or (503) 873-5463
cooleyiris@aol.com
www.cooleysgardens.com

DESERT NURSERY
1301 South Cooper
Deming, NM 88030
Cactus, including winter-hardy species
Send a U.S. stamp for plant list.

DIGGING DOG NURSERY
P.O. Box 471
Albion, CA 95410
(707) 937-1130
business@diggingdog.com
Plants for meadows, dry gardens, rock gardens, everlastings.
Free catalog.

FAIRWEATHER GARDENS
P.O. Box 330
Greenwich, NJ 08323
(856) 451-6261
www.fairweathergardens.com
Unusual trees, shrubs and perennials, including 36 viburnums. Catalog $4.

FORESTFARM
990 Tetherow Road
Williams, OR 97544-9599
(541) 846-7269
plants@forestfarm.com
www.forestfarm.com
Free catalog to U.S., $5 to Canada.

IMAGINE BACKYARD TREES
sales@backyardtrees.com
www.backyardtrees.com
Landscape trees. Retail arm of Sooner Plant Farm, Inc. Order online.

INTERMOUNTAIN CACTUS
1478 Ewe Turn
Kaysville, VT 84037-1256
(801) 546-2006
No website at time of publication.
Cold-hardy cacti and succulents.

LANGEVELD BULB CO.
725 Vassar Avenue
Lakewood, NJ 08701
(800) 526-0467 or (732) 367-2000
info@langeveld.com
www.langeveld.com
Free catalog.

LIMEROCK ORNAMENTAL GRASSES
70 Sawmill Road
Port Matilda, PA 16870
(814) 692-2272
Limerock@juno.com
www.limerockgrasses.com
Ornamental and native grasses and perennials. Order online.

MOUNTAIN VALLEY GROWERS, INC.
38325 Pepperweed Road
Squaw Valley, CA 93675
(559)338-2775
customerservice@
mountainvalleygrowers.com
Certified organic herbs. Free catalog.

OAKES DAYLILIES
P.O. Box 268
Corryton, TN 37721
(800) 532-9545
www.oakesdaylilies.com
Free catalog.
Daylilies and peonies.

OLD HOUSE GARDENS
536 Third Street
Ann Arbor, MI 48103
(734) 995-1486
newsletter@oldhousegardens.com
www.oldhousegardens.com
Heirloom bulbs. Catalog $2 or free newsletter.

PHOENIX DESERT NURSERY
3525 E. Southern Avenue
Phoenix, AZ 85040
(602) 243-7064
richard@getnet.com
www.phoenixdesert.com
Cacti and succulents. Order online.

PRAIRIE FRONTIER
Waukesha, WI 53189
(262) 544-6708
www.prairiefrontier.com
Seeds of wildflowers and prairie grasses. Free catalog to U.S. only.

PRAIRIE MOON NURSERY
31837 Bur Oak Lane
Winona, MN 55987-9515
(866) 417-8156
info@prairiemoon.com
www.prairiemoon.com
Seeds of native prairie and meadow plants; ecological lawn alternatives.

PRAIRIE NURSERY
P.O. Box 306
Westfield, WI 53964
(800) 476-9453
www.prairienursery.com
Plants and seeds of wildflowers and native grasses.

ROCK SPRAY NURSERY
P.O. Box 693
Truro, MA 02666
(508) 349-6769
question@rockspray.com
www.rockspray.com
Hardy heaths and heathers.
Does not ship to CA.

SCHREINER'S IRIS GARDENS
3647 Quinaby Rd NE
Salem, OR 97303
(800) 525-2367
iris@schreinersgardens.com
www.schreinersgardens.com
Free booklet.

SELECT SEEDS — ANTIQUE FLOWERS
180 Stickney Hill Road
Union, CT 06076
(800) 684-0395
info@selectseeds.com
Seeds of old-fashioned and rare annual and perennial flowers. Catalog $2.

SOURCES

SHOOTING STAR NURSERY
444 Bates Road
Frankfort, KY 40601
(502) 223-1679
shootingstarnursery@msn.com
www.shootingstarnursery.com
Plants and seeds of plants native to the
eastern U.S.

SISKIYOU RARE PLANT NURSERY
2825 Cummings Road
Medford, OR 97501
(541) 772-6846
customerservice@srpn.net
www.siskiyourareplantnursery.com
Rare perennials including a
selection for stone or concrete
troughs. Catalog $3.

VAN BOURGONDIEN
P.O. Box 1000
Babylon, NY 11702
(800) 622-9997
blooms@dutchbulbs.com
Free catalog.

VAN ENGELEN, INC.
23 Tulip Drive
P.O. Box 638
Bantam, CT 06750
(860) 567-8734
Customerservice@vanengelen.com
www.vanengelen.com
Flower bulbs.

WELL-SWEEP HERB FARM
205 Mt. Bethel Road
Port Murray, NJ 07865
(908) 852-5390
herbs@goes.com
Free catalog. No shipping of plants to
AZ, CA, OR and WA.

YUCCA DO NURSERY, INC.
P.O. Box 907
Hempstead, TX 77445
(979)826-4580
info@yuccado.com
www.yuccado.com
Rare drought-tolerant plants to
U.S. only.

EQUIPMENT AND IRRIGATION SYSTEMS SMALL AND LARGE

U.S. and International
DIG IRRIGATION PRODUCTS
1210 Activity Drive
Vista, CA 92081
Home gardeners phone
800-344-1172
or 760-727-0914
dig@digcorp.com
www.digcorp.com
Free planning and installation guide.

THE DRIP STORE
1145 Linda Vista Drive, Ste. 108
San Marcos, CA 92069
(760) 682-1580
orders@dripirrigation.com or
help@dripirrigation.com

DRIPWORKS
190 Sanhedrin Circle
Willits, CA 95490
(800) 522-3747
dripworks@pacific.net
www.dripworksusa.com

LEE VALLEY TOOLS LTD.
P.O. Box 1780
Ogdensburg, NY 13669-6780
(800) 267-8735
Canadian orders:
P.O. Box 6295, Stn. J
Ottawa, ON K2A 1T4
(800) 267-8761
customerservice@leevalley.com
www.leevalley.com
Garden tools and home watering
systems. Free catalog.

RAIN BIRD
877-727-8772
parts@rainbird.com
www.rainbird.com
Irrigation supplies including drip
retrofit kit for a popup sprinkler
system. Online only.

M.K. RITTENHOUSE & SONS LTD.
RR3, 1402 4th Avenue
St. Catharines, ON L2R 6P9
(905) 684-8122 or (877) 488-1914
consumersales@rittenhouse.ca
www.rittenhouse.ca
Gardening tools and watering
equipment.

THE SPRUCE CREEK CO.
P.O. Box 106
Warriors Mark, PA 16877
(800) 940-0187
info@sprucecreekrainsaver.com
www.rainbarrel.net
Rain barrels and other garden
equipment.

WEATHER MASS
P.O. Box 701
Franklin, MA 02038
(888) 430-8463
sales@weathermass.com
www.weathermass.com
Online sales of weather instruments
including rain gauges and soil-temper-
ature gauges for home gardeners.

PLANTS AND SEEDS

Canada and International
CANNING PERENNIALS
955309 Canning Road
RR 2
Paris, ON N3L 3E2
(519) 458-4271
info@canningperennials.com
www.canningperennials.com
Perennials, daylilies, ornamental
grasses and more. Minimum mail
order $25.

CHILTERN SEEDS
Bortree Stile
Ulverston, Cumbria
England LA1Z 7PB
info@chilternseeds.co.uk
www.chilternseeds.co.uk
Thousands of varieties of seeds of
all types.

GARDENIMPORT, INC.
P.O. Box 760
Thornhill, ON L3T 4A5
(905) 731-1950 or (800) 339-8314
flower@gardenimport.com
www.gardenimport.com
General plants, bulbs and seeds.

HOLE'S GREENHOUSES AND GARDENS
LTD.
101 Bellerose Dr.
St. Albert, AB T8N 8N8
(780) 419-6800 or (888)-88HOLES
www.holesonline.com
General plant nursery including hardy
cacti. Free catalog or order online.

HORTICO
723 Robson Road, RR1
Waterdown, ON L0R 2H1
(905) 689-6984
office@hortico.com
www.hortico.com
General plant nursery. Catalog $3 or
order online.

THE LILY NOOK
Box 846
Neepawa, MB R0J 1H0
www.lilynook.mb.ca
Lilies. Catalog $2 or order online.

THE PERENNIAL GARDENER
13139 - 224 St.
Maple Ridge, BC V4R 2P6
(604) 467-4218
info@perennialgardener.com
www.perennialgardener.com
Order online.

RICHTERS HERBS
Goodwood, ON, Canada L0C 1A0
(905) 640-6677
orderdesk@richters.com
Seeds and plants for hundreds of
herbs.
Catalog free to U.S. and Canada.

SWEET GRASS GARDENS
470 Sour Springs Road
RR 6
Hagersville, ON N0A 1H0
(519) 445-4828
info@sweetgrassgardens.com
www.sweetgrassgardens.com
Native seeds and plants including
grasses and cacti.

VESEYS
Box 9000
Charlottetown, PEI C1A 8K6
(800) 363-7333
Seeds, perennials, bulbs, shrubs,
supplies.
Catalog free to U.S. and Canada.

WILDFLOWER FARM
(866) GRO WILD
info@wildflowerfarm.com
www.wildflowerfarm.com
Wildflower and grass seeds and plants.
Demonstration garden. Pick your own.

INFORMATION WEBSITES

www.appletonridge.com
Maine organic gardeners describe how
to design a drip irrigation system.

**www.cactus-mall.com/whcsa/
index.html**
Winter Hardy Cactus and Succulent
Association, with information and
links.

www.climatechange.gc.ca
Government of Canada website with
links to newspaper reports, etc.

www.climatehotmap.org
Map created by the Union of
Concerned Scientists and World
Resources Institute illustrates the local
consequences of global warming.

www.desert-tropicals.com
An Arizona information service on
appropriate plants for the state.

www.gcrio.org/National Assessment
Website of the U.S. Global Change
Research Information Office, summary
report on potential consequences of
global warming in the U.S.
www.healthylawns.net
Website of Health Canada.

www.hotgardens.net
Guide to desert and drought gardens
in southern and southwestern U.S.
Free e-mail newsletter.

**http://invader.dbs.umt.edu/
noxious_weeds/**
University of Montana, Missoula,
maintains a list of invasive plant
species in all U.S. states and the six
southern Canadian provinces.

www.umassdroughtinfo.org
Website of the University of
Massachusetts Drought Information,
with links.

www.wmo.ch/indexflash.html
Website of the World Meteorological
Organization.

INDEX